European Monographs in Social Psychology
Nonverbal communication in depression

European Monographs in Social Psychology

Executive Editors:
J. RICHARD EISER and KLAUS R. SCHERER
Sponsored by the European Association of Experimental Social Psychology

This series, first published by Academic Press (who will continue to distribute the numbered volumes), appeared under the joint imprint of Cambridge University Press and the Maison des Sciences de l'Homme in 1985 as an amalgamation of the Academic Press series and the European Studies in Social Psychology, published by Cambridge and the Maison in collaboration with the Laboratoire Européen de Psychologie Sociale of the Maison.

The original aims of the two series still very much apply today: to provide a forum for the best European research in different fields of social psychology and to foster the interchange of ideas between different developments and different traditions. The Executive Editors also expect that it will have an important role to play as a European forum for international work.

Other titles in this series:

Unemployment by Peter Kelvin and Joanna E. Jarrett
National characteristics by Dean Peabody
Experiencing emotion by Klaus R. Scherer, Harald G. Wallbott and Angela B. Summerfield
Levels of explanation in social psychology by Willem Doise
Understanding attitudes to the European Community: a social-psychological study in four member states by Miles Hewstone
Arguing and thinking: a rhetorical approach to social psychology by Michael Billig
The child's construction of economics by A. Berti and A. Bombi

Nonverbal communication in depression

Heiner Ellgring
Department of Psychology
Max-Planck-Institute for Psychiatry

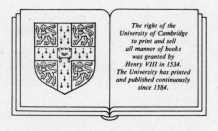

The right of the
University of Cambridge
to print and sell
all manner of books
was granted by
Henry VIII in 1534.
The University has printed
and published continuously
since 1584.

Cambridge University Press
Cambridge
New York   New Rochelle   Melbourne   Sydney

Editions de la Maison des Sciences de l'Homme
Paris

Published by the Press Syndicate of the University of Cambridge
The Pitt Building, Trumpington Street, Cambridge CB2 1RP
32 East 57th Street, New York, NY 10022, USA
10 Stamford Road, Oakleigh, Melbourne 3166, Australia
and Editions de la Maison des Sciences de l'Homme
54 Boulevard Raspail, 75270 Paris Cedex 06

First published 1989

Printed in Great Britain at the University Press, Cambridge

British Library cataloguing in publication data
Ellgring, Heiner.
Nonverbal communication in depression –
(European monographs in social psychology).
1. Man. Depression. Psychology).
interpretation of nonverbal communication.
I. Title II. Series
616.85'2706

Library of Congress cataloguing in publication data
Ellgring, Heiner.
Nonverbal communication in depression / Heiner Ellgring.
    p.   cm. – (European monographs in social psychology).
Bibliography.
Includes index.
ISBN 0-521-32310-X
1. Depression, Mental. 2. Nonverbal communication (Psycholgy).
I. Title II. Series.
RC537.E36 1988
616.85'27–dc 19   88-1725 CIP

ISBN 0 521 32310 X
ISBN 2 7351 0233 5 (France only)

Thanks to Dagmar, Jan, and Alina for their patience and support

Contents

Figures

Tables

Preface

The study of nonverbal communication attracted enormous interest during the 1960s and 1970s. Compared with this period, fewer studies are currently published which use behavioural observation in order to understand processes of communication. It seems as if more attention is being given to asking people about their perceptions and interpretations of nonverbal behaviour instead of studying conditions which actually elicit the behaviour. One can only speculate about the reasons for this development. One could be that a behaviour is difficult to observe and, moreover, may be caused by many conditions. In contrast, our perceptions tend to unify the phenomena around us and make them consistent. Thus, perception of behaviour yields a clearer picture of seemingly homogeneous phenomena whereas when they are systematically observed they confront the researcher with an awkward and disappointing variablity.

This book takes up the problem of how changing psychological states influence nonverbal behaviour. It stresses the analysis of behaviour as it occurs during dialogues and attempts to describe and explain the variety in nonverbal behaviour and its function during communication.

I would like to acknowledge the help of the many people who have contributed in various ways to this book. I would like to thank colleagues, friends and co-workers for their support, discussions and help with practical matters.

I thank Professor Dr D. Ploog, Director of the Max-Planck-Institute for Psychiatry, for his encouragement of my pursuit of the topic Nonverbal Communication. My interest in the topic was stimulated by his research in animal and human communication. Professor Dr J.C. Brengelmann, head of the Psychology Department, followed the undertaking with critical interest and advised me on behaviour theoretical issues.

I especially thank A.H. Clarke and H. Wagner, co-researchers in the DFG Project (part of the research was supported by the Deutsche Forschungs-Gemeinschaft, DFG, grant El67/1 and 2), S. Hieke and S. Zieglgänsberger, technical assistants, for their central and fruitful contributions and their continuous support.

I would like to acknowledge (in alphabetical order) the intensive, critical discussions and debates with P. Busch, P. Ekman, R. Krause, R. Lund, P.

Mangione, L. Meltzer, K.R. Scherer, H. Schulz, H. Wallbott, whose scientific integrity continuously gave me the courage to do the research.

I would like to thank the graduate and postgraduate students of the social psychology research unit for their interest and their creative involvement in the project: B. Agbede, M. Avarello, A. von Dewitz, B. Günthner, S. Hiebinger, S. Pattay, B. Regler participated in the research unit during this time.

I would like to acknowledge the patience shown by the secretaries, U. Golbs and K. Hollekamp, in deciphering my handwriting and during the many revisions the manuscript underwent. T. Hausen and V. Fowler helped to improve the English, which was not an easy task. The careful copyediting with additional clarification of linguistic idiosyncrasies carried out by M.J. Costa for the publisher is also gratefully acknowledged.

Important also was the help of the department for biostatistics and the computer center. I thank G. Dirlich, M. Federkiel and E. Hansert, H. Pfister and X. Rohde for their advice, their patience and their interest.

I would also like to acknowledge the willing, trustworthy collaboration of clinicians, psychiatrists and psychologists at the Institute. R. de Jong, J. Derbolowsky, D. von Zerssen and many others participated in the clinical interviews and contributed in many ways.

My special thanks go to the patients, without whom this work would not have been possible. Their willingness to take part in the investigation at a time when they were heavily burdened, their interest and openness were a very important basis for this project.

1 Introduction

To understand what man is experiencing, to recognize and discover the feelings and intentions of the other is essential for our existence as social beings.

In clinical psychology and psychiatry, observation and knowledge of affective states is a necessary basis for the therapeutic practice. For both the lay understanding and the clinical evaluation of affective states, nonverbal behaviour plays a major although mainly implicit role.

Investigating nonverbal behaviour in depression involves different closely related problems. From the perspective of clinical psychology it is of interest to what extent disorders become manifest in communicative behaviour. The question is whether this behaviour can reliably indicate changes in the emotional state. This problem is based on the widely discussed classical controversies about the expression of emotions. That is, the relationship between subjective experience or inner states and observable behaviour. Is there a differentiated "expression of emotions" as postulated by Darwin (1872), or does one have to continue to agree with Landis (1924), that behaviour does not allow specific and reliable inferences from behaviour to experienced emotions or affects.

From a social psychological viewpoint the communicative function of behaviour is of special interest. Behavioural signals contribute to our mutual understanding during social interaction.

Thus, from the clinical and social psychological perspective, two different functions of the behaviour are important regarding the expression of mood: the indicative function, i.e. its significance as a source of information, and the communicative function, i.e. its significance as a means of understanding each other.

1.1 Preliminary remarks on depression

Depression as a psychological condition is predominantly characterized by a depressed mood. Nearly everybody experiences such a depressed mood, more or less intensely, and more or less frequently. For a substantial part of the population, however, a clinically significant depressive disorder has to be expected at some point during their lifetime.

According to epidemiological studies, at a given point in time about

1

4-7% of the population suffer from a depression that needs professional treatment (Dilling & Weyerer, 1978; Boyd & Weissman, 1982; Weissman, Myers, Leaf, Tischler, & Holzer, 1986). There is evidence of an increase in the rate of depression in the western countries, especially in young adults (Klerman, 1986).

Point prevalence, i.e. the proportion of individuals at the point of time of investigation diagnosed as suffering from neurotic depression is, according to, for example, Dilling & Weyerer 12.8% of the population examined in southern Germany. There is agreement across various epidemiological studies that a significantly higher proportion of women than men suffer from depression.

Psychological functions are altered along with the depressed mood, in particular retarded thinking combined with negative thoughts and psychomotor retardation. These may be additionally accompanied by other physical and mental ailments.

It is to be expected that during depression changes in affective states, in cognitive and conative functions, are accompanied by changes or characteristics of nonverbal features. Considering the changes in wellbeing as they occur in depression, an association between subjective experience and behaviour should become clearly evident.

1.2 General outline of following chapters

Chapter 2 covers theoretical aspects of the relationship between nonverbal behaviour and psychological disorders. The clinical relevance of nonverbal behaviour, the differentiation of indicative and instrumental functions of behaviour, and the concept of multi-channel expression and impression are the main points to be discussed. Chapter 3 describes relevant studies on emotional experience and social interaction in depression. The question of "mood transference" and the instrumental and indicative functions of "depressive behaviour" seem of paramount interest to us .

In chapter 4, the general procedure of our longitudinal study, the characteristics of the examined individuals and the specific parameters of the measured behaviours are described.

Chapters 5 to 7 deal with the various nonverbal behaviours investigated. Although these behaviours, such as gestures, facial expression, etc. constitute as a whole what is understood under the general term "nonverbal behaviour". They have different functions and meanings and they require different methods of analysis.

Chapter 5 deals with facial expression in depression. The general quantitative results and the facial patterns as obtained through a cluster analysis are described.

In chapter 6, gaze and speech are examined as closely coordinated modes of behaviour. Individual time series correlations are used to encapsulate the individual specific relationships between behaviour and subjective well-being. In contrast, the coordination of this behaviour points to a stable control mechanism, unaffected by depression.

Chapter 7 looks at gestures, especially speech-related gestures in connection with depression.

Chapter 8 should clarify the individual relationship between nonverbal behaviour and the depressive state via examplary case studies.

The nonverbal patterns, which emerge when combining all these characteristics, are described in chapter 9.

In conclusion, chapter 10 discusses the implications of individual specific nonverbal expression for the inference of internal states and for interpersonal communication. Special reference will be made here to idiographic and nomothetic approaches within behaviourally oriented diagnostics. The findings will also raise the question as to how we communicate with others using non-verbal signals in an individual specific way.

Since different theoretical concepts and methodological approaches are required to account for the various phenomena one should not expect to find a unified theory of nonverbal communication. Our investigation of nonverbal behaviour during the course of depression should contribute to clarification of the following problems:

what is the relationship between psychological states and behaviour, i.e. to what extent can observed nonverbal behaviour be considered a valid indicator of mood states

what are the consequences for behavioural diagnostics using clinical observation of such nonverbal information?

Above all, how do individuals convey their psychological states nonverbally to their social environment and thus communicate their affective states?

2 Relating nonverbal behaviour to psychological disorders

One cannot expect that there exists a simple relationship between nonverbal behaviour and psychological disorders. Both nonverbal behaviour and subjective experience involve complex structures and processes and it is also likely that their relationship is of a complex nature.

Up to the present, it is not clear how close the relationship between internal processes and overt behaviour has to be considered, and to what extent nonverbal behaviour can validly differentiate between psychological processes. No close or unambiguous relationship between nonverbal behaviour and depression was found in most of the empirical and experimental research.

Before discussing specific clinical aspects, a closer look at some general characteristics of nonverbal communication seems appropriate. What are the functions of the behaviour and which theoretical concepts can be taken as a framework for our questions?

2.1 Communication

"Communication" denotes a process by which information is exchanged within or between biological systems.

A characteristic of human commmunication is the reduction of uncertainty (Berger, 1979). As we become more informed about an individual's state, feelings, intentions, and attitudes our uncertainty about the person is reduced. By stimulating the social environment through social behaviours, one elicits reactions from the other thus reducing one's own uncertainty.

"Communication" includes a directed transfer of information and thus an influx of a sending to a receiving system. An *interaction* is characterized by reciprocal transfer and influence between at least two systems.

Concepts of technical communication seem to be useful when representing interpersonal communication. According to the model of bi-directional communication (Neuburger, 1970), a message is "encoded" by a sender transmitted through a "channel" and "decoded" by a receiver (see Fig. 2.1).

Errors in this communication chain may occur during encoding as well as during decoding. When a person is not able to show that he is angry or cannot refuse anything, it can be regarded as an error of encoding. An

4

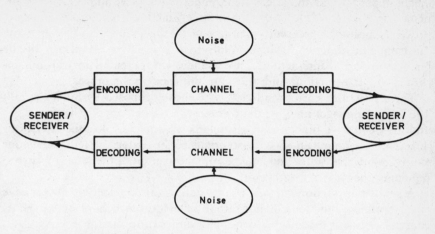

Fig. 2.1 Model of bidirectional communication

inability to interpret expressions of feelings or intentions can be seen as an error in decoding.

Notions like "sign", "signal", "code", "information" which are related to communication, will be used here in a way analogous to the terminology in technical communication (Cherry, 1957/1961; Klaus, 1969; Scherer, 1980; Ellgring, 1983). *Signs* denote the elements of a piece of *information*. In signals, this information is materially represented. Nonverbal behaviour may potentially be such a signal. As an example, the information of an emotion can be expressed in a facial behaviour which in this case would be a signal. A *code* matches signs of one set to the signs of another set. Since there rarely exists an explicit code for nonverbal behaviour, the meaning can hardly be defined unambiguously. A *message* generally denotes a piece of information directed towards another individual or a group of individuals.

Nonverbal communication
The concept of "nonverbal communication" is somewhat infelicitous since it describes both a class of behaviours (facial behaviour, gestures, voice, etc.) and their functions (transmitting information to others). A similar problem exists for the notion of "expression" or "expressive behaviour". Again, a behaviour is described, for example, facial activity together with its function, i.e. an externalizing of psychological processes into the behaviour.

Indicative and instrumental function of behaviour
Despite these ambiguities, we will maintain the concept of "nonverbal

communication" for the phenomena under study. Two important components are covered: One is the "indicative function" where psychological processes become potentially manifest in the behaviour. The other is the "instrumental function" which points to the social consequences of the behaviour during interaction. This includes the potential to transmit information via behaviour and, thus, an influence on the other.

These functions correspond closely to those proposed by Bühler (1934/1965) for language: namely, the communicative or "appellative function" and the expressive function. In a similar way, the twofold function of our means of communication is conceptualized by Ploog (1969). Behaviour expresses internal states and changes the motivation of the other by corresponding processes of impression.

A similar distinction is made by separating communicative, informative and interactive functions of nonverbal behaviour. A behaviour is seen as communicative if a sender intentionally directs information to a receiver, e.g. a gesture to show the way. An informative behaviour informs about the state of an individual without an intention to exchange information and without a reaction of the other as a necessary condition. Blushing is an example of this. Finally, a behaviour could be seen as interactive if it influences the other even though the information is not directed towards him. An example is unintentionally bumping into someone. Criteria proposed to differentiate these functions are: the presence of a common code (von Cranach & Vine, 1973); an intention to communicate (Ekman & Friesen, 1969a; Wiener, Devoe, Rubinow & Geller, 1972; Best, 1978, p 139 etc), or the presence of a goal-directed behaviour (MacKay, 1972; Scherer, 1980). None of these criteria is very satisfying. Distinctions which in principle may be possible are hard to ascertain for an actual behaviour.

Intention as a criterion for communication
Neither the "intention" of a message nor "goal-directedness" are criteria which unequivocally distinguish communicative from other behaviours. It appears not to be fruitful to equate nonverbal communication with linguistic communication which at the same time is conscious and mostly intentional. Only a narrow range of communication within a species would be covered. In addition, intentions are difficult to validate in subhuman species (Hinde, 1972, pp. 86-94). For the same reason, the criterion of goal-directed behaviour would only partly resolve the problem.

On the other hand, it seems to be of little value to encompass any kind of behaviour as communicative arguing that potentially it contains information (Watzlawick, Beavin & Jackson, 1968). Such a classification would lose any value for differentiating behavioural phenomena.

Behaviour as a directed signal

According to the ethologist, Altmann (1967, pp. 326ff) behavioural patterns are to be regarded as communicative if they influence the behaviour of other group members, i.e. if their occurrence changes the probabilities of reactions in other individuals. In a given situation a behaviour as part of a communication should transmit information and, thus, establish a relationship between a sender system and a receiver system.

Since it is impossible or at least requires great effort to specify intentions, etc. the nonverbal behaviours studied later are regarded as *potential bearers of information* in a social interaction. When investigating behaviour in this way as directed signals in social interaction, we refer to its *indicative* and *instrumental function*. Both functions play a role when asking what the relationship is between nonverbal behaviour and depression. The instrumental function points to the potential of an individual to communicate a depressive state to the environment, thus eliciting certain reactions such as increased attention. From the indicative function, on the other hand, it follows that related others or observers can infer the state from the behaviour. Both functions are simultaneously present in a behaviour proper. The momentary role of the interactants determines which functions are relevant.

2.2 Multimodal expression and impression

Characteristic for the concept of nonverbal communication is the assumption that various behavioural elements are working simultaneously in their respective channels forming a system. The different signals together constitute a message. During social interaction several modalities are simultaneously available for information transmission. We listen to somebody and see him at the same time. During talking we gesticulate and change our face. Even a blind person makes use of verbal content together with paralinguistic information. Various modalities are simultaneously activated during social communication, involving their respective effectors and receptors.

Effectors Following the general model of communication described above, modalities of expression can be described as effectors. These effectors are represented in the observable behaviour of the sender. Such effectors are facial behaviour, gaze, gestures, movements of feet or legs, body posture, physical distance to another individual, body or skin contact including haptic, temperature and moisture features and odours. Vocal nonverbal elements, loudness, intonation etc. of the voice and paralinguistic features, including pauses, are potential bearers of information as well (Duncan,

1969; Argyle, 1975; Wiener et al., 1972; see Handbooks edited by Scherer & Ekman, 1982 and Siegman & Feldstein, 1987).

Receptors and channels All sensual modalities – seeing, feeling, smelling, hearing – are to be considered as receptors of information that contribute to the impression of a receiver. Correspondingly, information is transmitted via the acoustic-audio, optic-visual, haptic, thermic, chemic-gustatonic and chemic-olfactory channels.

How these effectors, channels and receptors are to be studied is a matter of continuous scientific debate. The structural approach and the experimental quantitative approach may be regarded as two prototypes used in nonverbal communication research.

Structural and experimental-quantitative approach

Since during social interaction different modalities are involved in transmitting information simultaneously it seems obvious to analyse them within the context and with reference to each other. This has been attempted in the structural approach (e.g. Scheflen, 1966, 1973; Goffman, 1969; Kendon, 1970; Duncan & Fiske, 1977). The structure of various behavioural levels determines the meaning of single behavioural elements. The meaning is given by the context but is not accessible when one looks at the elements in isolation.

The experimental-quantitative or "external variable" approach (Duncan, 1969) recognizes the necessity of simultaneous analysis of different behaviours to understand the communicative meaning as well. However, it is aimed at systematically isolating defined external variables and their influence on the behaviour, namely operationally defined behavioural parameters (e.g. Mehrabian & Wiener, 1967; Ekman & Friesen, 1969a; Scherer, 1979a; Krause, 1981). The "Lens Model" for the perceptual phenomenon of size constancy, originally developed by Brunswik (1956) and expanded by Scherer (1978) for nonverbal communication gives a frame of reference for an experimental-quantitative approach that encompasses multimodal expression and impression processes.

On the sender's side, traits and states are expressed in a process of encoding by various distal indicators. On the receiver's side, judgement results from impression processes whereby various behavioural aspects are processed as proximal percepts. Thus, in a simplified way the state of the sender expands into a complex expression and is summarized by the receiver's impression (see Fig. 2.2, p. 9).

This model suggests a "multi-channel analysis" on both the sender's and the receiver's side since a state may be expressed in various behaviours simultaneously and the impression may combine a variety of aspects into a

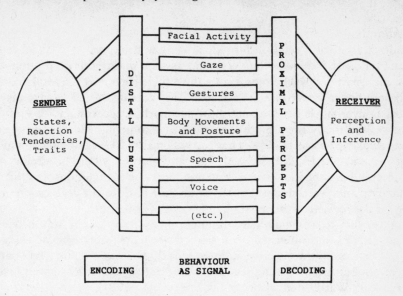

Fig. 2.2 Expression and impression in nonverbal communication

judgement. This model will be used in the following study as a frame of reference for the expression of a depressed state.

2.3 Relationship between psychological state and behaviour

The Lens Model does not explain how the relationship between a trait or state on the one hand and distal indicators on the other hand can be conceptualized. The same holds for a judgement or inference and its relationship to proximal percepts. Since it is impossible to discuss all possibilities fully, only three models directly relevant to our problem will be mentioned: a monotonous relationship model, an additive model, and a model of a "logical or-connection" of psychological state and behaviour.

Monotonous relationship model
A model of a monotonous relationship assumes that changes in the psychological state are linked to behavioural changes. As an example a more severe state of depression would result in less gaze at another person during a conversation; vice versa improvement of the state would be accompanied by more eye contact. Besides being intuitively plausible it is an open empirical question in which way such a model might be usable for nonverbal behaviour in depression.

Additive model

Another form of a relationship which does not necessarily contradict the monotonous relationship model would assume that the more pronounced the change of the psychological state the more elements of the total nonverbal behavioural repertoire are affected. The more depressed a person is the more nonverbal elements would show peculiarities according to this model. This would imply for a mild depression that some nonverbal components like facial expression could be changed, whereas in a severe depression more components like facial behaviour, gaze and gestures would be altered.

It would also be in accordance with a monotonous relationship model if all behaviours were changed at the same time to different degrees, depending on the severity of depression.

According to a widely held argument in psychology, the sum of single items defines the intensity of a general attribute. Concepts of classical questionaires follow such an additive model. The more items (with partly divergent contents) of a depression inventory (e.g. Beck Depression Inventory, Beck, Ward, Mendelson, Mock & Erbaugh, 1961) are answered in the direction of depression the more the person would be described as depressed. The sum or the weighted sum of the items indicates the degree of depression. For nonverbal behaviour, such a weighted sum of single behavioural elements has been proposed, for example, by Mehrabian (1969, 1972) to indicate a social status.

Again, it is an empirical question if this model adequately describes the degree of nonverbal changes depending on the severity of depression.

Model of "Logical or-connection"

As an alternative, the relationship between a psychological state and nonverbal behaviour may be described by a model of "logical or-connections" (more precisely: and/or-connections). According to this model a person may express a depressed mood in the face *or* in the gaze *or* may have a reduced speech rate. These nonverbal elements can express the state each on their own or in combination without the necessity of a hierarchical structure to exist. In contrast, a *hierarchical model* would assume that one behaviour dominates the other depending on the sensitivity to changes in inner states. Assuming a hierarchical model a depressed state would, for example, firstly be seen in the face, then in gestures and other behaviour. A hierarchical model would resemble in some respect an additive model described above. In contrast, a model of "logical or-connections" would allow behavioural components to vary independently of each other together with a psychological state. These considerations will be taken up in the discussion of the longitudinal study presented later.

Display rules and control of behaviour

The voluntary control of behaviour is to be seen as a major factor modifying the relationship between behaviour and psychological states. Thus, nonverbal behaviour may be regarded as an immediate expression of psychological processes and a controlled conscious display toward the other (Leyhausen, 1967; Ekman & Friesen, 1969a, Krause, 1981, pp. 22ff). A person smiles toward the other instead of letting the anger become apparent or tries to hide the bad mood in the presence of a superior yet allows this mood to come through at home.

Nonverbal behaviour conforms to social norms and rules (Wundt, 1905 p. 285; Ekman & Friesen, 1974), which determine when and how an emotion may be displayed. Depending on these rules, emotional displays according to Ekman & Friesen (1974), may be intensified, diminished, neutralized or masked by other emotions. The control of behaviour is part of learned social strategies which serve to build up our self-presentation to the outside world (cf. Goffman, 1959). An observation made by Kraepelin (1896) about the behavioural control of depressed patients shows the importance of this mechanism for our problem.

In his conduct the patient is orderly most of the time, is able to control himself when being with friends, is able to hold conversations and can be distracted for a short while by external stimulation... (p. 648, translated by H.E.)

Thus, the control of behaviour has to be taken into account when interpreting changes during depression.

Loss of redundancy

By control of behaviour the individual tries to resolve a conflict which emerges from antagonistic tendencies to give immediate expression, of its state on the one hand and behaving according to internalized social norms on the other. In emotional unaffected situations various nonverbal elements combined with verbal behaviour provide homogeneous and redundant information. A loss of redundancy characterizes a conflict situation (Krause, 1984). In this way, anger might be concealed in the verbal behaviour, and manifests itself, however, in parts of the nonverbal behaviour. This loss of redundancy can also be seen in a simultaneous expression of a conflicting motivational state. An example of this is a dog's expression displaying simultaneous fight and flight tendencies as described by Lorenz (1963). It is an open question whether the experience of conflicts during depression is expressed in complex behavioural patterns.

Even if one takes into account that display rules govern at least in part the behaviour during depression, one should expect a clear expression when the depressed mood becomes very intensive. There will not be enough energy left for the control of behaviour. Under these circumstances, the mood becomes the major influence on behaviour. As Wundt (1905) put it: "The influence of the will, however, generally fades when the emotion increases to high degrees. Also [cultural man] mostly succeeds in only veiling the inner state, rarely in totally hiding it." (p. 285, translated by H.E.).

On the whole, however, both factors have to be taken into account as one cannot simply expect a "pure" expression of mood. Control of one's own behaviour, display rules on the one hand, and the psychological experience on the other can counteract at a given moment.

2.4 Disorders in communication

Disorders in communication have to be studied along with the psychological problems during depression. Before describing these disorders of communication the concept of disorder as it is used here should be explained.

According to the general model of communication disorders in this domain refer to the processes of encoding, transmitting of information, and decoding. Given our problem, we will mainly analyse disorders of encoding from the position of the sender and on an individual level.

Disorders in communication can be described on various levels. A sender-receiver unit could be the unit of analysis. Here, one would assess a lack of correspondence between information sent and received. This, however, is only possible if the nature of the message itself as well as the way in which it is perceived, processed, and interpreted is known. The error in communication may then be deduced when comparing the sent with the received message.

Before analysing on a dyadic level it seems advantageous, from a clinical point of view, to explore individual determinants of the behaviour first in order to understand the operation of a disturbed interaction. Table 2.1 lists some aspects of disorders in communication as they appear relevant.

Social skills take a special place since a lack of social skills may be due to deficits in encoding and decoding of social signals (cf. Argyle, 1979). Various training procedures have been proposed to improve these skills for depressed individuals and others (Lewinsohn, 1974; Trower, Bryant, & Argyle, 1978). Our study of nonverbal behaviour should also contribute to some basic knowledge about social skills. The concept of "disorders" as it is used here applies to social skills as well as to other aspects of communication. Therefore it will be discussed with reference to the above mentioned general model of communication.

Disturbances of encoding
A changed or mutated usage of signals by the sender is the most striking

Table 2.1: *Disorders in nonverbal communication*

Signal usage	Sender (encoding)	Receiver (decoding)
Change of signal properties	Unusual or random usage of signals	Faulty inference
	Dissociation of otherwise coordinated behaviour	
Reduction (or increase)	Reduction of repertoire, amount or intensity of behaviour	Reduced capacity for processing nonverbal information (e.g., fewer signals are recognised because of constricted perception)
Retardation (or acceleration)	Reduced frequency of behaviour	Slowed processing (e.g. because of *slowed* perception and processing longlasting signals are perceived only)
	Elongated behavioural states	
Social Skills	Lack of nonverbal motor skills	Lack of differentation in perceiving social signals
	"too much" or "too little" behaviour	
	Inhibition of adequate behaviour, e.g. because of anxiety	Lack of sensitivity

characteristic for the receiver. This can be an unusual or a random usage of signals which then become incomprehensible. Or signals are displayed discrepant to the emotional state. An example would be a friendly expression, independent of the actual emotional state, be it angry, disgusted or whatever. Sudden changes in expressive behaviours without any obvious reason are another example where the signals become incomprehensible for the receiver because of an unusual usage by the sender. The sequential flow of a behavioural programme and of the corresponding affects may also be altered (Krause, 1984). Such a collapse of otherwise coordinated behaviours has been described by Ploog (1972) as a characteristic symptom of psychotic behaviour. Or a facial expression appears to be much stronger than would be adequate for the affect strength assumed to be present. Nonverbal signals in these cases are used in an unusual way.

For another person it is difficult or impossible to rely on these signals since the relationship between the signal and the transmitted information is unknown to him. It will be difficult to understand the behaviour if the signals are used in an unusual or random way. Behaviour, in this case, does not contribute to reducing uncertainty in the other.

Reduction and retardation

Using signals too frequently, rarely, slowly or too fast is another form of disturbed encoding in communication. However, only vague and implicit norms exist in everday life for a reduction or retardation of signals.

Reduction A reduction may refer to the variety of a behavioural repertoire as well as to the amount of behaviour displayed. During a psychosis, a reduction becomes apparent when comparatively rigid behavioural patterns are exhibited. Thus, motor stereotypes can be observed in the movements during psychosis (Ploog, 1958). A reduction is also present when little socially active behaviour is displayed during depression.

Retardation (or acceleration) in the production of behavioural signals is another dimension characterizing behavioural disorders. Retardation may be present, e.g. in slow gestural movements or prolonged phases of gazing at the other.

Criteria for reduction and retardation will be specified when dealing with the various behaviours analysed later. The following analyses will concentrate on the encoding and less on the decoding of signals.

2.5 Clinical aspects of nonverbal behaviour

In mental illness, nonverbal behaviour is relevant for several reasons:

> During social interaction it plays a central role in the mutual understanding between patients and others. Thus, disorders in communication also manifest themselves in nonverbal behaviour.
>
> Perceptible behaviour other than language plays an important, however frequently unreflected role, in clinical judgements and in clinical decisions.
>
> Nonverbal behaviour may be used as a criterion for diagnostic purposes or for the evaluation of therapies if reliable assessment is ensured.

Most of the studies on nonverbal behaviour during psychopathological states are aimed at finding valid behavioural indicators for altered psychological states (Ekman & Friesen, 1974; Jones & Pansa, 1979; Ulrich, Harms & Fleischhauer, 1976; Scherer, 1981; Pansa-Henderson, de l'Horne & Jones, 1982). Abnormal nonverbal behaviours can also be regarded as part of a mental illness itself (Ploog, 1964, 1972; Hill, 1974; Ruesch, 1980).

Behavioural diagnostic

Nonverbal behaviour is seen in psychiatry as an important source of information for clinical inference. Any description of psychopathological states includes notions of expressive behaviour (Kraepelin, 1896; Weitbrecht, 1968, p. 57; Bleuler, 1969, p. 63; Arieti, 1974, p. 456; Davison & Neale, 1986, pp. 193-226). Despite its clinical importance rating scales (cf. CIPS, 1981) or formalized systems like DSM III (American Psychiatric Association, 1980) only make minor use of nonverbal information. Probably this kind of information is implicitly included in clinical judgement, namely when emotional or affective phenomena are rated.

Psychology, especially experimental psychology generally has a rather sceptical attitude towards the validity of clinical judgements (Meehl, 1954; Sader, 1961; Wiggins, 1973, p. 182; Petrinovich, 1979; Szucko & Kleinmutz, 1981). Yet in practice the dispassionate remark of Hofstätter (1957) still holds:

Even a critical psychologist would be unlikely to believe in the result of an otherwise well examined test if this contradicts the immediate impression he gets from the client. (p. 39, translation H.E.)

By analysing nonverbal behaviour during the course of depression, the behavioural basis of clinical impressions can be empirically validated. The question of our study is: How can quantitatively assessed nonverbal behaviour contribute to behavioural inference and diagnostics?

Behaviour as indicator of a state
In order to assess the validity of nonverbal behaviours as indicators the association of behavioural changes with changes in the depressed state have to be determined. Behavioural parameters will not be used here to predict personality traits. In this case one would ask if there are differences between depressives and normals independent from the current state. In contrast depression is seen here not as a trait but as a dynamic state (cf. International Classification of Diseases, ICD-9, World Health Organization, 1978, and DSM III) which may change dramatically within a few days, weeks or months. As a consequence it appears necessary to study the behaviour over a time course and to intra-individually compare it given different psychological states of the individual. Thus, an important criterion for the validity of a behavioural indicator is its change over time corresponding with the change of the psychological condition.

2.6 Mood

A depressed mood signifies a form of an emotional state which lasts for a certain time – hours, days or weeks; it may even change during one day. Thus, a depressed state is neither a short affect nor a lasting personality trait but rather an affective basis which lasts a certain period of time. On this affective basis shorter emotional or affective events may occur.

Emotions and mood

Various authors regard emotions as an enduring, subliminal, active psychological process (cf. Tomkins, 1962, 1963, 1982; Izard, 1977; Scherer, 1984). These processes may become conscious and behaviourally operative when they are sufficiently strong. In general, theories on affect and emotion do not refer specifically to moods like depression (cf. Zajonc, 1984; Lazarus, 1984). It seems plausible to assume that mood levels remain over a period of time. Yet their duration and intensity differ. Sometimes mood resembles short-term affects or emotions. Wessman (1979) defines mood:

…as shifting yet pervasive emotional feeling states of varying duration – usually not as intense nor as clearly related to a specific provoking object or situation as is the case with a fully developed emotion. (p. 74).

Very little empirical material can be found to shed light on the relationship between mood, emotion and affects. Classical psychological literature regards mood as a general state of an individual which is not associated with a specific experience elicited by specific stimuli as for the emotions (Rubinstein, 1959, pp. 615-16). Emotion, on the other hand, is seen as a psychological reaction to outer or inner stimuli and their evaluation. Affects are seen as emotions of greater intensity (Rohracher, 1963, pp. 400-49).

Yet another distinction refers to the Latin roots of the words "emotion" and "affect". According to this, an emotion is a motivational state which activates movement energy. In contrast, affect refers to conditions of being touched or "affected". In our case, the important variable is the mood state of depression. Short-term affects or emotions may occur on this basis.

Mood as a behavioural readiness

Ethology regards "mood" as a preparedness for behaviour or action, i.e. a motivational state. An individual is, for example, in a sexual mood or sexually motivated. Mood is thus seen as a motivating factor. Given a high behavioural readiness or motivation, even weak stimuli may release an action. The transference of mood states between individuals is an important function of social communication (Eibl-Eibesfeldt, 1978, p. 457). By expressing one's own mood state it is transferred to the other. This expression in turn changes the mood state of the other. While the psychological concept of mood stresses the subjective experience, the ethological concept emphasizes the potential influence on the behaviour of oneself and of others. Therefore, both concepts give necessary clues to our problem.

From the discussion above we infer that depression is characterized by a relatively enduring, intense depressed mood which by far exceeds normal strength. Given this depressed mood as a general affective-emotional state or base level, specific and discrete emotions may develop in addition. These emotions should also become noticeable in the behaviour during social interaction.

Depression is also seen as a mood in an ethological sense: Regarding its activating influence on nonverbal behaviour it may stimulate the occurrence of specific behavioural patterns. These can be perceived as the expression of a depressed mood by others.

2.7 Summary and Consequences

Underlying our study is an "expression" hypothesis: A psychological state – mood, emotion, or affect – potentially activates behaviour, which thus expresses the actual state. Changes of psychological states are associated with changes in nonverbal behaviour. Within this frame nonverbal behaviour has various functions:

Expression of psychological processes and states
Source of information which can be perceived by others
Medium of interpersonal communication.

As an expression, changes in the psychological state manifest themselves in the behaviour. Changes in the state are communicated by the behaviour as a signal to the social environment, thus enabling a mutual understanding.

Nonverbal behaviour as it is analysed below is regarded as a potential signal during an interaction. The question is what kind of relationship can be assumed between a depressed state and these behaviours. As discussed above, various models may be appropriate to describe such a relationship, like a simple additive model or a "logical or-connection". A "logical or-connection" would imply that one *or* the other part of a behavioural repertoire rather than a sum of changed elements indicates the depressed state.

From a clinical point of view, disorders in communication are of special interest. During depression, retardation and reduction in the behaviour of the sender would be expected at first. When concentrating on these aspects of communication, we select a few components of an interaction omitting other important parts. This might well be criticized as a reductionist approach leaving the essentials of communication aside. The reason for our approach is, however, that we might be able after all to differentiate the concept of disorder in communication, to operationalize some of the constituting components, and to better understand how nonverbal signals are used.

3　Social interaction and affective states of depression

Numerous clinical descriptions of "depressive" behaviour, systematic observations, and judgement studies show that there are consistent changes in nonverbal behaviour during the state of depression. Before dealing in detail with the various modes of behaviour some general aspects of emotions and interaction related to depression will be summarized. Psychological theories describing emotions during depression are also of interest.

3.1 Symptoms of depression influencing behaviour

Since the symptoms of depression are thoroughly described in all psychiatric and psychological text books (cf. DSM III American Psychiatric Association, 1980; Davison & Neale, 1986, pp. 193-226) only those aspects that have an influence on nonverbal behaviour will be mentioned.

The basic symptoms are characterized by Bleuler (1969) as the "depressive triad" with (a) depressed mood, (b) inhibition of thought processes and (c) inhibition of centrifugal functions.

(a)　The dysphoric depressive state: The patient is sad, depressed and dysphoric; he feels anxious, with an inner restlessness, and at times an empty indifference and callousness. This emotional part of depression will be more fully described later. Mimic and maintenance of eye contact are the nonverbal aspects that are relevant for this part of the disorder.

(b)　Inhibition of thought processes: Thinking is slowed down, laborious and often fixated on one basic pessimistic idea. This inhibition of thought manifests itself in language and should be recognizable in a slow manner of speech.

(c)　Inhibition of centrifugal functions: Drives and desires are inhibited. The patient is indecisive, passive. His voice is soft and monotonous. The muscle tone is reduced and movements are slowed down and vigorless. The body posture appears uniform, limp, bent with the tendency to tighten the limbs. In some cases, particularly during states of anxiety there is, instead of motor inhibition, an urge to physically work out the inner unrest. Gestures are probably the central indicator of this inhibition.

18

All three basic symptoms are indicated in altered means of nonverbal behaviour implying a reduction of the individual's potential.

Endogenous and neurotic depression

It is acknowledged by all schools of psychiatry and clinical psychology (Kendell, 1976; DSM III, 1980; Davison & Neale, 1986) that depression occurs in individuals with different degrees of severity. There is, however, controversial discussion whether it is necessary to differentiate between various forms of depressive disorder.

In a one dimensional concept endogenous depression (which mostly corresponds to psychotic depression) is a more severe form of neurotic depression. This theoretically implies a greater change of nonverbal behaviour in endogenous depression. Ekman & Friesen (1974) presume that psychotic depressive patients display the culturally expected social smile less frequently than neurotic depressive patients. They are suspected to adhere less stringently to the social rules of "normal" nonverbal behaviour. If, however, other forms of conflict are involved, then one would expect qualitative differences in the nonverbal behaviour of neurotic and psychotic depressed patients.

It cannot be determined whether it is useful to distinguish between neurotic, psychotic or endogenous depression. This distinction should, however, not be discarded, as long as there exists no contradictory empirical evidence with regard to nonverbal behaviour.

3.2 Emotions as part of psychological theories of depression

Affective states of depression as defined in diagnostical systems like the Impatient Multidimensional Psychiatric Scale (IMPS) (Lorr, McNair, Klett & Lasky, 1962) appear to be highly specific compared to those of other clinical groups. They are characterized as sad and depressed (82%-86% of 125 depressed patients studied by Mombour, 1974) without hope, desperate (63% or 58%) and anxious (57% or 73%). Figures refer to IMPS resp. the documentation system AMDP (Angst et al., 1986).

However, the various currently most influential theoretical approaches – cognitive, behavioural and psychoanalytical theories (see Hautzinger, 1979; Davison & Neale, 1986, pp. 198-210) contain quite different views on emotions and their expression.

Cognitive theory (Beck, 1974) states that the depressive mood is a consequence of a cognitive disorder. This disorder is characterized by a negative image of oneself, the world, and the future. This theory gives no decisive and differential statements about emotional processes and their transmission.

Behavioural theories (Ferster, 1973; Blöschl, 1978; Lewinsohn, 1974) also regard the negative evaluation of external events and of one's own behaviour as central in depression.

The loss of reinforcement value is a central concept here. At the same time, the communication of affects has an important part in developing and maintaining depression. The deficits in social skills include, according to Libet and Lewinsohn (1973), Hinchliffe, Vaughan, Hooper & Roberts (1977), Blöschl (1978) that "positive" social behaviour is rarely exhibited (Vanger, 1984). Therefore, little positive reinforcement is elicited from others.

According to behavioural theory the expression of the depressed state elicits differentiated reactions from others. Initially, attention and positive consequences occur. Rejection, frustration, negative emotions and negative consequences follow. These reactions maintain a vicious circle of withdrawal and passivity in the depressed individual (Klerman, 1974, p. 135, etc.; Costello, 1977).

Psychoanalytic theory regards "inward directed hostility" and emotions of fear, anxiety and anger as the central psychodynamic factors for depression.

According to Karl Abraham (1912, 1968) the basic dynamic of depression is hostility associated with the loss of a loved object. Most psychoanalysts regard aggression and hostility as central to depression (see contributions in Gaylin, 1968). Rado (1928) recognized depression as a "cry for love". Its function is to re-establish an emotional security which has been threatened by an actual or imagined loss. The depressed individual feels responsible for the loss and feels guilty. The result of this complex psychodynamic process is a conflict between fear, enhanced guilt and compulsive anger (Rado, 1928). The predominance of fear would characterize a retarded depression whereas the predominance of anger would be prominent in agitated depression.

Izard (1972, p. 195, etc.) factor analysed a questionnaire administered to depressed patients. He found a factor which was interpreted as inward directed hostility. Gershon, Cramer & Klerman 1968, in an investigation of six female depressed patients found a correlation of $r = 0.45$ between inward directed hostility and the extent of depression. Suicide is also regarded by the psychoanalytic view as an extreme form of autoaggression and as evidence for inward directed hostility.

Research on this concept cannot be considered conclusive. Above all it appears that this construct can only be partially tapped by questionnaires and other surveys. It is important to note from the psychoanalytic approach that it postulates a psychodynamic differentiation of emotional states in depression. The two dominating emotions are anger and anxiety. It is of interest to us whether these emotions can be observed in nonverbal behaviour, particularly in facial expression.

Expression of subjective experience

Both the behavioural and the psychoanalytic approaches emphasize the "expression of subjective experience" in depression. From a behavioural point of view at least two consequences for non-verbal behaviour can be deduced: (1) The loss of experienced reinforcers should lead to a reduction in active social behaviour, also including nonverbal behaviour. (2) This reduction should become apparent during social interactions in facial expression and other nonverbal behaviour. Yet another consequence can be deduced from the assumption that behaviour, including nonverbal components, has an instrumental function even during depression (request for attention and positive responses from others). It can be concluded from the specific reactions of others that depressed mood is behaviourally expressed in a clearly recognizable way.

3.3 Clinical descriptions of nonverbal behaviour during depression

The psychiatric literature describes nonverbal behaviour during depression in accordance with the triad of psychological symptoms mentioned previously. Facial expression and posture show the depressed mood. Language and speech point to the inhibition of thought processes. The manner, the movement and gestures indicate the psychomotor retardation.

In Doctor Diamond's "portraits of the insane" (about 1860; Burrows & Schumacher, 1979, see Fig. 3.1) melancholia is depicted with remarkable expression in the face, the head posture and direction of gaze. (In the older literature melancholia refers to the sad state of depression as well as to the depressive part of a manic depressive cycle.) Mayer-Gross, Slater & Roth (1969) describe the behaviour of the depressed patient in the British Handbook of Psychiatry as follows:

"Sad people tend to be more silent than their wont" (p. 194). From the general appearance alone the beginning of depression is not difficult to recognize. The patient looks tired and self-concerned. Often the sadness of mood is reflected as much in posture and movement as in facial expression. With the appearance of retardation the normal wealth and freedom of expression and gesture diminish. An expression of indifference may disguise the real mood. An "omega figure" between the eyebrows and Veraguth's Fold of the upper lids have been considered characteristic" (p. 207).

The diagnostic and statistical manual of mental disorders (DSM III, American Psychiatric Association, 1980, pp. 210-24), stresses the symptoms of psychomotor retardation or agitation and the withdrawal from friends. Psychomotor retardation is defined as slowed speech and body movements, long hesitation before answering, reduction in the quantity of speech and

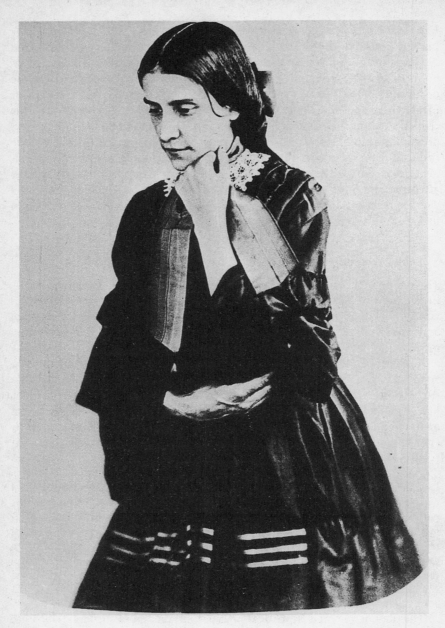

Fig. 3.1 Melancholia (from Dr Diamonds's pictures of the insane [*c.* 1855]).

impoverished language or silence. A general depressed appearance is also typical.

It seems worth noting that DSM III only mentions explicitly speech and voice as nonverbal criteria. Facial expression, gestures and gaze are totally omitted. This is even more astonishing when considering that clinical descriptions emphasize nonverbal indicators. Most probably these indicators play an implicit role in clinical diagnosis.

3.4 Rating and systematic observation of nonverbal behaviour

Despite numerous and extensive concurrent descriptions of the clinical picture of depression, empirical and quantitative data about nonverbal behaviour are rare. Various reasons could account for that.

Since clinical rating scales and self-rating scales were introduced, nonverbal behaviour has received less attention (Hill, 1974). In addition, nonverbal changes may be more subtle and therefore more difficult to describe and to rate than verbalizations and statements.

Rating of wellbeing probably makes implicit use of behavioural cues. It is difficult to determine, however, to what extent facial expression or other nonverbal behaviour contribute to clinical judgements.

In any case, nonverbal aspects currently fall behind the verbal information as being explicitly recognized diagnostic and prognostic indicators.

On the other hand, numerous studies have shown that the relationship between nonverbal behaviour and state of depression can be systematically observed and assessed (Williams, Barlow, Agras & Jackson, 1972; Waxer, 1974, 1976; Ulrich, Harms & Fleischhauer, 1976; Renfordt, Busch, Fähndrich & Müller-Örlinghausen, 1976).

Williams et al. (1972) obtained data on social and other aspects of behaviour of depressed patients through observations and records of nurses. It was found that social behaviour still changed substantially while self-rating in the Beck-Depression-Inventory and interviewer-rating on the Hamilton scale had already suggested a stable state.

In order to determine whether depressive conditions can be rated on the basis of nonverbal behaviour alone Waxer (1974, 1976) presented videotaped sections of standardized interviews. Untrained observers were able to identify depressed individuals and also the extent of their depression using nonverbal information only.

Renfordt & Busch (1976) and Renfordt et al. (1976) presented video clips without sound from interviews with depressed patients in a "time blind" sequence. Using the video information alone, raters were able to identify beginning, middle and end of a therapy far above chance.

Although the depressed state can be judged from visible behaviour, depressed patients in an experimental situation seem to display less clear

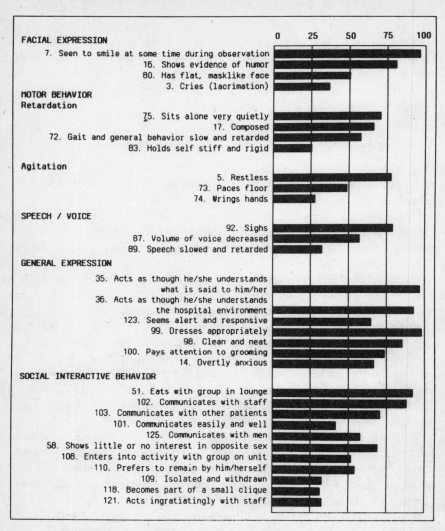

Fig. 3.2 Nonverbal and social interactive behaviour of depressed patients. (Adapted from Grinker et al., 1961). Percentages of patients (n=96) showing behaviour. Selected items according to a percentage ⩾ 25%.

nonverbal information than controls. Prkachin, Craig, Papageorgis & Reith (1977) found that depressed patients performed like normals when judging nonverbal signals but for others their behaviour in the same situation was more difficult to interpret. The behaviour of depressed patients gave little information as to whether they expected a positive, neutral or negative stimulus.

A similar result has been reported by Miller, Ranelli & Levine (1977) who in addition found that some of the patients could be judged more clearly later in therapy while for others the reverse was true. Unfortunately, no information on subjective wellbeing was given and no data of control groups were reported here.

One can only speculate as to what impedes judging depressed patients in these experiments. They might have displayed a reduced variety or intensity of nonverbal signals but also an ambiguous, i.e. random relationship between experienced state and behaviour. To further explain these results on indirect ratings, more information on the actual behaviour of patients is needed.

From detailed observations of 96 depressed patients, reported by Grinker, Miller, Gabshin, Nunn & Nunnally (1961) some indication of frequent and infrequent nonverbal behaviour can be obtained (see Fig. 3.2). Figure 3.2 summarizes those of the 139 items of their "current behaviour check list" which refer to nonverbal and interactional aspects and which, in addition, have been observed to occur in at least 25% of the patients.

As can be seen from this table, a substantial proportion of behaviours presumably characteristic for depression were recognized for only less than half of the patients (e.g. "cries" or "speech slow and retarded"). Other behaviours, generally considered as "normal" occur with a frequency of more than 75% (e.g. "shows evidence of humor", and especially items labelled here as "general expression" and "social interactive behaviour".)

In their study of body movements during interviews from depressed patients, Fisch, Frey & Hirsbrunner (1983) found significant differences during antidepressant treatment: "Upon recovery, patients spent more time in motion, displayed a more complex pattern of movement, and initiated and terminated movement activity more rapidly than when they were depressed" (p. 316). There were significant correlations with the doctors' rating of depression. However, the authors stress the fact of considerable individual differences of behaviour. Some patients were in motion for 50% of the time during their depressed state whereas others spent only 25% of time in motion during their recovered state.

Obviously, changes of specific behaviours are apparent for part of the depressed individuals only and thus could hardly be considered as general indicators. On the other hand, "normal" behaviours, especially social interactive ones point out that patients exhibit a social "responsiveness" that can be recognized by others.

It follows from the decoding studies that depression can be validly inferred from the visible behaviour. This corresponds to clinical impression although it seems as if the picture is less clear from systematic studies. It appears contradictory at first sight that it is more difficult to infer from the behaviour of depressives in what kind of (experimental) situation they are currently in. From their behaviour it cannot be inferred what kind of stimulus, positive or negative, they received at a given moment. This contradiction is resolved if one considers a general reduction in their nonverbal behaviour. This means a constant low amount of behaviour during depression, unaffected by external stimuli. This in turn makes it difficult for an observer to differentiate between reactions. Nevertheless, this low amount of behaviour would be in accordance with the depressed state.

Systematic behavioural observations are needed to specify the kind of reduction in nonverbal behaviour. The figures given by Grinker et al. (1961) point out that despite various deficiencies there remains a great deal of social responsivity in these patients.

3.5 Social interaction and transference of mood

Social environments recognize the symptoms of depression and react to them. Social interactive behaviour of depressed individuals is frequently seen as an attempt to communicate one's state and needs. Psychoanalysis as well as behavioural theory assume an instrumental function of behaviour during depression. The "cry for help" that is expressed according to psychoanalytical views (Rado, 1928; Arieti, 1974, p. 451) corresponds to the appellative, hostile and deprivation components seen from a behavioural standpoint (Linden, 1976). The patient appeals by displaying his helplessness; he shows hostility by demanding and accusing behaviours. With deprivation behaviour, apathy, slowed reactions and expression of dullness he refuses to give the normal reinforcement to others during interaction.

According to Forrest & Hokanson (1975) the instrumental function of depressive behaviour is to induce sympathy and attention and to reduce social withdrawal. Systematic studies in this area mainly deal with lack of social skills, reactions of others and the family climate. They will be discussed briefly in the following.

Social skills and interaction

Depressives generally have less contact outside the family, but more contacts inside the family (Blöschl, 1976). This could be due to lack of social skills (Blöschl, 1978; Lewinsohn, 1974; Lewinsohn, Youngren, & Grosscup, 1979). They exhibit less general and specifically social activities, such that e.g. the rate of interpersonal activities in a group is half the rate of controls (Libet & Lewinsohn, 1973). From a social skills perspective, depressives elicit very little social reinforcement which indirectly leads to depression (Vanger, 1984).

Especially for the nonverbal part, behaviour as an expression could also be the consequence or merely a concomitant of depression. In this case, behavioural peculiarities would not be caused by a lack of social skills but rather be induced by reduced availability of a repertoire or a reduced proneness to use it in a given psychological state. Behaviours would then change together with the state.

Interaction of depressed individuals with their partner or within the family appears to be characterized by specific patterns of communication. These are considered as partial causes for depression or as risk factors for relapse (Weissman & Paykel, 1974). The extent of "expressed emotions", which denotes an excessive critique of relatives about the patient, has been shown to predict the relapse of depressed as well as schizophrenic patients (Brown, Birley & Wing, 1972; Vaughan & Leff, 1976; Leff & Vaughan, 1985). "Incongruent" nonverbal behaviours during interaction of depressed patients and their relatives have been reported by Hinchliffe, Hooper, Roberts & Vaughan (1975). Compared to controls, couples with one depressed partner gave a high amount of negative affective evaluations during interaction (Hinchliffe, Hooper & Roberts, 1978).

Generally reaction of long-term partners (i.e., mostly relatives) are described as rejecting and hostile. In a study of Dutka, Hartmann-Zeilberger, Linden & Hoffman (1978) short-term partners tended to avoid qualitative negative evaluations and to express own needs. In contrast, long term partners tended to express negative feelings, put frequent demands and evaluated the patients negatively.

According to Coyne (1976a and b) a lack of reciprocity leads others to avoid communication with depressed individuals. When getting to know others depressed individuals tended not to reciprocally self-disclose on personal problems.

There is some evidence that family interaction might influence the probability of relapse in depressed patients. Yet it is unclear as to how cause and effect can be seen. Is it the lack of social skills or the low amount of social active behaviour that induces hostile reactions from long term partners, thus leading into a vicious circle? Or is the depressed behaviour "adaptive" by temporarily protecting the individual from social overstimulation or overcharge?

Transference of mood in depression

If behaviour during depression has an instrumental or adaptive function it should influence feelings, attitudes and behaviours of others. In the previous section, behaviour of partners was analysed as a potentially harmful agent. Assuming an adaptive function the patient's behaviour is to be examined as to what kind of reaction it elicits in others. Is there a transference of mood?

When subjects (students in an experimental situation) are asked to get to know others by telephone they react to depressed patients (or faked depression) in a specific way. According to Coyne (1976a), subjects felt more anxious and hostile after having spoken with depressed individuals. Contrary to their subjective indication, no behavioural differences, such as frequency of agreeing responses were observed. Subjects were less likely to want to get to know the depressed person than subjects talking with a non-depressed person. Activity level in depressed individuals was not lower than in normal individuals. From this, a reduced activity could, according to Coyne (1976a) be caused by a withdrawal of the partner rather than an expression of lacking social skills.

In a similar way, using standardized answers in a telephone conversation, Hammen & Peters (1978) found that subjects speaking with a presumably depressed person regarded themselves as more depressed and rejecting than those interacting with a normal person. In addition, subjects tended to react more negatively to "depressed" males than to females. The last finding, however, could not be replicated by Howes & Hokanson (1979), who observed students' reactions to a confederate other (depressed or non-depressed) when waiting for an experiment. Behaviour during interaction with a "depressed" confederate had a higher proportion of pauses, direct negative comments, and lower rate of verbalization. The "depressed" confederate was rejected more and described in more negative terms. Here, no difference with regard to induced mood could be found.

The quality of the faked "depression" is obviously a central point in these experiments in addition to the duration of actual interaction and whether the interactants knew each other. These variables must account for some of the discrepant results from these studies.

The question whether the influence on the behaviour of others depends on the state of depression, i.e. changes over time, has been studied by Pattay (1982), Regler (1982) and Avarello (1983) in their unpublished diploma and doctoral theses. They used video material of the longitudinal study described later analysing behaviours of interviewers or therapists interacting with the same patients during depression and recovery. The question was, whether observers could determine from the visible and audible behaviour of the interviewer that he was interacting with the same patient in a depressed or a recovered state. In the study of Avarello (1983) raters had to compare pairs of silent video clips of about 20 seconds duration. The video showed the interviewer's head and shoulders only (see chapter 4). The task was to decide which of the video clips showed the interviewer interacting with the patient in a better state. Of each patient-interviewer dyad video clips were taken from relatively bad, middle and good states of wellbeing. Paired comparisons revealed a significant point-fourfold correlation of $r = 0.77$ ($p<0.05$) between rated visible behaviour of the *interviewer* and selfrated subjective wellbeing of the *patient*. Raters generally could not tell which behaviour their judgement was based on. They could, however, significantly differentiate "better" or "worse" by immediately comparing the video clips of the same interviewer.

In a similar way, Pattay (1982) had subjects decide from two audio-taped standard questions given within the interview whether they were given to the patient in a better or worse state. Again raters were able indirectly to infer the patient's state from the acoustic behaviour of the interviewer. 9 out of 10 voice experts and 13 out of 15 lay judges were correct in more than half of the 16 paired comparisons (Fischer Exact Tests, $p < 0.05$).

In both studies, behaviour of the interviewer turned out to be dependent on the state of the patient. Very short segments of behaviour (about 20 seconds or two standard questions) seemed to be sufficient to make valid indirect judgements on the patient's behaviour. There were, however, marked individual differences in the recognizability of these behavioural differences.

The "back channel" behaviour of interviewers during various states of the patient's wellbeing was found by Regler (1982) to be dependent on the patient's state as well. In general, interviewers double their back channel behaviour (nodding, "mm" etc.) during improvement in the patient. From Mdn (f) = 4 back channel behaviours per minute in the depressed state over Mdn (f) = 9/min during a medium state of wellbeing to Mdn (f) = 7/min during relatively best state of wellbeing. From a behavioural point of view these results deserve special consideration: "Nonverbal reinforcers" of the interviewer tend to increase during improvement and there is obviously less opportunity for the interviewers to display back channel behaviour during the depressed state.

Generally these studies give evidence that the state of the patient also influences nonverbal behaviours of others and that a transference of mood takes places. This points to the social operation of the behaviour during depression. The depressed state becomes apparent in the behaviour and leads to specific reactions by others which include positive and negative emotional reactions.

With regard to the expression and communication of depression the question arises which emotions or affects of patients are involved and how the depressed state becomes apparent in specific behaviours.

3.6 Specific questions and hypotheses

Given the observations and theories mentioned before the general question regarding the relationship betwen nonverbal behaviour and depression has to be specified:

Is there a reduction or retardation of nonverbal behaviour to be observed during depression and does this change over time?

Do various aspects of nonverbal behaviour change together or independently?

Are there indications of different negative affects to be found in the nonverbal behaviour?

Nonverbal behaviours will be analysed according to two hypotheses:

The *reduction-hypothesis* assumes that (a) the amount, (b) the variety and (c) the coordination of communicative behaviour is reduced.

The *retardation-hypothesis* refers to the amount, variety and coordination as well, in that these aspects could occur in a slowed down manner.

It is expected that a reduction appears in nonverbal behaviours, i.e. a reduced amount during depression of facial, gestural, speech activity, and gaze at the other. For specific behaviours, variety and coordination may also be reduced or disturbed. These hypotheses will be specified further when dealing with the respective behaviours.

Duration, frequency and variety A reduced amount of behaviour may refer to frequency, to duration, or to intensity. One or the other aspect can be a more appropriate parameter for a specific behaviour. So, for gestures frequency measures are probably appropriate and their duration less so. Duration in turn is a more appropriate parameter for gaze. In our study, frequency and duration measures will be applied to the various behaviours under study. Variety refers to the domain or range of a behavioural repertoire. For facial behaviour, the variety of the elements used or activated within a situation can be analysed.

Coordination refers to internally or externally triggered temporal contingencies between different behaviours. In our study, coordination of speech and gaze as it occurs during dialogues (cf. Kendon, 1967) will be studied in some detail. A reduction of such a capacity would result in a disintegration of the behaviours otherwise coordinated. Furthermore, with regard to retardation, one would expect prolonged latencies in the coordinated behaviours.

Since for various aspects, the necessary methodological tools are limited and in order to keep analyses in the measure of the possible, "variety of the repertoire" and "coordination" are analysed for single nonverbal features only. For all of the behaviours, however, the hypothesis of a reduced amount of behaviour will be investigated.

Summary

Though they are not as unequivocal as clinical observations suggest, systematic studies give evidence of changes in nonverbal behaviour during depression. Generally, these changes are in accordance with changes in psychological functioning, i.e. behaviour is described as reduced or retarded. However, even during depression, individuals appear to be susceptible to social stimuli. This becomes evident, for example, in "normal" social reactions such as smiling or active communicative behaviours.

Furthermore, from theories of depression and clinical observations, it follows that not only a sad, depressed mood dominates the affective experience. It may also be accompanied by emotions like anger, hostility and fear. One would expect that on the basis of a general depressed mood level which extends over a considerable period of time, such single affective or emotional events may occur during short moments. These short events, as well as the general mood are expected to manifest themselves in various nonverbal behaviours.

Retardation and reduction of psychological processes are seen as the main factors influencing the behaviour during depression. With that, mainly changes in the encoding processes, i.e. in the behaviours displayed are to be expected, since depressed individuals are as good as controls in judging nonverbal behaviours in an experimental task. Their behaviour, however, appeared to be less easily decoded which might be due to less variation in their own behaviour.

A behavioural indicator for depression, thus, has to be tested in various directions: as to how unequivocally the behaviour indicates the state; whether changes occur generally or in a few individuals only; how consistently the behaviour occurs during a stable psychological state; and how much it changes over time.

4   Longitudinal study during the course of depression – Methodological aspects

A total of 36 depressed patients and 9 controls at the Max-Planck-Institute for Psychiatry participated in the longitudinal study described below. From these individuals, standardized interviews and subsequent free dialogues were repeatedly videotaped in regular intervals during their clinical stay and during a post-control period. Observations and video recordings were made between 1976 and 1980. Reports on selected aspects of this study have been given by Ellgring & Clarke (1978), Ellgring, Wagner & Clarke (1980), Ellgring (1984), Ellgring & Ploog (1985), Ellgring (1986). In the following a comprehensive presentation of the methods and the results of the longitudinal study will be given in context. A total of 510 video recordings of the standardized interviews or 502 of the free dialogues is the basic material for the behavioural analyses.

4.1 Patients and controls

A total of 20 endogenous depressed patients (9 male, 11 female, ICD 296.0/2/3) and 16 neurotic depressed patients (7 male, 9 female, ICD 300.4) were studied during their clinical stay. Patients were independently diagnosed by two experienced psychiatrists according to ICD criteria. After their clinical treatment patients participated in follow-up interviews when being without symptoms of depression and without medication. Nine controls (4 male, 5 female) matching the endogenous depressed patients for age, gender, and socioeconomic status also took part in the investigation during a one to two week clinical stay under comparable conditions. (A tenth control subject could not be used because of prior knowledge as a psychologist).

The endogenous depressed patients and controls participated also in a project on biological rhythms during depression (Dörr, von Zerssen, Fischler & Schulz, 1979). The neurotic depressed patients were systematically treated in a behaviourally oriented study (de Jong & Ferstl, 1980; de Jong, Henrich & Ferstl, 1981). No medication was given to these patients during their treatment. An overview of the individuals, duration of clinical stays, etc. is given in Fig. 4.1.

Medians of age distributions were between 31 to 33 years. The higher age of female endogenous depressed patients and female controls is due to the

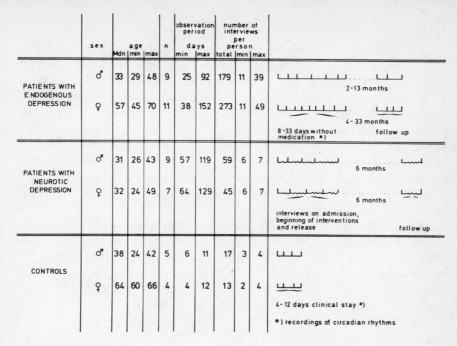

	sex	age			n	observation period days		number of interviews per person			
		Mdn	min	max		min	max	total	min	max	
PATIENTS WITH ENDOGENOUS DEPRESSION	♂	33	29	48	9	25	92	179	11	39	2-13 months
	♀	57	45	70	11	38	152	273	11	49	4-33 months
											8-33 days without medication *) follow up
PATIENTS WITH NEUROTIC DEPRESSION	♂	31	26	43	9	57	119	59	6	7	6 months
	♀	32	24	49	7	64	129	45	6	7	6 months
											interviews on admission, beginning of interventions and release follow up
CONTROLS	♂	38	24	42	5	6	11	17	3	4	
	♀	64	60	66	4	4	12	13	2	4	4-12 days clinical stay *) *) recordings of circadian rhythms

Fig. 4.1 Patients and controls. Overview of subjects, interviews, and periods of observation in the longitudinal study.

interdisciplinary project on biochemical parameters and circadian rhythms, where females could only participate after their menopause. For detailed descriptions of patients and ICD criteria see Appendix B 4.1.

Follow-up of neurotic depressed patients was done after six months independently of their subjective state. For endogenous depressed patients, a precondition for follow-up was a state without clinical signs of depression and without medication. Under these conditions, 14 of the endogenous depressed patients agreed to participate after variable intervals.

Although differentiating between endogenous or psychotic and neurotic depression is a controversial issue these two groups will be treated separately in our data analysis for various reasons. Symptomatology may differ, especially the severity of depression and also its treatment. Without necessarily accepting the etiological assumptions with regard to the impact of different external or internal factors associated with this distinction, a differentiation seems preferable given the present state of our knowledge. It leaves open the possibility for differences in the behaviours which might be obscured by simply merging these individuals. Besides this, the main focus will be on the intra-individual comparisons of subjective wellbeing and nonverbal behaviour.

4.2 Dialogue situation and course of the study

Patients were interviewed with a standardized interview for the course of depression. Interview sessions lasted between 15 minutes to an hour depending on the length of the free dialogue following the standardized part. To account for possible fluctuations during the day, the video sessions took place in the morning between 8.30 and 10.30 a.m. Patients knew about the video recording and gave their consent. A written consent to use the video recordings for scientific purposes was given by the patients at the end of their clinical stay. In order to minimize any psychological pressure the end of clinical treatment was chosen to ask patients for their written consent.

At the beginning of each session, patients indicated their subjective well-being on a Visual Analogue Scale (VAS, see below). The following interview (Standardized Interview for the course of Depression-SID, Ellgring, Derbolowsky & von Dewitz, 1977; Ellgring, Derbolowsky, von Dewitz & Hieke (1978) (see Appendix A1) lasted for about 10 to 15 minutes and the free dialogue for at least another five minutes.

For the interviewer certain behaviours were prescribed during the standardized part (not for the free dialogue). Therefore, interviewers were instructed and trained beforehand. They had to learn, for example, to be visually attentive, to lower their voice at the end of a question in order to avoid monotonous questioning etc. Endogenous depressed patients were interviewed by different interviewers, if possible alternating between the therapist and a research psychologist.

Patient and interviewer sat at a 90° angle towards each other. This seating position was chosen in order to build up some kind of "comfortable" dialogue situation and at the same time to have optimal recording conditions for two cameras (see Fig. 4.2). The total situation was recorded from the right side with a visibly open remote control camera. A second camera behind a one-way screen (not visible to the patient) was used to record head and shoulders of the patient. The mixed picture was recorded on a 1' Grundig video tape recorder with a SMPTC time code recording 25 frames/sec. (see Fig. 4.3).

Using this technique, the whole situation including the gross behaviour of the interviewer and the enlarged face of the patient could be recorded.

Experiencing the interview

Patients appeared to be essentially undisturbed by the situation. During depression they were primarily preoccupied with their state or were interested in discussing their problems. When improved, some interest in the recording was expressed. Very few incidental refusals to take part in the interview occurred during severe depression. Once a female patient felt too weak to endure the interview; another male patient was paranoically an-

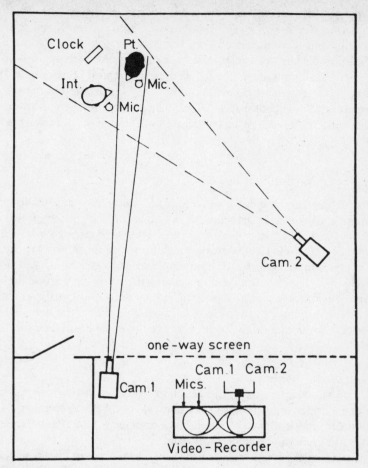

Clock
Pt.
Int.
Mic.
Mic.
Cam. 2
one-way screen
Cam.1 Cam.2
Cam.1 Mics.
Video - Recorder

Fig. 4.2 Recording situations and camera angles

xious on one day. He feared that the interview would be too costly and that he would financially ruin his family by having it. Some reservations about video recordings appeared primarily in new therapists cooperating in the work. These reservations disappeared as soon as therapists got used to the situation. It seemed that therapists felt uneasy during their first video session because they did not know what kind of impression they gave.

At the end of an investigation, patients were asked if they would like to look at parts of the recordings. At the beginning of this study, we tried confronting the patients with parts of the recordings of their depressed state compared with those of their improved state. Interestingly enough, patients indicated that the video picture did not reflect their state as intensely as they had experienced it.

However, because of the possible negative effects of such self-confrontation (see Ellgring, 1982) only parts from the improved state were shown later and were discussed with the patients.

At this point it has to be acknowledged that patients were highly cooperative in each case and were interested in these dialogues. For example, on the occasion of a later relapse one patient expressed his disappointment that the interviews were not continued. I would like to express my gratitude and respect for their willingness to cooperate even under conditions of extreme distress.

4.3 Single case longitudinal study

The general methodological approach in this study aims at intra-individual comparisons over time. Generally two video recordings per week (on Mondays and Fridays) were taken with endogenous depressed patients and controls. For neurotic depressed patients, a maximum of 6 recordings was taken at certain points during a therapeutic program (see figure 4.1). Economical reasons led to fewer recordings during the study of neurotic depressed patients which started later. Also, for endogenous depressed patients, the initial three interviews were reduced to two per week. From Figure 4.1 it can be seen that some individuals were observed over a period of up to several months.

Methodological problems
There are various methodological problems emerging from this approach of single case longitudinal studies under clinical conditions: Missing data, lack of statistical independence of single measurements, and effects from repeated observations of the same individual.

Confounding effects of medication and other treatment effects which lead to improvement of wellbeing seem to be especially problematic. During their treatment, neurotic depressed patients in this study received no psychoactive medication at all. Endogenous depressed patients received no medication during their first 10 to 14 days in the clinic and during a post control period. This was followed by medication according to clinical necessity. At the end of their clinical stay these patients received low doses of antidepressants and Lithium. Withholding of medication for these patients at the beginning was part of the necessary preconditions for studying circadian rhythms. Medication was given earlier if clinical symptoms required it.

Given these conditions, medication effects should not play a major role in our results when comparing behaviour on admission, release from the clinic and during post control.

Fig. 4.3 Mixed video still on the monitor

Group comparisons

Although intra-individual comparison is the leading methodological strategy, the groups of neurotic and endogenous depressed patients, male and female alike, will be compared. A higher expressivity of female individuals would be expected from the literature (Hall, Rosenthal, Archer, DiMatteo & Rogers, 1978; Hall & Braunwald, 1981; Vrugt, forthcoming). From clinical impression, neurotic depressed patients are expected to show their depressed mood clearly in their nonverbal behaviour. Besides these group comparisons, intra-individual changes of the behaviour associated with mood changes, however, will be our main source of reference.

4.4 Variables assessed

Information with regard to various psychological and behavioural variables was gained from each video session (see Fig. 4.4).

Behavioural features

Nonverbal behaviour was assessed in two ways: Firstly, by behavioural measurements as described in the following chapters: Secondly by rating on various scales (see Appendix A2). It can be anticipated here that behavioural

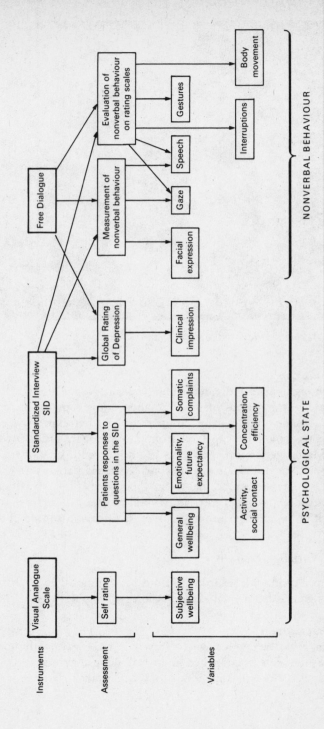

Fig. 4.4 Variables assessed from a video session

ratings, as they were used here, can be taken as substitutes for behavioural measurements to a limited degree only. In the following we will focus therefore on the behavioural measurements.

Defining 'reduction' and 'substantial change'

For each of the various behavioural measures, these two criteria will be defined with reference to the measures from the normal controls. *Reduction* means that a given value is below a limit defined by at least 16 out of 18 control values, two for each of the controls. *Substantial change* means that a given change ratio exceeds a criterion value. The criterion is defined by 8 of the 9 controls having a lower value, i.e. showing a higher stability of behaviour on repeated measurements.

Mood and wellbeing

A self-rating scale and a global clinical rating are used as the main criteria for changes in subjective wellbeing and the depressed state.

As a self-rating, the patient indicates on a visual analogue scale (Folstein & Luria, 1973) his state of wellbeing. Values on a "Zustandsbarometer", i.e. a "state barometer" vary between 0 = extreme wellbeing to 113 = extreme distress. Generally, these measures are highly correlated with other measures of self rating and clinical ratings (Zealley & Aitken, 1969). Moreover, they discriminate better than various other indications of wellbeing (Little & McPhail, 1973). In our data, a high correlation ($r = 0.84$, $n = 305$ interviews) to a Scale for Wellbeing (Befindlichkeitsskala, Bf-S, von Zerssen, Köller & Rey, 1970), a mood adjective check list was found. From these results the use of the Visual Analogue Scale (VAS), especially for intra-individual comparisons, seems to be justified.

A Global Clinical Rating (GR) developed by Schwarz & Strian (1972) was used to assess the degree of depression in a general way (see Appendix A2). This clinical impression was rated after the answers of the interview were analysed and by using the video recording. This clinical impression thus summarizes all of the information available to the interviewer. According to Schwarz & Strian (1972) this scale correlates highly with other rating scales.

For correlations with behavioural measures these scales are reversed, if not explicitly noted otherwise: thus positive correlations indicate a higher incidence of behaviour, i.e. more gestures, more facial expressions, or more gaze when their wellbeing improved.

Answers on behaviour and subjective experience in the SID

Answers during the interview were rated according to various criteria on 9-point scales. For comparison, parts of these scales were combined into 5 general aspects (see Appendix A2). By this, differentiated information on

Table 4.1 *Intercorrelations of phychological variables*

		SID components						
		VAS	GR	GEWE	ALSO	EMFU	CONE	SOSL
Subjective wellbeing	(VAS)	–	.82	.80	.65	.63	.77	.55
Global Clinical Rating	(GR)	.74	–	.78	.75	.70	.79	.63
General wellbeing	(GEWE	.76	.78	–	.64	.64	.81	.70
Activity, social contact	(ALSO)	.58	.72	.64	–	.71	.67	.52
Emotionality, future expectations	(EMFU)	.65	.70	.70	.67	–	.64	.49
Concentration, efficiency	(CONE)	.72	.78	.79	.65	.69	–	.63
Somatic symptions, sleep	(SOSL)	.48	.55	.65	.42	.45	.53	–

Notes:
VAS = Visual Analogue Scale of subjective wellbeing, GR = Global Clinical Rating of depression.
SID components:
GEWE = General wellbeing
ACSO = Activity and social contact
EMFU = Emotionality and future expectations
CONE = Concentration and efficiency
SOSC = Somatic symptoms and sleep

Upper half: n = 120 interviews (dataset GEFA)
Lower half: n = 573-581 interviews (dataset ALL)

"General wellbeing", "Activity and social contact", "Emotions and future expectations", "Concentration and efficiency" and "Somatic complaints" was available.

Intercorrelations of psychological features
Generally, the various features from the SID are highly correlated (see Table 4.1).

The upper part of the table contains correlations based on all of the available interviews (about 500), the lower part shows those based on a selection of 120 interviews (see below). Correlations of r>0.70 correspond to a common variance of 50% and more. It would be inappropriate to establish levels of significance when describing these data sets. Therefore, correlations should be taken as descriptive parameters here, indicating the amount of common variance.

From the various aspects of the SID, the extent of "somatic complaints" correlates the least whereas "Concentration and efficiency" correlates highest with subjective wellbeing. The generally high correlations are partly due to the broad range of values from patients and controls. In the single case, however, the various aspects may be affected differently by depression.

Taken as a whole, the high correlations suggest that it is a rather homogeneous distortion or syndrome patients suffer from: when general wellbeing is bad, efficiency and concentration are low, social activity and concentration are problematic, and there is a tendency towards somatic complaints.

Furthermore, as a methodological consequence one would not expect differential correlations of behavioural measures with the various SID features simply for statistical reasons. Therefore, subjective wellbeing from the Visual Analogue Scale (VAS) and the Global Clinical Rating (GR) will be taken as main references of the depressed state and its changes.

4.5 Selection of interviews for behavioural measurements

All of the technically sufficient interviews were taken for the analysis of gaze and speech behaviour, i.e. five minutes from the standardized and five minutes from the free part. From this, a total of 510 (standardized) or 502 (free part) five minute video-taped segments were available (Dataset: "All").

Because analyses of facial behaviour and gestures are by far more time consuming than analyses of gaze and speech, they were obtained from only a selection of 120 interviews (Dataset "GEFA"). For the 36 depressed patients one interview (a) from the beginning of the clinical stay, (b) one from the time shortly before discharge and (c) one from a post control period were analysed. To allow for accommodation to the situation the second or third of all the interviews was chosen, if possible (i.e. for 38 of the 45 individuals) as the initial one.

Fourteen of the twenty endogenous depressed patients took part in the post control study so that for six of them facial behaviour and gestures were analysed only from two interviews. For controls, only two interviews, preferably the second and third one, were taken for facial and gestural analysis. Interview numbers are listed in the data tables of the Appendix.

High correlations of those variables which were assessed in the selected as well as in the total general data pool justify regarding this selection as being representative (see Table 4.1).

Facial behaviour and gestures were analysed with only few exceptions from the first five minutes of the free part of the interview. This section was chosen because it was assumed and incidentally observed that more active behaviour occurs during the free dialogue than in the highly structured part of the interview. To decide whether this assumption is justified or not would

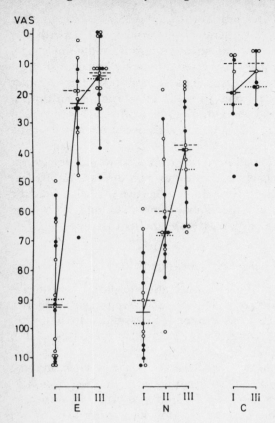

Fig. 4.5 Subjective wellbeing of different states. Visual Analogue Scale (VAS) measures for individuals from selected interview. *Groups*: E = endogenous (n = 20 in I and III, n = 14 in state II), neurotic (n = 16) depressed patients, C = controls (n = 9). ● : males, ○ = females. *States of wellbeing*: I = depressed or relatively worst state, II = intermediate state, III = recovered or relatively best state of wellbeing. *Median values* are connected (— = for each subgroup; median values for males (. . . .) and females (-----) marked separately. *Ranges* cover all values except the highest and lowest value of each subsample.

require a systematic comparison of different parts of the interview. This enterprise did not appear to be a primary need at this stage especially when considering that analysis of a five minute tape needs several hours of observation.

Taking into account the high correlations of variables from the dataset "All" and "GEFA" the selection of interviews for the systematic analysis of gestures and facial behaviour can be justified.

4.6 Changes of subjective wellbeing and clinical impression

As might be expected, subjective wellbeing of patients changes considerably over their clinical stay whereas controls stay in a stable state. This is recognized in the global clinical rating as well (see Fig. 4.5 and 4.6).

The description of the formal aspects in figure 4.5 also applies to similar figures in the next chapters. Marking of the ranges is similar to the procedure in box plots proposed by Emerson & Strenio (1983). As has to be expected, patients' subjective wellbeing covers the whole range of the Visual Analogue Scale. For controls these values remain in the upper half indicating a good state of wellbeing. Their values remain within a comparatively small range. Similar trends can be observed in the Global Clinical Rating (see Fig. 4.6).

It has to be kept in mind that wellbeing does not in any case change continuously or in a monotonous way from the beginning towards the end of the clinical stay and towards post control (see also chapter 8 on single cases). Especially for neurotic depressed patients, there were deteriorations during the post control phase. Therefore interviews with a *relatively bad condition* (ı), an *improved condition* (ıı) and the *relatively best condition* (ııı) were defined for each individual according to his/her subjective wellbeing. For 16 out of 20 endogenous and for 5 out of 16 neurotic depressed patients this corresponds to the temporal sequence. For the other patients, the interview from the end of the clinical stay instead of the interview of the post-control period was the relatively best one. Since our study aims at investigating the relationship of mood and behaviour, the subjective experience seems to be the more important criterion over the purely temporal one.

Given the aforementioned selection, subjective wellbeing increases necessarily from state ı over state ıı to state ııı. In contrast control values – and this justifies assuming a comparatively stable state of general wellbeing – remain nearly constant.

There are no substantial differences between males and females with regard to subjective wellbeing and global clinical rating. There is a remarkable difference between endogenous and neurotic depressed patients. Whereas changes appear nearly linear over the three interviews for neurotic depressed patients values for endogenous depressed patients from the "medium" state ıı are already close to the relatively best in state ııı. Moreover, improved wellbeing of neurotic depressed patients was not as close to the point of extreme wellbeing, compared to the other groups.

Assuming a monotonous relationship between mood and behaviour, one would expect pronounced changes in endogenous patients' behaviour when comparing states ı and ıı, whereas for neurotic depressed patients this would not be the case until comparing states ı and ııı. One has to keep in mind,

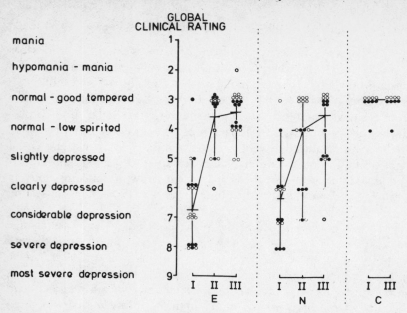

Fig. 4.6 Global Clinical Rating at different states (further explanation at Fig. 4.5).

however, that a Visual Analogue Scale is primarily suited for intra-individual, not inter-individual comparisons.

A similar picture of changes for patients and stability for controls appears for the Global Clinical Rating (see Fig. 4.5). Values for the clinical rating are quite similar for endogenous and neurotic depressed patients, medians nearly identical. There is a slight tendency for more endogenous depressed patients being rated as considerably or severely depressed during state I whereas ratings for neurotic depressed patients have a broader range at state III. Controls were generally rated as "normal to good tempered". Two exceptions have to be mentioned. In each subgroup one patient received a rating of "normal to good tempered" during state I, during their second resp. third interview. Nevertheless, when comparing their values on the Visual Analogue Scale, these were their *relatively* worst states (see Appendix B, table B.3). Their self rating can still be regarded as clearly on the lower part of wellbeing.

On the whole, values of subjective wellbeing and clinical rating from selected interviews indicate clear differences in the state of depression be-havioural measures can be related to. Values during depression change towards a range corresponding to stable control values.

5 Facial expression of mood and emotions

Psychological processes appear to be easy to discover by facial expression. There are few other parts of the behaviour where we can observe phenomena as manifold as in the movement of the facial musculature.

Facial musculature is innervated by the facial nerve, nervus facialis, which in turn is controlled by the facial motor nucleus. This motor nucleus is connected with various other areas of the brain – colliculus superior, oliva, formatio reticularis, but also with the hypothalamus (Rinn, 1984).

Especially the associations with the limbic system, that part of the brain mainly involved in the generation of emotions (Ploog, 1980), suggest a close link between emotional processes and facial activity (Ekman & Oster, 1979). By this, facial behaviour should be especially suited to studying the association of subjective experience and behaviour.

On the other hand, facial muscles are controlled by various, functionally different parts of the brain. They are partly under voluntary control by their cortical connections. Thus an activation of facial muscles may express an affective state immediately but it can also be used in a conscious display.

Both immediate expression of an emotional state and controlled display may be present in a current facial behaviour.

5.1 Facial behaviour as a social signal

Facial behaviour appears as a universal signalling system in various higher mammals by which motivations may be expressed and informations can be directed towards others (van Hoff, 1967; van Lawick-Goodall, 1968; Chevalier-Skolnikoff, 1973; Redican, 1982). Although it can be assumed that facial signals are inborn expressive movements at first, i.e. instinctive behaviours, *sensu* Lorenz (1965, p. 281) and Tinbergen (1951), learning plays a substantial role for humans.

Between the ages of 9 to 13, skills in expressing emotions consciously and voluntarily are still imperfect. Even 13 year olds have difficulties in displaying at will certain negative emotions, such as fear, sadness and anger (Ekman, Roper & Hager, 1980).

The conscious display of negative emotions and voluntary control of facial behaviour seems to be a capacity which is acquired rather late during ontogenesis and which is possibly only mastered in part (cf. Ekman &

45

Friesen, 1969b; Ekman, Hager & Friesen, 1981). It can be assumed that under conditions of a higher load during depression, control of facial behaviour in conscious display would require too great an effort.

Facial behaviour is primarily activated during social interaction. The smile, for example, appears very often, independent of a "happy" emotion. It is elicited mainly by social conditions, i.e., when orientating towards another person (Kraut & Johnston, 1979). Brunner (1979) deduced a "back channel" function of the smile from observing that listeners frequently display this behaviour at points during conversation where other back channel behaviours, such as "yes" or "hm", etc. also tend to appear.

A considerable number of conversational signals are displayed in the brows area. For brows behaviour, Ekman (1979) differentiates between (a) speaker's signals like "batons", "underliner", "punctuation", "question mark", "word search", (b) turntaking signals like "agreement" and emblems, i.e. (c) conversational signals without language, like the eye flash (Eibl-Eibesfeldt, 1972), "disbelief", "mock astonishment", "affirmation", "negation", "sophisticated skepticism". Even for the few possible facial actions in the forehead area a considerable variety of meanings for social interaction becomes evident from this.

Although the meaning of facial signals, as elements of social interaction, goes beyond pure expression, there is still a link with the basic emotions. Even with a voluntary smile during greeting, an individual undoubtedly does not signal anger or sadness but rather a positive affective attitude towards the other.

The problem is to decide whether a behaviour is a "true" expression of an emotion or a social display. To infer a "true" emotion from a sender is complicated by the conscious and voluntary control of the behaviour. However, if one does not claim to describe a "true" emotion, the smile can be regarded as a signal in the communication system between sender and receiver which is associated with a positive affect. Other functions like a conversational signal or a means of deception may be present independently.

Investigating the association of facial expression and mood does not need the presumption of detecting a "true" emotion. A more simple question should be sufficient: what kind of facial behaviour is activated within a social situation given a specific affective or mood state.

5.2 Simultaneous expression of different affects

Despite the relatively homogeneous appearance of the depression syndrome, complex affective processes have to be taken into account. Besides sadness or grief, emotions like anxiety and, from a psychoanalytical view, anger may be important (cf. chapter 2). Up to now, little has been known about the temporal flow of different affects and about the interplay with the corresponding expression. A simultaneous expression of different emotions presupposes discrete, distinguishable processes (Scherer, 1984) in contrast to general dimensions. Furthermore an association of these emotions with specific muscular action, resulting from single or simultaneous muscle innervations, has to be assumed given a simultaneous occurrence of emotions.

Various studies indicate such simultaneous expressions of different affects or emotions. As has been observed by Ekman & Friesen (1969b) a "leakage" in part of the behaviour takes place when subjects try to deceive and withhold their felt emotions. When commenting in a prescribed positive way on a negative film this was accompanied by frequent "negative affect smiles". This "negative affect smile" contains facial elements of a smile together with facial indicators of negative emotions (Ekman, Friesen & Ancoli, 1980). In a study on stuttering, Krause (1978, 1981) found such simultaneous positive and negative (mainly disgust) facial elements as "affective blends" when analysing dialogues of stutterers with normally speaking individuals.

"Leakage theory" can be traced back to Darwin's (1872) principle of antithesis, i.e. that opposite emotions lead to opposite expressions. Extending this principle, it is claimed by Leyhausen (1967) that given two contradictory motives, the weaker one will result in an expression whereas the stronger one will lead to an action. With regard to the experimental situation in Ekman & Friesen's (1969b) study, the intention to deceive as the stronger motive determined the consciously controlled behaviour, whereas the "weaker motive", i.e. the negative emotion felt was expressed in a less controlled way as disgust when watching the unpleasant film.

When studying the expression of mood by facial expression one has to take into account two processes possibly interfering with each other. An immediate, direct expression of emotional processes has to be expected given the universality of facial behaviour, its phylogenetical and ontogenetical traces as instinctive behaviour. This immediate expression may be counteracted by cultural influences whereby during ontogenesis a control of affective expressions is built up (Ekman, 1973). This means that the face will express an emotional state only as far as it is tolerated by specific cultural norms. The strain resulting from such a control will be endurable up to a certain degree only so that an immediate expression might "leak" through. Which one of these two tendencies dominates at a given point in time during an ongoing interaction, can very rarely be decided in an unambiguous way.

5.3 Facial expression during depression

Because of the depressed mood as a central feature, one would hardly

Fig. 5.1 Patient in hypomania and depressed stupor (from Weygandt, 1902).

associate a happy facial expression with depression. One would rather expect a state-congruent expression as the natural behaviour in a depressed condition.

Correspondingly, with improvement or with an elated mood, a change in facial behaviour should occur. This contrast is depicted in traditional textbooks on psychiatry like that of Weygandt (1902) in an impressive way (see Fig. 5.1).   Clinical descriptions frequently point to the sad facial expression but also to a total lack of facial expression corresponding to the lack of affective experience as one of the symptoms during depression.

Systematic observation of facial features
There is little quantitative information available on the actual facial behaviour during depression. From the study of Grinker et al. (1961) the following figures refer to facial aspects:

Item	Content	% patients showing behaviour
3.	Cries (lacrimation)	37%
6.	Never smiles	6%
7.	Seen to smile at some time during observation	97%
80.	Has flat masklike face	51%

In only about 50% of the patients the flat masklike face (Item 80), i.e. a lack of facial expression has been observed. This corresponds to figures of Mombour (1974) who reported that 43% of 125 depressed patients show a rigid facial expression. This, however, is also the case for 47% of patients suffering from an organic psychosyndrome and for 51% of schizophrenic patients.

Several points should be stressed: Observers register a lack of facial expression as an important feature. None the less, it is observed in about 50% of the patients only and does not seem to be specific to depression. It is interesting to observe that in the study of Grinker et al. (1961) nearly all patients happened to smile at one time during observation. This phenomenon seems important when later discussing the homogeneity of an affective level. Nevertheless, facial behaviour appears to be generally in accordance with the psychological disorders, specifically a lack of emotional variability, during depression.

According to Bunney & Hamburg (1963) nurses are able to evaluate verbal and facial expression of anger and anxiety in newly admitted patients, when observing over a period of 8 hours. Even though inter-rater reliabilities turned out to be only moderate (r = .45 for an angry and r = .60 for a sad facial expression), the differentiation between these two emotions in depression deserves attention.

More specifically, facial expression has been examined in studies by Ulrich et al. (1976), Waxer (1974, 1976), Jones & Pansa (1979) and Pansa-Henderson, et al. (1982). Rating of reduced facial behaviour turned out, according to Ulrich et al. (1976) to be a valid indicator for depressive retardation but also for agitation.

The feature "depressed" is mainly inferred by raters from mouth corners angled down (Waxer, 1974) whereas a lip bite or pressed lips are taken as indicators for anger in a group of patients with mixed diagnoses (Waxer, 1976). In a study of Jones & Pansa (1979) quantitative aspects, i.e. frequency and duration of facial behaviours, are presented for those features which significantly differentiated between depressed and schizophrenic patients or controls. A lower frequency and duration of the smile appeared to be the most distinct feature for depressed patients at the beginning of their clinical stay, a result that Jones and Pansa themselves comment as being of little surprise when considering clinical observations and expectations. They also found a reduced frequency of eyebrow movements, i.e. speaker signals for depressed patients. This could be regarded as an indicator for motor retardation.

There is very little information about the simultaneous expression of different emotions in depressed patients. In a paper of Matsumoto, Ekman & Friesen (1983) that came to our knowledge after the completion of our study, "felt" and "unfelt happy" expressions significantly correlated with depressed mood on admission and improvement of neurotic depressed patients. For psychotic depressed patients, this was the case to a minor degree and only for "unfelt happy" expressions.

It is unclear why in this study for psychotic patients (corresponding to endogenous in our case) the correlation was not significant for "felt happy" expressions. From the low average values and the proportionally large standard deviations one would suppose bottom effects to play a role. This suggests that a substantial part of the 17 patients showed little or none of the specific behaviour defined. Individual comparisons would probably help to explain this result further. Nevertheless, it points to the usefulness of measuring facial behaviour to expand rating procedures and the necessity of differentiating between various forms of depression.

From the systematic studies of visible facial behaviour, significant effects for differentiating depression from a normal state can be found. When critically analysing these effects however, they appear to be weaker than one would expect from clinical or everyday life experience.

Various reasons could be responsible for this discrepancy between data from systematic observation and the homogeneous impression gained from clinical experience. Social psychological mechanisms like selective perception, expectancies, over-generalization, implicit theories on behaviour and personality could produce a homogeneous picture of depression, not present in actual life. Also, from a methodological point of view, rating and measurement techniques might not be sensitive enough for subtle facial phenomena.

Electromyographical studies
Electromyographical registration of muscular activity does not suffer the flaws of ratings and observation with regard to sensitivity. Instead there are other problems like spillover of electrical activity from different muscles which, however, will not be discussed here. Primarily an increased activation of the musculus corrugator and a reduced activation of the musculus zygomaticus as measured in the electromyogramme (EMG) appear to be characteristic for negative thoughts. A clear differentiation between various clinical and normal groups using EMG measure, however, is still equivocal (Fridlund & Izard, 1983). Schwartz, Fair, Salt, Mandel & Klerman (1976a

and b; Schwartz & Weinberger, 1980) found different activation in the EMG when subjects imagined "happy" situations compared to other emotional contents, like anger. No substantial differences were found between depressed and non-depressed subjects. In their thorough review on this and other studies, Fridlund & Izard (1983) discuss the importance of a baseline EMG measure which could be on a higher level for depressed individuals.

In a replication by Oliveau & Willmuth (1979), again differences in the EMG level turned out to depend on the kind of imagination (happy or sad daily events), whereas no differences were found between depressed and non-depressed subjects. The correlation between negative thoughts and higher level activity of the musculus corrugator has also been found by Teasdale & Rezin (1977). Again, no significant correlation was found with the extent of the depressed mood.

Even though EMG levels do not significantly differ between groups, it appears to be predictive of improvement when compared on an individual basis. For five clinically depressed patients Teasdale & Bancroft (1977) obtained a correlation of r = 0.70 with subjective wellbeing. Schwartz, Fair, Mandel, Salt, Mieske & Klerman (1978) found more improvements on a Hamilton rating for those patients with an initially higher activity of the musculus corrugator. According to Carney, Hong, O'Connell & Amado (1981) those of the 21 clinically depressed women, which showed higher initial activity of the musculus corrugator at the beginning of their clinical stay, showed greater changes in the Beck Inventory later. Other than Schwartz et al. (1978) no relationship appeared in this study with changes of clinical symptoms. Predictive validity of the activity of the musculus corrugator and the musculus zygomaticus has been replicated by Greden and his group (Greden, Price, Genero, Feinberg & Levine, 1984; Greden, Genero & Price, 1985, cf. section on Veraguth fold below).

In their review, Fridlund & Izard (1983) hypothesize that an "over arousal" during depression (cf. Goldstein, 1965) might be responsible for a higher EMG level, rather than the expression of a sad face. From this, the base level seems to be a crucial variable in EMG studies on depression. For the facial expression of emotions, however, EMG studies provide indirect evidence. It is not indicated whether changed frequencies, intensities or qualities of emotions during depression are communicated to others. Nevertheless, the high EMG levels during depression are of interest. They point to possible facial actions which could contradict the assumption that there is a total lack of facial expression during depression.

5.4 Summary and hypothesis

Particularly in clinical descriptions, facial expression seems to correspond to the state of wellbeing and emotions during depression. To a lesser extent, this is confirmed by the few studies using systematic observations. Generally, a reduction of facial behaviour has been found, particularly for the smile. Thus in the face affective disorders appear to be expressed in a way which meets our expectations about behaviour in a depressed mood.

Electromyographical studies are partly in accordance with, and somewhat in contradiction to, observational data. High levels of musculus corrugator activity predicted later improvement. This points to an increased facial activity or tension with a negative affective content during depression. This is contrary to reduced facial activity as expected from clinical observation. A higher level of musculus zygomaticus activity, i.e. the muscles responsible for the smile, has been found for depressed patients as well (Carney et al., 1981; Greden et al., 1984). This suggests a generally high tension in facial muscles. It still has to be investigated whether this is due to an unspecific high activity of facial muscles corresponding to an over-arousal or to specific reactions. From a communication point of view, the visible facial behaviour is of special interest. It is still unclear to what extent the electromyographically measured muscular activity becomes apparent on the facial surface.

Systematic observations revealed comparatively weaker association of facial behaviour with depression than would be expected from clinical impression. The question arises whether clinical impression exaggerates factually low correlations. Is it possible that clinical descriptions are derived from special significant cases which exhibit, for example, a facial torpidness? The impression could be gathered from rare but impressive events. The use of more sensible methods for observing and coding facial behaviour should help to give a clearer view. Beyond global ratings it is necessary to gain differential information on facial expression during depression. This behaviour may not only be indicative of a depressed mood, but also of negative emotions, presumably present during the illness.

Reduction hypothesis for facial expression

From clinical and the few systematic observations and also from learning theories, a reduction of facial activity and a predominance of negative affective expression has to be expected for depression. This hypothesis can be specified as follows:

Facial activity and the repertoire of its elements will be reduced during depression and will expand with improvement of subjective wellbeing.

Facial actions which become apparent on the level of a generally depressed mood should represent negative emotions. Whether these resemble expressions of sadness, distress, anger or fear will not be tested in a strict sense but rather studied in an exploratory way.

5.5 Methods of facial analysis

Facial behaviour was analysed from videotapes with variable speed (slow motion, frame by frame analysis). The occurrence of facial movements was coded according to the Facial Action Coding System (FACS) by Ekman & Friesen (1978). Upper and lower face were analysed in separate runs.

The coding system is based upon a notation system of the Swedish anatomist Hjortsjö (1970). He described the muscular basis of facial expression and classified the appearance changes on the surface of the skin caused by different muscular actions. The system allows the description of facial behaviour in an "analytical" way using 44 Action Units (AU) or Action Descriptors (AD). The Action Units of the frontal area are depicted in Fig. 5.2.

Additional code numbers can be used to describe eye and head positions. These were not used in our study since gaze was assessed separately as an on-off pattern (see chapter 6).

Action Units, single or in combination, describe visible changes in the face without giving qualitative interpretations about possible emotions at this stage. Visibility of muscular activity is an important criterion, since we are interested in the potential communicative aspects of the behaviour. Communication requires that changes in muscular activity can be observed by others.

Selected elements used for coding

In our analysis an event was coded near the "apex", i.e. the maximum of a movement without temporal and intensity qualifications. The intensity of a movement had to fulfil the criterion of showing at least a "trace level", defined in the FACS manual, i.e. a trace of the movement had to be apparent.

The most important modification of FACS was a selection of the elements to be coded. This selection was obtained after analysing 40 interviews with 20 endogenous depressed patients. The resulting frequency distribution of single Action Units is shown in Figure 5.3.

The distribution is clearly skewed to the left. This had to be expected from prior knowledge on systematic observation of behaviour. Generally, within a categorial observation system, few behavioural categories occur with high frequencies whereas for most of them low frequencies are obtained. This distribution is in accordance with the "principle of least effort", postulated by Zipf (1949/1965) for the use of words. It states that few elements of the behavioural repertoire are used quite frequently whereas most of the available elements are used rarely. According to Zipf (1949/1965) this use of verbal elements enables us to communicate with the least amount of effort.

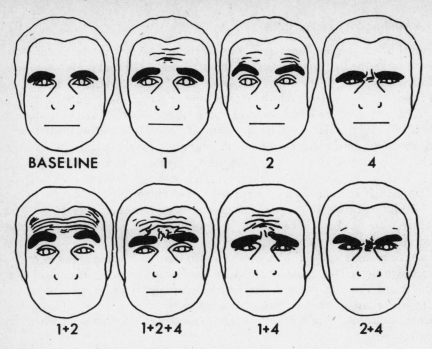

BASELINE   1   2   4

1+2   1+2+4   1+4   2+4

Fig. 5.2 Action Units of the brows (from Ekman, 1979).

Regarding the frequency distribution in Fig. 5.3, the "principle of least effort" seems to apply to facial behaviour as well. Given this result, 13 Action Units or Action Unit combinations were taken for the analysis of the total sample of interviews (see table 5.1).

For Action Units 1+2 (lifting the eyebrows) and 6+12 (smile) no differentiation was made, since the single elements AU1 or AU2 rarely occur separately and AU6 (cheek raise) is mostly combined with AU12 (lip corner pull) in the smile. The AU28 (lip suck) and AU32 (lip bite) were taken together because of their similar appearance and functional equivalence.

As can be seen from Table 5.1 our selection (except for the last three AUs) corresponds to EMFACS, a simplified version of FACS. This simplification has recently been proposed by Friesen & Ekman (1984) after our analysis had been terminated.

Action Unit 5 (upper lid raise) is the only AU excluded in our selection but included in EMFACS. It was excluded here because of its very low frequency of occurrence. Whether this was due to the difficulty in detecting it on the video screen or to its actually rare occurrence, could not be decided. We also omitted coding of mouth openings (AUs 24, 25, 26). This would have been of interest, for example, in evaluating the intensities of smiles or laughter. Since our study, however, did not aim at differentiating

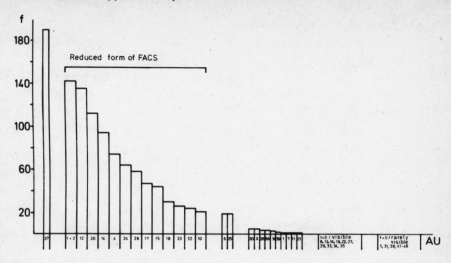

Fig, 5.3 Frequency distribution of various Action Units (AU): From 40 clinical interviews of 20 endogenous depressed patients; 5 mins. duration each.

in this respect, these codes were not used. Also a mouth-opening (AU25 or AU26) simultaneously occurring with other facial action or in a specific context, could be part of a "surprise" expression. Such an event, however, has not been observed in the whole material.

Our selection does not imply any rank order with regard to the importance of single elements. In particular, events occurring rarely may be highly important for gaining a specific impression. Nevertheless, in comparison to frequently occurring behaviours, these elements would not be identifiable as indicators of change in a quantitative analysis.

It has always been a controversial issue in psychological literature to infer an emotional meaning from facial actions. Therefore, the references to emotions in table 5.1 cannot be used as a definite guideline for interpretations. Taken from the proposals of Ekman & Friesen (1975, 1978) they point to possible interpretations only. They were validated mainly by studies on the recognition of emotions. The Action Units can be thought of as possible elements in a complex facial expression. Generally, several elements act together in producing an expression.

It has to be stressed that not the emotions but the facial elements were observed and coded according to the criteria of the coding system.

Reliability
Reliability of coding was assessed in various ways. First, the author took the final test of the Human Interaction Laboratory in San Francisco, directed by

Table 5.1: *Selection of facial elements*

AU	EMFACS	CONTENT	Surprise	Fear	Happiness	Sadness	Disgust	Anger	Contempt
1+2	+	Inner and outer brow raise	×	×		×			
4	+	Brow lower		(×)		(×)		×	
9	+	Nose wrinkle					×		
10	+	Upper lip raise					×	×	×
(6+)12	+	Lip corner pull (cheek raise)			×	(×)			
14	+	Dimpler							×
15	+	Lip corner depress				×	×		
17	+	Chin raise				×	×	×	
18	+	Lip pucker							
20	+	Lip stretch		×					
23	+	Lips tight						×	
24	+	Lip press						×	
28/32	+	Lip suck/bite							

Note:
Reduced form of FACS with elements of EMFACS marked. Content description and hypothetical relations to emotion.

Ekman. Second, inter-rater reliability with another trained observer was determined by coding 6 interviews with depressed patients. Reliability of the two independent coders was 79% (Cohen's kappa = 0.75, p<0.05, cf. Asendorpf & Wallbott, (1979)). Third, a repeated coding, after a one month period, revealed an intra-rater reliability of 88% (Cohen's kappa: r = 0.87, p<0.05). These figures refer to a point-to-point agreement for the single events. Agreement for coded events had to be within +/−10 video frames, i.e. 400 msecs period of time. Regarding the complexity of the behaviour, the reliability of coding appears to be sufficient or good.

5.5.1 *Parameters of facial behaviour*

"Activity", "repertoire" and "patterns" were defined as parameters of facial behaviour. These parameters could be chosen with certain freedom, since little experience was available from the literature at that time. Parameters were selected on the basis of the general hypothesis that there is a reduction of nonverbal behaviour during depression.

Facial activity, general and specific
Facial activity is defined by the frequency of Action Units within an observa-

tional period of five minutes. General and specific facial activity were differentiated.

General facial activity (MIAK = Mimic Activity) is defined by the total number of Action Units coded within the five minute interval.

MIAK = f(AUs in five minutes)

This parameter does not distinguish whether few AUs occur frequently or many different AUs occur infrequently. Combinations of AU1+2 resp. 6+12 were counted as one action since they occur together in nearly every instance.

Specific facial activity is defined by the frequency of occurrence for each single AU within a five minute interval. Here, in particular, the smile, i.e. AU(6+)12 will be analysed. Criterion for coding was the occurrence of AU12 (activation of musculus zygomaticus) with an optional activation of AU6 (cheek raise).

Repertoire

The facial repertoire is defined by the number of different AUs which were coded within a five minute interval. To reduce random variation those action units occurring at least twice will be included in the parameter REP2. This parameter is taken for further analyses. It is the number of different AUs occurring at least two times within the five minute period.

REP2 = Number of different AUs with f$\geq$2 within 5 minutes

The repertoire is limited by our selection of AUs, i.e. by a maximum of 13. Generally, it turned out to be much lower, with a median value of Mdn = 4 AUs. Obviously, the repertoire REP2 is lower than the repertoire REP1, where AUs are included occurring only once. REP1 has a Mdn = 5.8, i.e. 2 AUs higher than REP2. Taking the total of 120 measurements, correlation between REP1 and REP2 is high (r = 0.78). The repertoire is defined here quantitatively as the domain of facial actions used two or more times. The parameter REP2 does not refer to the content. It represents the variety of facial signals used.

"Reduction" and "substantial change"

Parameters of facial behaviour, MIAK, f (AU12), and REP2 are characterized, as for the other nonverbal behaviours, by two qualifications with reference to normal values. For each individual (a) presence of a reduction compared to control values, and (b) presence of substantial changes, i.e. changes exceeding normal variations of behaviour over the time course (see chapter 4) will be stated. Reduction is thus defined according to inter-individual variation of control values. Substantial change takes intra-individual variation of control values as a reference. Apart from these direct parameters, *patterns of facial activity* will be described as they were obtained from a cluster analysis in order to comprise the variety of phenomena observed.

5.6 Results on facial behaviour

During depression, patients exhibit considerable reductions in their facial behaviour. Facial behaviour was also qualitatively different from that of controls. Marked changes occurred with improvement. However, at a state of relatively best subjective wellbeing, part of the patients values were still considerably below those of controls. Since general correlations insufficiently represent the associations between psychological measures and behaviours in our case, descriptions of individual values and changes will be accentuated in the following.

5.6.1 *General facial activity*

For a considerable part, particularly of the endogenous depressed patients, general facial activity is reduced compared to that of normal controls. Facial activity increases with improvement of subjective wellbeing. For part of the neurotic depressed patients, however, facial activity decreases with improvement, thus showing changes contradictory to expectation (see Fig. 5.4).

On the average, patients showed between Mdn = 16 – 25 Action Units, i.e. 3 – 6/min., whereas controls had Mdn = 27 – 35 Action Units, i.e. >5/min. Even during the remitted state, patients show significantly lower values than controls (U-Test: p<0.01; cf. table B.13 in the appendix).

As a counter trend, median for neurotic depressed patients at state II is *below* the critical value of f = 22 whereas the median of the endogenous patients is in the normal range.

Reduction

During depression (state I), 15 out of 20 (= 75%*) of the endogenous depressed patients have reduced values whereas this is the case for 7 out of 16 (= 44%) of the neurotic patients only (see table B.14 in the appendix).

Even during their relatively best state (III) 7 (= 35%) of the endogenous and 10 (= 63%) of the neurotic depressed patients still had reduced facial activity.

A divergent trend appeared in both subgroups. For endogenous patients the proportion of reduced values decreased significantly from 75% to 35% whereas it increased for neurotic depressed patients from 44% to 63%.

---

* Although it might be regarded as problematic because numbers of subjects within subgroups are small, percentages are given here for the sake of easier comparison.

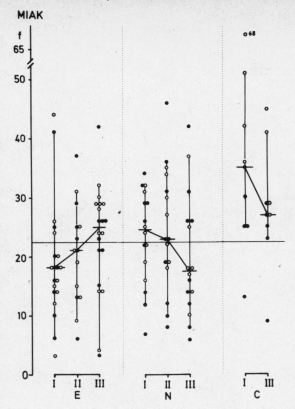

Fig. 5.4 General facial activity (MIAK). Individual frequencies (f) of coded Action Units within a 5 minute interval. Horizontal criterion (defined according to controls) separates *"reduced"* from "normal" values. (For further explanation see Fig. 4.5.)

Individual changes

For 11 out of the 36 patients (= 31%) facial activity increased substantially, i.e. for more than one third of the initial values with improvement (see Fig. 5.5 and table B.14 in the Appendix). The critical value for substantial change is CR = .33, i.e. 33% of the initial value. The reference is 8 out of 9 controls which have lower values, i.e. a more stable behaviour on repeated observations.

While a larger part of endogenous depressed patients has a substantial increase in general facial activity with improvement, the contrary holds for 5 out of 16 (= 31%) neurotic depressed patients (Fisher Exact Test: p<0.05).

From these intra-individual comparisons it can be seen that *consistency* of changes is high (see Fig. 5.5). For 14 out of the 17 (= 82%) cases where a

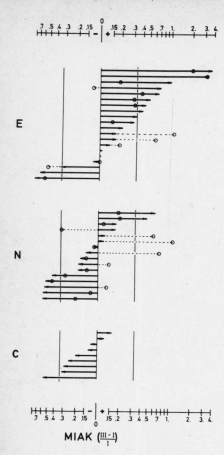

Fig. 5.5 Individual changes of general facial activity (MIAK). Semi-logarithmic scale with linear low values for change ratios: [f(III)-f(I)]:f(I). Endogenous (E), neurotic (N) depressed patients and controls (C). + = increase, − = decrease of MIAK with improvement of subjective wellbeing. *Arrows* indicate amount and direction of change ratios. *Circles* give amount and direction of change to intermediate state: [f(III)-f(I)]:f(I). *Consistency* of change is given when arrow and circle point in the same direction. (Exception: controls and 6 endogenous depressed patients have only two measures). Vertical criterion line defines "*substantial change*" according to controls.

substantial change took place (and three observations were available) both change ratios point to the same direction, thus being consistent. This is evidence that the substantial changes of general facial activity obtained here have not to be attributed to random variation of behaviour, but rather to changes in psychological conditions.

Generally, more than half of the patients showed reduced facial activity during depression. Despite increases with improvement for 10 (= 63%) of the neurotic and 7 (= 44%) of the endogenous depressed patients reduced values remained even at a state of relatively best wellbeing. This result is not easy to explain.

It is possible that the reduction in behaviour represents a depressive tendency as a personality trait or a lack of social skills. Another cause may be the repetition of interviews. This could have induced a "habituation" of facial behaviour. The increasing rates of behaviours in most cases, however, contradict this surmise.

Another explanation is that patients are able to control their behaviour better when improving and follow the display rules of showing little affect. This cannot be excluded but from the therapeutic interventions one would argue against this presumption. In the behaviour therapeutic program in particular, expression (although mainly verbal) of emotional contents was forwarded. This group of patients with neurotic depression showed least facial activity at state III. One could also think of an enduring "labile state" in these patients where depression has been overcome only in part.

It should be reminded that both explanations – labile state and disposition as a cause for this continuously reduced behaviour – would only apply to some of the patients.

For a considerable part of the patients general facial activity is in accordance with the reduction hypothesis. This holds for the two subgroups at different states of wellbeing. Whereas general facial behaviour is reduced for a considerable part of the endogenous depressed patients during depression and increases with improvement, the reverse holds for the neurotic depressed patients. Thus, for both subgroups, there are different trends in this parameter of facial behaviour, for endogenous in accordance with, for neurotic in contradiction to prior expectation.

5.6.2 *Specific facial activity*

Except for the smile (AU12) single facial elements are not unequivocally related to the depressed state. The smile and the lifting of the eyebrows (AU1-2) occur frequently enough to compare it within and between individuals. Except for the smile, frequencies of changes and their direction in relation to subjective wellbeing will be presented only.

The smile (AU12)
As expected, this behaviour was considerably reduced during depression. It frequently remained in the reduced range even during recovery. For most of the patients, however, the frequency of AU12 increased with improvement of subjective wellbeing (see Fig. 5.6).

f.(AU 12)

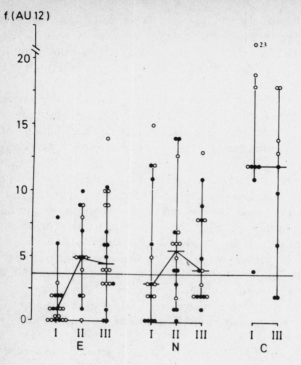

Fig. 5.6 Action Unit (6+)12: Smile. Individual frequencies within a five-minute interval (For further explanation see Fig. 4.5).

For patients median values vary between Mdn 1 to 7, i.e. 0.2 to 1.4 per minute whereas for controls median values are about Mdn = 12, i.e. 2.4 per minute or roughly double the amount of the patients (see Table B.13 in the Appendix).

Compared with general facial activity, control values have a higher variability. At all states of subjective wellbeing, patient values are significantly lower than control values (U-test: p<.05). Generally, patients have significantly lower values during depression (state I) compared to the intermediate state (II) and recovered state (III) (Wilcoxon tests: p<.01). During the depressed state, endogenous depressed patients show significantly lower values than neurotic depressed patients (U-test: p<.05). Other than in the general facial activity, no reverse tendencies were observed for the two patient subgroups.

Reduction
According to control values, the critical level for "reduced values" of AU12 is f<4, i.e. less than 0.8 per minute. During the depressed state 18 (= 90%)

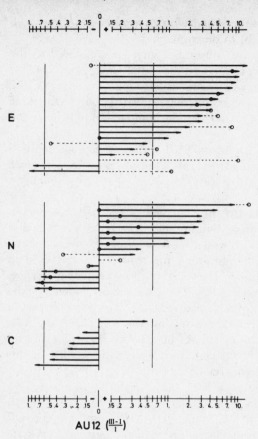

Fig. 5.7 Individual changes for smile. Change ratios for the frequency of AU (6+)12. (For further explanation see Fig. 5.5).

of the endogenous and 10 (= 63%) of the neurotic depressed patients had reduced values. Even when recovered (state III) this is still the case for 7(= 35%) of the endogenous, and 7(= 44%) of the neurotic depressed patients. At the intermediate state (II) of wellbeing the proportion of reduced values clearly declines, (see table B.14 in the appendix). Even at the relatively best state of subjective wellbeing a considerable proportion of the patients (14 = 39%) has reduced values and medians are still below the median of the controls.

Individual changes
The smile increases substantially for 22 of the 36 patients (= 62%) with improvement. For some of the patients, particularly neurotic depressed

ones, a substantial decrease was observed with improved subjective well-being (see Fig. 5.7) and table B.14 in the appendix.

Most of the patients exhibited a substantial increase compared to the limits of CR>0.6 (corresponding to 60% of the initial value) set according to the control values. *Consistency* of change is very high. In 18 out of 22 cases (= 82%) change ratios for the intermediate state (o) point to the same direction as the substantial changes given by the comparison of states ɪ and ɪɪɪ.

Behaviour of AU12 increased for 14(= 70%) of the endogenous depressed patients. This was also the case for 8(= 50%) of the neurotic depressed patients in which case, however, they were opposed by 4(= 25%) having a substantial decrease.

As for the general facial activity median values for patients remain considerably below those of controls. Display rules could play a role in that the interview touched on problems taken more seriously by the patients, whereas the contents had another meaning for controls. Stable median values for controls could also point to the social norms set by the interview, which requires a certain amount of friendliness. The state dependency of the patients' behaviour is clearly given considering the frequent substantial increases with improvement. Certainly the low initial values during depression have to be taken into account. Nevertheless, the highly consistent changes over the three measurements give evidence for the validity of this behaviour as an indicator of the depressed state.

Occurrence of single Action Units
Besides the frequency of smiles (AU12) only AU1+2 (lifting the eyebrows) and AU24 (lip press) do change for at least part of the patients in a state dependent way. Other Action Units neither increase nor decrease unequivocally with improvement. The number of patients and controls for whom the frequency of occurrence changed in one way or the other is depicted in Fig. 5.8. Only the fact of change, not the amount, is registered in this figure.

It is noticeable that AU24 (lip press) decreased with improvement for endogenous and neurotic depressed patients in 15 out of 36 cases (= 42%). AU24 may be regarded as part of negative emotions, such as anger or tension. Frequency of AU1+2 (lifting the eyebrows), a conversational signal, increased in 11 (= 55%) and decreased in 2 (= 10%) of the endogenous depressed patients whereas for neurotic depressed patients, increases and decreases appear to be balanced (each 7 out of 16 = 44%). This is somewhat similar to the state dependent changes of the smile discussed above. No clear direction of changes can be seen for the other AUs. It should be noted that changes for single Action Units were highly consistent as can be seen from the lines within each column in Fig. 5.8.

Generally, AU12 (smile), AU1+2 (lifting the eyebrows) and AU24 (lip

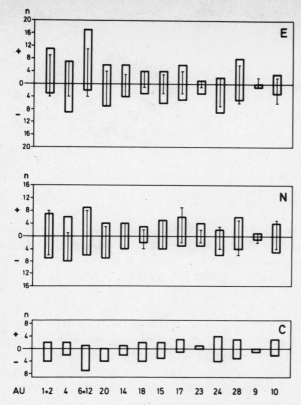

Fig. 5.8 Increase (+) and decrease (−) of Action Unit (AU) frequency with improvement of wellbeing. Number of patients and controls (n) for whom frequencies of Action Units (AU) increased (+) or decreased (−) with improvement from depressed state I to recovered state (III). Lines within columns refer to changes to intermediate state II. Bottom and top lines limit the maximum change within each subsample (E, N, and C).

press) occur frequently enough to determine state dependent changes on a group level. While AU12 and AU1+2 tend to increase with improvement, AU24 (lip press, suggesting an expression of tension and anger) tends to decrease. In the single case, however, other action units may be important, too, as will be shown below in the patterns of facial activity.

Veraguth fold

A characteristic form of the eyelid, the "Veraguth fold", is regarded as a sign of depression or depressive tendencies in traditional psychiatric textbooks (see Fig. 5.9).

From our observations, the specific fold of the upper eyelid, with the characteristic sharp arch appears when the inner eyebrows are slightly lifted

Fig. 5.9 Veraguth fold (left) and normal fold (right) of upper eyelid (from Bleuler, 1969).

and pulled together (AU1+4). This simultaneous activation of musculus frontalis, pars medialis and musculus corrugator supercilii can be done by will given some practice. A stronger activation leads to the "omega sign" of depression, described already by Darwin (1872).

Studies on electromyographically measured activation of this area (Greden et al., 1985) have already been discussed above. Even a very slight activation of both muscles not codable according to the FACS criteria can produce the Veraguth fold. The Veraguth fold could point to a complex facial muscular activation associated with the emotion "grief" or "sadness". Since there are to our knowledge no quantitative data on this phenomenon, the occurrence of the Veraguth fold was determined in a post-hoc analysis. *Results on the occurrence of the Veraguth fold.* It turned out that this feature was present in 8 out of 10 (= 75%) female endogenous depressed patients. In 7 out of these cases, the Veraguth sign was associated with a habitual (i.e. continuously present) AU4 or AU1+4. For the rest of the patients as well as for controls, this feature was present in about one third of the subjects. In particular this was the case for 3 out of 9 male endogenous depressed patients and 5 of the 16 neurotic depressed patients. Four of the controls also showed the Veraguth fold. This, however, was associated with a habitual AU4 or 1+4 in one case only. It seems noteworthy that Greden et al. (1985) found an increased EMG corrugator activity in this group of female patients with an average age of 43 years, having psychomotor agitation.

These observations clearly need to be replicated also whether this sign (and higher corrugator activity too) is specific to female depressed patients of a higher age. For EMG studies, a selection of subjects according to the Veraguth criterion could be helpful for differentiating between subgroups, since it would predict a habitual tension in the corrugator muscle. It would be worth testing whether this is associated with a generally increased arousal.

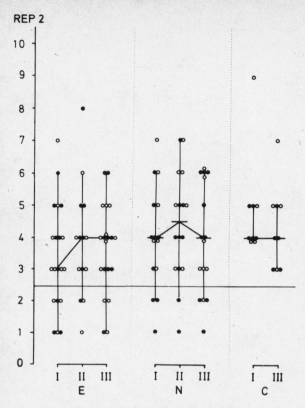

Fig. 5.10 Facial repertoire. Individual number of different Action Units (= repertoire) occurring ⩾ 2 times (REP2) during a 5-minute interval. (For further explanation see Fig. 4.5).

5.6.3 *Facial repertoire*

There is no clear relationship between subjective wellbeing and the width of the facial repertoire as defined here (see Fig. 5.10).

There are no marked differences between patients and controls and no clear changes in the average repertoire occur when subjective wellbeing improves. On the average, 4 to 5 out of the possible 13 different Action Units are observed at least twice for a person during the five minutes analysed (see table B.13 in the Appendix).

Reduction

At the various points in time, 15% to 30% of the patients have a reduced facial repertoire compared to the normal range. This appears independent of the state (see table B.14 in the Appendix). Criterion for reduced values

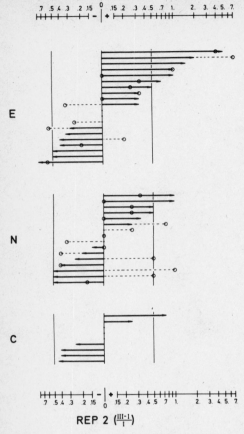

Fig. 5.11 Individual change ratios for the facial repertoire. Change ratios for the repertoire of Action Units occurring ≥ 2 times (REP2) during a 5-minute interval. (For further explanation see Fig. 5.5).

according to control values is set to REP2 <3, i.e. less than three different Action Units within the five minute period.

Individual change
For some of the patients, mainly endogenous depressed, substantial changes in the facial repertoire occur with improvement of subjective wellbeing (see Fig. 5.11).

    Compared to normal variation of the repertoire, a change ratio of CR>0.50 is defined as "substantial". For 6 (= 30%) of the endogenous and only 2 (= 13%) of the neurotic depressed patients a substantial increase of the facial repertoire occurs with improvement. Compared to the other facial parameters, consistency of these substantial changes is somewhat lower, i.e. 6 out of 8 (= 75%) substantial changes from I to III also have a consistent change with regard to the intermediate state III.

It should be noted that both patients and controls activated only a quarter to a third of the possible facial repertoire at least twice during the observed period. This again is in accordance with Zipf's (1949/1965) principle of least effort which obviously holds for the facial behaviour as well. Only a few elements of the behavioural repertoire are frequently used.

5.6.4 *Comparison of facial parameters*

While the frequency of smiles was reduced during depression and mostly increased with improvement, general facial activity seems to differentiate between the two groups of patients. Endogenous depressed patients exhibited the expected reduction followed by substantial increases, whereas for a considerable part of neurotic depressed patients general facial activity tended to decline with improvement of subjective wellbeing. The least association with subjective wellbeing was found for the facial repertoire.

Reduction
With one exception, a reduced repertoire occurred together with a reduced general facial activity (8 out of 9 cases) and this in turn occurred together with a reduced smile (19 out of 21 cases). During improvement (state II and III) this dependency resolves: in 10 out of 15 or 8 out of 17 cases, a reduced general facial activity is *not* found together with a reduced smile (see values in Table B.4 in the Appendix). Even during the improved state there were frequently reduced values in general facial activity *or* frequency of smiles. Assuming this "logical or-connection", 19 out of 30 (= 63%, state II) or 23 out of 36 (= 64%, state III) patients still had reduced values when their depression had already improved.

The proportion of patients with 3 or 2 reduced facial parameters, however, declined for about 22% with improvement (see Table 5.2).

Most of the *substantial changes* occurred already at the intermediate state II whereas few shifts only took place from state II to III.

Furthermore, Table 5.2 indicates that only about 10% of the patients had substantial changes in all of the three parameters; about 60% had an increase in one or two parameters. On the other hand, it is for about a quarter of the patients only that none of the facial parameters substantially increased with improvement.

Frequency of AU12 substantially increased most often (for 60% or 61% of the patients). It is followed by general facial activity with 27% to 31% patients substantially increasing. Here the reverse tendency for neurotic depressed patients has to be remembered. The facial repertoire increased

Table 5.2: *Reduced facial parameters and their change*

	Reduction						Substantial increase			
	I		II		III		I → II		I → III	
m										
	n	p	n	p	n	p	n	p	n	p
0	6	(.17)	11	(.37)	13	(.36)	8	(.27)	9	(.25)
1	9	(.25)	11	(.37)	10	(.42)	15	(.50)	17	(.47)
2	13	(.36)	6	(.20)	10	(.28)	3	(.10)	6	(.17)
3	8	(.22)	2	(.07)	3	(.08)	4	(.13)	4	(.11)
Sample (n)	(36)		(30)		(36)		(30)		(36)	

Note:
Number (n) and proportion (p) of patients showing reduction respectively substantial increase of facial parameters.

less frequently with improvement (23% or 22% of the patients, see Table B.14 in the Appendix).

Initial values and substantial changes
Generally, substantial changes emerge from reduced initial values. Correlations between initial values and amount of change are for patients $r = -.59$ (MIAK), $r = -.53$ (AU12) and $r = -.50$ (REP2); corresponding correlations for controls are $r = -.52$, $r = -.16$ and $r = -.48$.

On the other hand, only part of the reduced values during depression increased substantially with improvement: 9 of 22 (= 41%) for MIAK, 22 of 28 (= 79%) for AU 12 and 6 of 9 (= 67% for REP2). A low initial value appears to be a necessary, however not sufficient condition for a substantial change.

General descriptions
Sex differences No statistically significant differences between males and females were found, neither for average nor for reduced values nor for substantial changes (U-tests: p>.10). Only general facial activity of female controls tended to be significantly higher than that in male controls (U-test: p<.05). It could be presumed that for patients the influence of the illness superimposes that of gender, i.e. mood is the predominant factor in the patient's facial behaviour. However, a larger sample of controls would be needed to corroborate this finding on sex differences.

Intercorrelations General associations of psychological and behavioural measures were not very high when taking a data pool of 90 interviews as the basis (one measure from state I respectively state III for each individual in the respective variables). Frequency of the smile (AU12) correlated fairly high with the Global Clinical Rating (GR: r = .60) respectively the subjective wellbeing (VAS: r = .49; p<.01; see general correlation Table 9.1, chapter 9). For general facial activity (MIAK), correlations with the depression rating or mood are r = .26 (GR) or .17 (VAS), for the repertoire (REP2) r = .17 (GR) or r = .08 (VAS).

These correlations, however, only insufficiently reflect the clear changes in facial behaviour found in the individual.

5.7 Patterns of facial activity

Despite its general reduction, facial behaviour appeared in a variety of patterns even during depression. Some of these patterns are represented in Fig. 5.12 for four endogenous depressed patients. Their other nonverbal behaviours are also described in more detail as single cases in chapter 8.

As can be seen from this figure, patterns varied considerably when comparing their changes over time or between individuals at comparable states. In these cases the depressed state ı, the intermediate state ıı and the recovered state ııı correspond to admission, release, and follow up.

For the male patient EM5, frequency of AU12 (smile) increased from admission to follow-up whereas AU-group 23, 24, 28, 32 (tension and pressure of lip area) decreased. For the female patient EW11, AU12 did not increase before the follow-up interview. However, the AU group 23, etc., indicating tension and pressure in the lip area, increased in this patient as well.

These descriptions could be continued. Given this variety, comparison of facial patterns within or between individuals are difficult to make. Therefore, patterns were clustered according to their similarity. This should reveal whether there are common forms of facial reactions and whether individuals or states of wellbeing can be grouped according to their facial patterns.

Similarity of patterns

A pattern of facial activity was defined as the individually standardized frequency distribution of Action Units occurring during a five minute period of observation within one interview. To explain the procedure a fictitious example will be used. Theoretical frequency distributions of Action Units from three different interviews are shown in Fig. 5.13.

In order to compare these frequency distributions, relative weights for each AU are determined as a first step. This is done by standardizing each distribution to 1. Relative frequencies indicate the relative strength or weight of an AU in relation to the others. Then a similarity of distributions is defined as the Euclidian distance by the sum of absolute differences between corresponding relative frequencies of AUs.

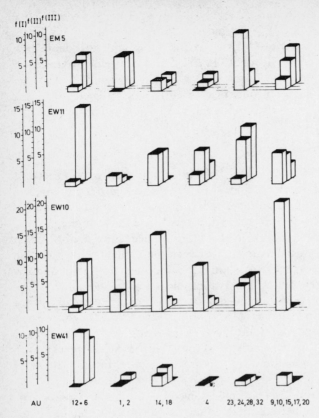

Fig. 5.12 Patterns of facial activity for individual patients. Frequencies for groups of Action Units (AU) within 5-minute intervals during states I, (depressed), II (intermediate) and III (recovered) for four endogenous depressed patients (EM5 to EW41). Action Units are grouped according to similar emotional content.

From the right part of Figure 5.12, Euclidian distances would be $d = 0.2$ when comparing A-B; $d = 0.7$ for $A - C$ and $d = 0.7$ for $B - C$. $A - B$ are obviously more similar than $A - C$ or $B - C$.

This measure of similarity adjusts for different general levels of facial activity and mainly accounts for the configurations, i.e. the relation of frequencies within a distribution.

From the resulting matrix of similarities, the 120 interviews were grouped by a cluster analysis according to the Ward procedure (Steinhausen & Langer, 1977; SPSS-X, 1986, pp. 777-90). Since no optimizing effects were obtained by applying a "hill climbing method", the initial solution of the Ward procedure was taken. It suggests a grouping according to 5 clusters to which each of the 120 interviews is assigned. The different

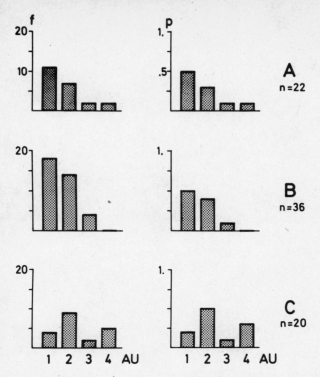

Fig. 5.13 Fictitious distribution of Action Unit frequencies. Frequencies (f) and relative frequencies after individual standardization (p).

interviews of a person may be located in the same or in different clusters depending on the respective similarity of their AU patterns.

5.7.1 *Assignment to clusters*

Some of the clusters turned out to be specific for facial patterns of depressed patients. With changing wellbeing, individuals were assigned to different clusters whereas with few exceptions controls remained in one cluster. In Fig. 5.14, the various clusters are shown representing the individuals and their "migration" from admission to discharge and follow up. Numbering of clusters is taken from the computer analysis and has no specific meaning.

Striking at first sight is the clear-cut assignment and stability of facial patterns for controls. In contrast, patients are represented in a variety of patterns being more or less depression specific. In two of these, clusters I and V, no control interview is to be found. In cluster III, only one control interview is represented. No initial interview of endogenous and only three of neurotic depressed patients is assigned to cluster IV. Since control inter-

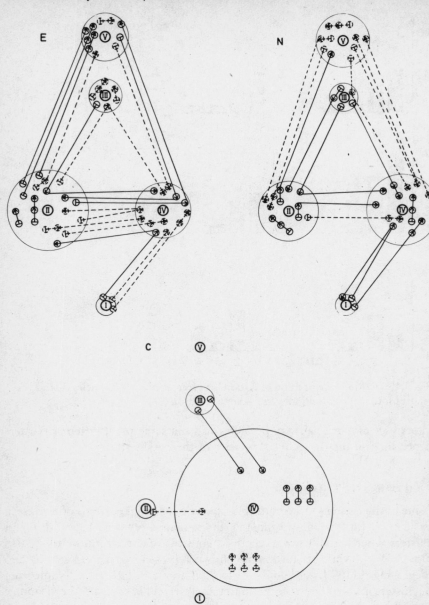

Fig. 5.14 Clusters of facial patterns. Location of each individual pattern (o) within clusters (I to V). Individual patterns are connected (——— = male, ---- = female subjects) in their temporal sequence (→) *Diameters* of cluster circles correspond to proportion of interviews covered by a cluster within the respective subgroup (E, N, C).

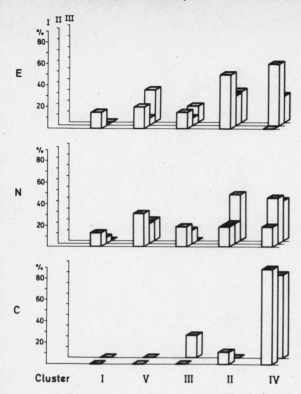

Fig. 5.15 Distribution of facial patterns across clusters. Proportions (%) of individual patterns in clusters I to V within each subgroup (E, N, C) at different states of wellbeing: depressed (I), intermediate (II) and recovered (III) state.

views (15 out of 18 = 83%) are mainly represented in cluster IV, the corresponding pattern of facial behaviour may be regarded as "normal" for the situation given.

Changes of an individual between clusters reveal another interesting result: Clusters I, III and V apparently represent exclusive domains. Except for one neurotic depressed patient, patients change with improvement either to clusters II or IV. They do not change between I, III or V. The individual facial patterns are exclusively either in cluster I *or* III *or* V before changing to II or IV. There is no clear indication of male or female patterns forming a specific cluster. Proportions of clusters at different states of wellbeing are summarized in Fig. 5.15.

An opposite tendency can be seen for cluster II where the proportion of endogenous depressed patients decreases with improvement whereas it increases for neurotic depressed patients.

The most noteworthy finding here is the relative homogeneity and stabil-

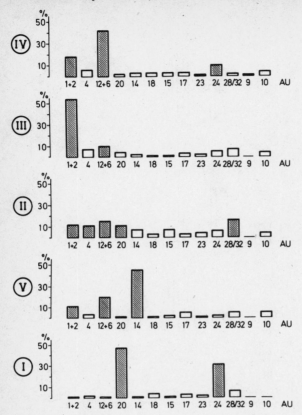

Fig. 5.16 Patterns of facial activity. Relative weight (% = centroid value) of Action Units (AU) within clusters I to V. Values ≥ 10% marked.

ity of facial patterns in normals compared to the heterogeneity and variability in patients.

5.7.2 *Description and interpretation of patterns*

Each cluster represents a pattern of facial activity characterized by the relative weight of single Action Units. The centroid values of the single elements define the average reaction pattern represented within a cluster.

In order to interpret these patterns, one needs to make reference to the possible emotional content of each element. This is a critical point which requires some additional remarks. It would be of low risk to restrict oneself to the numbers of AUs, the number of clusters, and to give the quantitative figures avoiding any interpretation of emotional contents.

On the other hand, facial expression is investigated at least to promote hypotheses about emotional and communicative processes although emotional content of facial behaviour is still insufficiently validated.

There remains a dilemma: Restricting oneself to the absolutely safe leads to anaemic reports on the results; they could eventually be brought to life by a reader who takes the trouble to reformulate numbers into content. Interpretations, on the other hand, are open to debate and – this has to be taken seriously – are susceptible to the flaw of being insufficiently validated. Therefore, interpretations are offered here in order to stimulate hypotheses and contradictions. It is not pretended that they are based on direct and sufficiently validated access to emotions. These preliminary interpretations are based on proposals given amongst others by Ekman & Friesen (1978) for Action Units and their combinations as parts in emotional expressions. They could contribute to expanding hypotheses on emotional processes during depression. Fig. 5.16 shows centroid values as percentage weights of single Action Units for each of the five clusters.

As can be seen from Fig. 5.16 single Action Units have different relative weights within the five clusters. A level of >10% is marked to accentuate the important proportions. The centroid values do not indicate the striking single event but rather the relative weight of AUs within an average pattern.

Cluster IV

The average pattern of facial behaviour represented in this cluster can be labelled "normal" since it covers most of the control interviews and very few of neurotic patients during depression. It is dominated by frequent smiles (AU(6+)12) and lifting of the eyebrows (AU1+2). In addition, lip press (AU24) occurs with an average of 10%.

The behaviour could be interpreted as a friendly-interested pattern. According to Ekman (1979) facial activity in the frontal area can be emotional, as well as purely conversational signals. As an emotional expression, AU1+2 occurs together with "surprise" or "interest" (Tomkins, 1982). Given the asymmetric interview situation, this behaviour is primarily to be regarded as a conversational signal of the speaker, which could underline or punctuate the spoken content, occur as a question mark or when searching for words (Ekman, 1979). The dominating smile (AU12) in this pattern can also be regarded as a conversational signal (Kraut & Johnston, 1979), which in addition communicates a positive affect. At the same time some tension stemming from the asymmetric situation might be reflected in AU24 (lip press) with an average representation of 10%.

In sum, this cluster IV is characterized by a behavioural pattern "normally" displayed in such a situation. It mainly contains the smile and the lifting of the eyebrows as elements. They include positive affective expressions and interest or can be regarded as positive facial conversational signals during the dialogue.

Cluster III

This pattern could be characterized as "actively interested" and partly "friendly". Here 14 of the 120 interviews are represented including two initial interviews with controls. The pattern is dominated by a relatively high amount of eyebrow activity (AU1+2). In addition, the smile (AU12) is represented with 10%.

In this pattern, the relative weight of AU1+2 and AU12 is interchanged compared to cluster IV. Cluster III has a more frequent usage of speaker signals, indicating an active interest combined occasionally with friendly signals. Compared to Cluster IV the kind of conversational signals could be interchanged between AU1+2 and AU12. In sum, active interest seems to be the dominant feature of this pattern.

Cluster II

Variable facial activity, where 5 out of the 13 coded AUs appear with a proportion of more than 10% characterize this pattern. It represents 34 (= 28%) of the interviews including one initial control. None of the AUs dominates the pattern. AU1+2 and AU12 occur above the limit in all other clusters except cluster I. AU20 (lip stretch) as a possible indicator of fear is more clearly present in cluster I. Specific features of this cluster are the activations of AU4 (brow lower) and AU28/32 (lip suck, lip bite). Both can be regarded as indicators of tension or suppressed anger. AU4 is also part of the emotion sadness, grief or fear when combined with other AUs (cf. section on Veraguth fold).

AUs 28/32 are mostly associated with negative affects and general tension. This pattern thus could be regarded as representing mildly negative affective states and tension blended by some positive components.

Cluster V

This facial pattern could be characterized by emotional ambivalence with a predominance of AU14 (dimpler), an inward pulling of the mouth corners. This cluster represents 22 (= 18%) interviews, none of them controls.

The inward pulling of mouth corners (AU14) sometimes combined with dimples, partly resembles a smile, partly the appearance of AU15, depression of lip corners or AU20, stretching of the lips.

Since AU12 and AU1+2 are also present with considerable relative weights of 20% resp. 11% one could presume an ambivalence of positive and negative facial expressions. Ekman & Friesen in their proposals for affective interpretations relate AU14 to contempt. By the occurrence of

AU12 resp. AU1+2, this negative affective expression would be assuaged by displaying friendly and interested behaviour. From this, ambivalence could be regarded as the characterizing feature of this pattern.

Cluster I

This depression specific pattern, covering 6 interviews of depressed patients, is characterized by the predominance of AU20 (lip stretch) and AU24 (lip press).

Both Action Units point to negative affective tension. According to Ekman & Friesen, AU20 occurs with the emotion of fear, AU24 with the emotion of anger. In contrast to all other patterns, positive affective signs (AU12, AU1+2) are nearly lacking. Thus, this pattern is characterized by the expression of negative affects without conversational signals or indications of positive affects.

Comparison of clusters

Patterns of facial activity obtained by cluster analysis are characterized by the predominance of different Action Units, presumably associated with specific emotions.

A friendly, actively interested behaviour is present in the "friendly normal" pattern of cluster IV and the "actively interested" pattern of cluster III, with different weighting of the positive elements. In contrast, the pattern of cluster I is dominated by facial indicators of "fear and anger". Indicators of positive affects are lacking. The pattern of cluster V is dominated by an indicator for the emotion contempt, attenuated by a considerable proportion of smile and eyebrow lifting. This led us to denote this cluster as representing "ambivalence of emotional expression". Variable facial activity given in the pattern of cluster II combines a broad repertoire of AUs. This pattern specifically contains indicators for "anger, sadness and tension" which are not represented as clearly in the other patterns. This cluster, however, is not dominated by a few Action Units as is the case for the others.

It should be noted that some of the AUs do not appear with a relative weight >10%, like AUs 10, 15, 17. AU15 (lip corner depress) would be regarded as an indicator for sadness.

It has to be emphasized that the relative weight of the single elements from the facial repertoire assessed clearly distinguishes between the various patterns. These in turn could be assigned differentially to controls and to patients during depression and recovery as has been shown above. By this, these facial patterns can be regarded as state specific but also depending on individual behavioural tendencies.

5.8 Discussion of results of facial behaviour

Facial behaviour is obviously associated with the state of subjective well-being in an individual specific way. There are characteristic patterns of facial behaviour as well as reduced general and specific facial activity. The repertoire, i.e. the variety of facial elements displayed, however, turned out not to be affected by depression to any considerable degree. For individuals state dependent changes occur in part, rarely in all of the facial parameters. Unexpectedly, substantial decreases of facial behaviour occur, especially for part of the neurotic depressed patients, with improvement. This is evidence against a universal validity of the reduction hypothesis for depression with regard to facial behaviour. Some of the methodological and conceptual consequences suggested by these results will be discussed in the following.

Patterns of facial activity
The variety of facial patterns for the depressed patients compared to the homogeneity of controls was an unexpected result of this analysis. According to these findings even during depression a differentiated expression of affects takes place. The content of these affect displays can be interpreted as pointing to emotions of anger and fear. There were no clear indications for sadness or grief. Moreover, the patterns suggest a combined occurrence of positive and negative facial components. These interpretations were drawn from proposals of Ekman (1980), Ekman & Friesen (1978), Kraut & Johnston (1979) and Krause (1981). They must remain preliminary and hypothetical at this point. A behaviour like AU24 (lip press) could indicate inner tension as well as controlled expression of anger (Krause, 1981). The same behaviour may have a different meaning depending on the context etc. Further empirical evidence is needed to gain a firm basis for these or similar interpretations. But even with better knowledge, interpretations of emotions from naturally occurring behaviour must remain ambiguous to some extent because of the probabilistic nature of meaning given by behavioural signs during social interaction (Scherer, 1980, cf. chapter 2).

Various clusters are clearly specific for depressed patients, whereas one cluster represents a "normal" pattern of facial behaviour. With few exceptions, control interviews were represented in this cluster together with those of patients when being improved.

Discrete emotions
From the patterns of facial elements it follows that discriminable expressions occur as behavioural tendencies in a state dependent way. This study was not intended to be a comparison of dimensional approaches (Schlosberg, 1952; Osgood, 1966) or discrete approaches (Izard, 1972; Plutchik, 1980; Tomkins, 1982; Scherer, 1984) to emotions.

The clusters of facial patterns found here obviously do not support any system of 4, 5, or 7 classes of emotions.

Nevertheless, given these clusters, it seems inappropriate to apply a priori a dimensional concept for facial behaviour. More has to be known about the actual co-occurrence of elements during emotional situations. Given these results it is to be expected that during social interaction affects and affective blends are conveyed by discriminable facial patterns suggesting a variety of emotional states.

Facial expression of affects and mood in depression

While the variety of facial action patterns of depressed patients was an unexpected finding, the reduction expecially of the smile during depression and its increase with improvement is not surprising. This result corresponds to the expectation that depressed people do not display a happy face and it can be regarded as some kind of validity check for the observational method. The significant correlations of "felt" and "unfelt happy" expressions reported by Matsumoto et al. (1983) are in accordance with this result.

The smile which according to Grinker et al. (1961) can be observed occasionally in more than 90% of depressed patients, need *not* be equated with the presence of positive affects. This is especially the case when it occurs together with negative facial elements such as a "negative affect smile" (Ekman, Friesen & Ancoli, 1980; Krause, 1981). From the report of Matsumoto et al. (1983), however, no clear evidence is given that either psychotic or neurotic patients show more of this behaviour.

But even as a conversational signal (Kraut & Johnston, 1979) the smile conveys some positive attitude which is displayed to a minor degree by patients.

The association of general facial activity with subjective wellbeing is not as clear as for the smile. Fewer patients show reduced values compared to those of controls. For part of the neurotic depressed patients, general facial activity unexpectedly decreases with improvement. This can be regarded as evidence against the suppressant effect of medication for facial activity. Since medication was given to endogenous depressed patients only, one might have expected a decline in facial activity mainly in these patients. However, the contrary was the case.

Reduction persists for a substantial part of the patients even during remission. This points to either a still labile state or a persistent deficit, possibly apparent as a lack of social skills. The problem of disorders in communication will be discussed in chapter 10 with reference to all the observed nonverbal behaviour.

For only few individuals the repertoire, i.e. the number of different facial actions activated by an individual, appeared to be influenced by depression. Patients and controls activate on the average Mdn = 4 AUs out of the 13

AUs coded at least two times during a five minute period. For a few patients there is a substantial increase of the repertoire with improvement.

General correlations between facial parameters and subjective wellbeing turned out to be too low to enable valid inferences on the subjective state of an individual. However, for the single subjects, incidents of reduction and substantial changes clearly show the state dependency of facial behaviour. It is important to note that 30 of the 36 patients (= 83%) have at least one reduced facial parameter during depression and 27 (= 75%) show a substantial increase in at least one of the parameters. Thus the reduction hypothesis is valid, though in a way specific for the individual.

For part of the neurotic depressed patients, unexpected decreases are found with improvement, especially for general facial activity. It should be noted that there is rarely a total lack of facial activity during depression. It may be reduced in individual cases but some facial actions can be observed in all cases.

Principle of antithesis in facial expression?
We can only speculate as to why indicators of sadness or grief are rarely to be found in single Action Units or facial patterns. One is inclined to refer to Darwin's (1872) principle of antithesis, expanded by Leyhausen (1967). The central affect of depression, grief or sadness would result in actions like withdrawal and passivity. The affective minorities or minor motivations (like anger or fear) which supposedly are also present during depression would be expressed in facial actions.

In these behaviours, a "leakage" of inner directed hostility together with fear as postulated by Abraham (1911/1968) for depression could have occurred. Evidence for inner directed hostility in depression has been found by Izard (1972) and Gershon et al. (1968) using content analysis. Facial behaviour suggests further evidence. In addition, tendencies for affect control could be active. Probably the central negative affect would be most controlled whereas minor affects would be less controlled and then become apparent in expression. With the controlled affect of grief, other negative affective components could "leak" through in the behaviour (Ekman & Friesen, 1972; Krause, 1981).

The depressed mood, thus, may become apparent in other negative expressive elements. It is obvious in the reduced behaviour too. Given the reduced level of facial activity, the negative elements probably add to the impression of a depressed affective state.

Methodological consequences
It is by intra-individual comparison that changes of individual specific facial reactions can be discovered. Furthermore, definition of reduced values and substantial changes according to inter-and intra-individual variation of

behaviour in controls gave some normative basis to evaluate individual behaviours. By this, persistent behavioural deficits in patients even during remission and independent changes in individual behavioural parameters could be determined. These phenomena would have been obscured when comparing on a group level only. A group comparison or a general correlation lumps together individuals for whom a state dependency of a specific behaviour is present with those for whom this is not the case. An average low association would result.

Individual associations of facial parameters and subjective wellbeing seem to be described appropriately by "logical or-connections" between the single aspects. This is to assess the association as it is probably done in everyday life, where we recognize specific changes in individuals we know. This aspect will be discussed further in the final chapter 10.

For the problem of comparing patterns of facial activity individual standardization and clustering proved to be useful. By this, the total of analysed interviews could be grouped according to the similarity of the facial activity on the basis of individual frequency distributions. From the centroid values for facial behaviours an average pattern characteristic for individuals in the respective cluster could be deduced. Complex Action Units or AU combinations were not specifically analysed here since most of the combinations occurred with very low frequencies. Nevertheless, the patterns obtained by cluster analysis already give some insight into the complex facial behaviour.

In sum, patients' facial behaviour tends to reflect the subjective state by reduced values during depression and substantial increase with improvement. This holds, however, only when allowing "logical or-connections" between variables and taking individual specific reactions into account. Whereas the frequency of smile turned out to be more generally changed with mood in the expected way, general facial activity tended to discriminate between subgroups of patients. Some of the neurotic depressed patients unexpectedly decreased their facial activity with improvement.

Differentiated affective processes can be deduced from the variety of facial patterns found for depressed patients during depression and recovery. It would be of diagnostic and therapeutic interest to further validate these differences since distinct diagnostic and treatment approaches could be conceived depending on the predominant affects being involved during depression.

6　Gaze and speech

Gaze and speech are analysed here as behaviours whose temporal structure provides clues to the readiness or capacity to receive and produce social information. Both behaviours are dealt with together since they are highly coordinated during conversation and comparable methodological approaches can be applied to each of them. These behaviours are also frequently studied simultaneously and reported on together in the literature (Kendon, 1967; Argyle & Cook, 1976; Exline & Fehr, 1982; Rutter, 1984).

For their relation to depression, two complementary functions of gaze and speech are especially relevant. On the one hand, it is assumed that the extent of gaze at the other indicates the readiness or capacity to *receive* social nonverbal information from the partner. On the other hand speech during social interaction can be regarded as an indicator of the extent to which an individual is ready or able to *produce* partner-directed information. During depression, a clear decrease in emotional and cognitive capacity and thus a reduction in both behaviours is to be expected.

6.1 Gaze during social interaction

The eyes are of special relevance for human interaction. Since the beginning of the systematic study of human behaviour attempts have been made to understand the "language of the eyes" (Magnus, 1885). The eyes were frequently regarded as "the mirror of the soul". The most immediate and purest interrelation emerges, according to Simmel (1921), from the mutual gaze. In contrast to a simple viewing or observation, the eye contact constitutes a totally new and unique relation between individuals.

The region around the eyes is a prominent area of the face. As has been shown by Yarbus (1967) the eyes and the mouth are the areas most looked at within the face. In many cultures, the eyes are accentuated by make-up, and eyes can be found in many of their symbols (König, 1975). By using an eye-schema it is possible to elicit a smile very early in infancy (Ahrens, 1954; Ambrose, 1961) and the eyes are an important part in the communication between adults and infants (Papousek & Papousek, 1977). Thus, from early infancy on there are indications of the high social relevance of gaze. Unless

84

otherwise stated, the term gaze will be used here to refer to gazing or looking at the other's face or just at the eye region.

6.1.1 *Functions of gaze*

Various aspects of nonverbal communication can be illustrated most distinctly in the gaze. By looking at the other one signals attention. At the same time information from the other is received.

Within the temporal structure of looking at and away from the other, one's own planning of speech and speech preparation is reflected. To accomplish this, gaze regulates the kind and the amount of incoming visual information. At the same time these alterations of gaze at or away from the other regulate the flow of the dialogue. One will be less likely to be interrupted when looking *away* than when looking *at* the other at the end of long utterances (Kendon, 1967; Beattie, 1978a and b; Ellgring, 1981, for a review cf. Rutter, 1984).

During face-to-face interaction, gaze may have various functions: monitoring the behaviour of others, regulation or coordination of behaviour during a conversation, expression of a preparedness for or avoidance of communication (Kendon, 1967; von Cranach, 1971b; Rutter, 1984).

The regulative function of gaze has been postulated by Kendon (1967) from the finding that individuals tend to look away from the other at the beginning of long utterances and to look back at the other again towards the end of these utterances. Looking away would be a signal for the partner not to interrupt, whereas looking at the partner would be a signal to take the turn. Gaze behaviour would, thus, be a "floor yielding cue" by which turns during dialogue are signalled and regulated (Kendon, 1973; Duncan, 1972; Duncan & Fiske, 1977).

However, this regulating function has been questioned in two studies of Rutter, Stephenson, Aylling & White (1978) and Beattie (1978a and b). They found that gaze at the other is frequently absent in these turns during conversation. Moreover, the other is often not able to perceive the gaze since he is looking away at this moment. Thus gaze would not be so much a way of synchronizing the speech flow of two individuals as a way of enabling interactants to monitor each other. Kendon (1978) argues against this interpretation. He claims that it depends on the kind of interaction, the kind of turns each speaker takes and the intentions in the moment of the interactants as to which behaviour may serve as a floor yielding cue. Since various other behaviours could function the same way one single behaviour could not be investigated apart from the others in terms of a turn taking signal.

The coordination of gaze and speech could be regarded as a mechanism which enables short term discharge from the task to process social information. Various studies showed that the other is looked at less during speaking than during listening (Nielsen, 1962; Kendon, 1967; Argyle & Ingham, 1972; Argyle & Cook, 1976, p. 98ff; Ellgring, 1975, 1981). Argyle, (1975, p. 229) gives the following figures for individuals talking about a neutral topic at a distance of about 2 metres: general gaze at the other in 60% of the time, when listening 70%, while speaking 40%. Mutual gaze occurs during about 30% of the time.

Various phenomena are in accordance with the assumption of an un-burdening effect of looking away. Turning the gaze away, i.e. the mainly lateral eye movements as a reaction to various kinds of tasks (Day, 1964) can be regarded this way. The arousal reducing effect of "cut-off" be-haviour which has been postulated by Chance (1962) can be observed in various species. The reduced amount of gaze during speaking would also fit in with this assumption.

In contrast, gazing at another individual may increase the level of arousal (Nichols & Champness, 1971; Kleinke & Pohlen, 1971; Bond & Komai, 1976) and may function as an aggression releasing signal between humans as well as between animals (Ellsworth, Carlsmith & Henson, 1972; Ellsworth & Langer, 1976; Thomsen, 1974).

It could be shown experimentally that this coupling of gaze and speech occurs independently, whether a person or another object provides visual information (Ellgring, 1981). This linkage of gaze to the various phases of speech preparation and speech is represented in changing probabilities over time (see Fig. 6.1).

The minimum of gazing at the information source occurs shortly before the beginning of the talking (see Fig. 6.1). Probability of gazing at an information source increases again toward the end of the verbal output. This pattern of gaze probability remains the same given some lamps as a visual information source instead of the face of the other.

Generally, probability of gazing away increases with difficulty of the task (Duke, 1968; Ellgring, 1981). This indicates that with higher cognitive load there is a tendency to cut off meaningful information. Comparable to attention theories (Broadbent, 1958; Treisman, 1964) an upper limit for the capacity to process information is assumed. Visual information is not pro-cessed above this limit. By reducing the load within one channel, as is the case for receiving visual information by gaze, an overload can be avoided. Given this assumption, other phenomena of gaze, like the gaze avoidance of autistic children may be explained as a reduction of their excessive level of arousal (Hutt & Ounstedt, 1966; O'Connor & Hermelin, 1967).

Thus, during various phases of a speech process, different conditions exist for the associated gaze. Firstly, there is a coordination performed by the individual for both of these behaviours. Secondly, there are intervals where there is more or less cognitive load for the individual. An increased

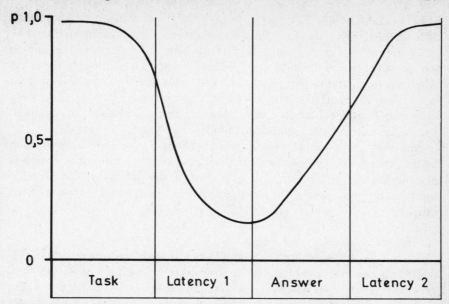

Fig. 6.1 Probability of gaze during a task-answer sequence. Probability (p) of gaze at a source of visual information during a standardized sequence of task, latency, and answer (from Ellgring, 1981).

load is probably given when social information is produced, i.e. when there is talk. This is also the case during gaze at the other, when relevant nonverbal information from the partner is processed at the same time. Thirdly, by gazing away, a general unloading of the information processing task can be accomplished. Given the hypothesis of a general reduction of performance capacity in depression, it has to be expected that states of increased strain as they are given when gazing at the other are less likely or will be avoided.

Gaze as part of the intimacy equilibrium

Gaze is regarded as a component of nonverbal behaviour which, according to the equilibrium theory of Argyle and Dean (1965; Argyle, 1970) contributes to intimacy and social distance. With decreased spatial distance, as is the case, for example, in an elevator, the higher tension resulting from social closeness is reduced by gazing away. By this, an equilibrium of intimacy is maintained. The "cut-off" behaviour (Chance, 1962, 1967) may be regarded correspondingly.

The finding of Ellsworth & Ross (1975) that a dialogue is rated as more "intimate" when there is more gaze at the other would, however, challenge a simple model of equilibrium. Moreover, reciprocal relations between the extent of gaze at the other have been reported by Schneider & Hansvik

(1977) and Coutts & Schneider (1975, 1976). According to Coutts, Irvine & Schneider (1977) there is some compensatory adjustment as predicted by the equilibrium theory. Subjects reacted with fewer smiles when being looked at more. On the other hand, subjects tend to look more at the other when the other smiles. According to Patterson's (1976) "arousal model" it is a change in spatial distance which has a stronger effect on increasing arousal than a higher amount of being gazed at. Gaze alone is, according to Patterson, not sufficient to induce compensatory actions.

Although some studies provide arguments against a simple equilibrium theory, there is no evidence for the reverse. A reduced amount of gaze will not induce a higher arousal. A reduction of arousal and a discharge of information processing is the more probable effect of gazing away from the other.

Seeking and avoiding of eye-contact

Up to now there is no convincing evidence that during conversation eye-contact between individuals, i.e. mutual gaze at the face or at the eyes, generally is either sought for or avoided. Exceptions are autistic children (Hutt & Ounstedt, 1966) or incidental observations of schizophrenics (Argyle & Cook, 1976). Contrary to the assumptions of Strongman & Champness (1968) and Argyle & Ingham (1972) postulating tendencies to seek or avoid eye contact above chance, it turned out that when testing with appropriate probability models, no significant deviations from chance could be found (Ellgring, 1975; Rutter, Stephenson, Lazzerini, Ayling & White, 1977; Lazzerini, Stephenson & Neave, 1978; Dabbs, Evans, Hopper & Purvis, 1980; Wagner, Clarke & Ellgring, 1983). From these studies it follows that except for specific individuals or groups a model of interpersonal independence of gaze has to be maintained. This means that internal conditions of the individual like the depressed state in our case become more important as a regulating factor for the gaze.

Expressive components of gaze

Some phenomena are to be described here which refer to expressive components of the gaze. They have little to do with the eye itself and the direction of gaze, but nevertheless contribute to impressions about the "way of looking". They partly describe aspects of the lid widening, partly temporal features of gazing, as in the stare.

A classification of abnormalities of the gaze proposed by Riemer (1955) contains these temporal and also complex expressive features. According to this classification, the "excessive blink" is used by hysterics to limit the span during which they perceive others. The "dramatic gaze" or stare can be used according to this view by exaggerating the "meaningful" gaze in order to increase the self-image. The "dull" absent gaze of depressives can indicate their hallucinations. The "cautious" gaze on the other hand is described as over-alert and symptomatic of paranoid ideas whereas continuous gaze avoidance is supposed to be typical of schizophrenia and autism.

These qualitative descriptions point to phenomena whose validity, however, has still to be tested.

Phenomena like "friendly" or "sad" gaze or stare are based mainly on changes of the facial musculature around the eyes. Thus, the "sad" expression which may also be seen in the Veraguth fold (cf. chapter 5) is given by the configuration of the upper eyelids. Lifting the upper eyelid contributes to the impression of a "surprised" or "fearful" gaze. Raising the cheeks gives the impression of a "friendly" but also of a "sad" gaze, depending on additional features, whereas contracting the lower eyelids leads to perceive an "angry" or "aggressive" gaze. The "eye flash" (Eibl-Eibesfeldt, 1972) describes a complex behavioural pattern which contains a lifting of the eyebrows, slow nodding of the head together with a smile.

Diameter of the pupils and direction of gaze are the main changing features which can be perceived from the eyes. The extent of the pupil size and its changes depending on the arousal level is assumed to influence evaluation of sympathy (Hess, 1965). The meaning of various directions of gaze is not investigated here since this field with its richness of hypotheses (Ehrlichman & Weinberger, 1978) does not immediately contribute to our present problem.

In our study observation will be confined to looking at or away from the other, i.e. the direct social and communicative aspect of the behaviour.

Personality factors and short term influencing factors
The extent of gazing at the other was found to depend on various factors like personality features, social needs and elements of the situation (cf. Argyle & Cook, 1976; Rutter, 1984). The extent of gaze in turn influences the judgement of intimacy between individuals (Thayer & Schiff, 1974, 1977; Kleinke, Meeher & La Fong, 1974). "Machiavellianism", i.e. the need to control others, as a personality trait is regarded as an influencing factor on gaze in a study of Exline, Thibaut, Hickey & Gumpert (1970), together with situational components like the possibility to behave in a dishonest way. On the other hand, females tend to look at others more frequently and for longer duration (Exline & Winters, 1965). Dominance and Machiavellianism would hardly be regarded as the influencing factors being especially high in females.

A variety of relatively stable factors has been found so far to influence gaze behaviour: sex of subject and interviewer (Exline, Gray & Schuette, 1965), personality factors like affiliative motivation (Exline & Winters, 1965), need for approval (Rosenfeld, 1966), abasement and nurturance needs (Libby & Yaklevich, 1973), attractiveness and attraction between partners (Exline, Gray & Schuette, 1965), status and power differences (Exline, 1972). If all these different variables influence gaze behaviour to a considerable extent, one would have to expect, according to Jones & Pansa (1979), psychopathological states to dominate overwhelmingly all these general factors in order to alter this behaviour significantly.

According to various studies, indication of momentary states seems to be an important aspect of gaze behaviour. The readiness to communicate indicated by gazing at the other substantially increases the probability of a discourse taking place (Cary, 1978). Looking at the other during a dialogue functions as a reinforcer (Holzkamp, 1969). It intensifies a positive evaluation of a positive content and a negative evaluation of a negative content (Ellsworth & Carlsmith, 1968). According to Stephenson, Ayling & Rutter (1976) gazing at the other prompts spontaneity, a broader discussion and facilitates the adoption of conventional role relationships. However, no clear influence on the content itself is given (Rutter, Stephenson & Dewey, 1981). Thus, except for an excessively long-lasting and intense stare, normal gazing at the other has positive and facilitating effects for an interaction.

Generally, situational factors and interpersonal relations appear to influence gaze behaviour at least as much as personality factors. From this it has to be expected that an extremely altered state of psychological functioning during depression will affect gaze behaviour to some extent.

6.1.2 *Gaze in depression*

Studies on gaze in relation to depression provide no consistent results even though they generally point to a reduced amount of gaze. Like the studies on speaking described below they appear to give only weak support to the clinical expectation of a clear reduction in these behaviours. On a group level, depressed patients like other groups of patients tend to exhibit less gaze than controls.

For depressed patients, Waxer (1974) found significantly less eye contact. Eye contact of depressed patients increased when treated by medication compared to a placebo group (Miller et al., 1977). In this study, however, quantitative data on subjective wellbeing and on the behaviour observed are missing.

In a study of Rutter & Stephenson (1972a) schizophrenics on average gazed at the other for 43% of the time. Depressives gazed at the other for 52% of time whereas for the respective control groups this was 67% or 71%. Studies reported later by these authors, however, revealed less clear results. In a study of Rutter (1976) schizophrenics as well as controls gazed 55% of time, depressives 45% of time, whereas patients with neurotic and personality disorders showed only 35% to 40% gaze at the other. Further interesting data are reported from comparing long stay with recently admitted schizophrenics (pp. 301-3). Rutter found 31% or 28% gaze, i.e. considerably lower figures than in the above study. Since in both studies different topics were discussed during the observed`session, Rutter concludes that the content might be a main factor in influencing gaze. This would be in accordance with the notion that dealing with personal problems induces a higher mental load. This would reduce the capacity for looking at the other, as was the case in the latter study. For a longitudinal study, where the influence of a depressed state changing over time has to be analysed it follows that observations should be made in comparable social situations thus holding this influence constant.

Comparison of pooled studies

When comparing quantitative data on gaze from various studies, surprisingly homogeneous average figures emerge for the various groups. In a meta-analysis data from 11 studies were compiled: Kendon (1967), Strongman & Champness (1968), Hinchliffe, Lancashire & Roberts, 1970 and 1971a), Rutter & Stephenson (1972a and b), Ellgring (1977), Rutter (1976 and 1977a), Rennschmid (1979). Excluded is a study by Hinchliffe et al. (1970) because of unclear data. These data were also neglected by the authors in subsequent reports.

As can be seen from Fig. 6.2 schizophrenic and depressive patients do not differ substantially with regard to their average amount of gaze.

The small variations within groups show that gaze behaviour, at least the average values for depressives and controls, reveal similar results in different studies. Gaze appears lowest in the group with neurotic and other disorders (N+0). It has to be stressed that the difference of about 10% which shows between depressives and controls would be too small to support the clinical impression of a clearly reduced gaze.

Also, in a study of Jones & Pansa (1979), depressive patients on admission showed on the average less gaze than controls. This held, however, for the last two minutes of an interview only but not for its other parts. Comparisons between interviews of depressives on admission and on discharge as well as of schizophrenics revealed no significant group differences with regard to gaze.

As a parameter for a differential diagnostic of depression gaze appears to contribute insufficiently regarding the results presented so far. In depression, gaze appears to be somewhat reduced. The extent of reduction, however, is small. Some studies even found no significant differences compared to controls. Is the depressed mood therefore not expressed in the gaze and does clinical impression exaggerate an in fact quite weak relationship? Both questions will be pursued in the longitudinal study below.

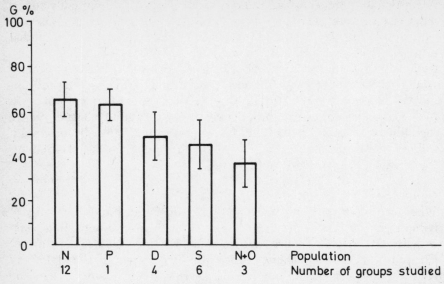

Fig. 6.2 Amount of gaze in clinical populations. Meta-analysis of the relative amount of gaze (G%) from 11 studies with a total of 26 different groups. Averages and their standard deviation for normals (N), psychiatric patients except depressives and schizophrenics (P), depressives (D), schizophrenics (S), neurotic and organic disorders except depression (N+O) (for further explanation see text).

Gaze during speech

It is not surprising that results are no more consistent when comparing the relative amount of gaze during speaking, i.e. a state of increased cognitive load. If a study found that the single behaviour was reduced in depression this was also the case for the proportion of gaze during speech (Hinchliffe et al., 1971b; Rutter & Stephenson, 1972a). If it was found that the single behaviour was not reduced, the combined parameter of gaze during speech did not significantly differ between depressives and controls either (Rutter, 1976). The proportion of gaze during speech is, however, confounded with the two single behaviours so that these results have to be expected on a group level. On the other hand, it should be possible that an individual shows reduced gaze without decreasing verbalization.

From the studies on the relationship between both behaviours and the concept of reducing visual information by gazing away it has to be expected that a negative correlation exists between the amount of gaze and speech activity. If gazing away leads to a decrease of the mental load, a reduced amount of gaze could enable a higher amount of speech.

6.1.3 *Consequences*

Two important functions for communication are clearly to be seen in gaze behaviour: Firstly, a selection of incoming information is accomplished by the direction of gaze. Secondly, by gazing away, a discharge of information processing takes place, but also a loss of information which presumably is kept as low as possible. During a conversation it is to be expected that gaze will be substantially reduced only when it is required by a higher internal load.

Obviously, gaze may have various other functions. The individual may consciously display interest, readiness to communicate etc. For the receiver, on the other hand, gaze would have various other functions and meanings. It may function as a turn-taking cue, may regulate social distance, or communicate interpersonal attitudes. For our problem regarding the relationship between the behaviour and the subjective wellbeing, the expressive function of a momentary state, i.e. willingness or capacity to receive social information, is the most important at this point.

6.2 Speech

As a vocal nonverbal component of communication the course and the amount of talk and silence during dialogue are analysed. Since content aspects of speech are excluded we deal with vocal nonverbal elements of communication. With regard to the mediation of internal states by nonverbal behaviour, special regard is given to the expressive function of speech. Specifically a readiness or capacity to produce social signals and to direct information towards the partner is assumed as a main process underlying speech activity. This assumption holds for normals and most probably for depressed patients, but not necessarily for all clinical groups. From incidental clinical observation of schizophrenic patients, for example, it may be concluded that an excessive speech production can also function to prevent communication during psychosis.

In this section, some formal aspects of speech and their functional meaning will be described first. In the following, studies of speech with regard to depression will be reviewed together with the aspect of anxiety also relevant for depression. In order to keep this study within a reasonable framework, aspects of voice will not be dealt with even though they reflect emotions and psychopathological states (cf. Ploog, 1979; Scherer, 1985). We restrict the analysis to the patterns of speech activity which are characterized according to Norwine & Murphy (1938) as follows:

> In the simplest case of conversation interchange, each party speaks for a short time, pauses, and the other party replies. The time intervals are then

simply the lengths of time each party speaks and the lengths of pauses between speeches. (p. 282)

According to the "interaction chronography" introduced by Chapple (1940, 1949) patterns of speech are registered as a sequence of speech and silence of an individual or of participants in a dialogue, independent from content.

Clinical implications of these temporal structures have already been stressed by Chapple and Lindemann (1942), who described the relative amount of "actions" and "inactions" during clinical interviews by means of their "interaction chronography". Speech-pause behaviour is regarded as an objective measure for psychotherapeutic interviews to assess synchronicity and congruency of individuals (Matarazzo & Wiens, 1977), conflict actualization (Siegman, 1978a), success of psychotherapeutic sessions (Zenz, Brähler, Braun, 1974; Brähler & Zenz, 1977) or conflicts during family interaction (Schuham, 1972). Its relevance for assessment of depression is acknowledged increasingly in recent studies as will be described later.

Parameters of speech

On closer inspection, numerous parameters can be deduced from a simple sequence of "actions" and "inactions". In their "chronography of conversation", Jaffe and Feldstein (1970) define "pauses, switching pauses, and vocalizations" as the main parameters of speech, as do Feldstein & Welkowitz (1978). Matarazzo & Wiens (1972) in their "anatomy of the interview" primarily consider the relative amount of speech, i.e. the relative duration of time an individual vocalizes during a certain part of the conversation.

Various other, mostly interrelated parameters can be found in the literature. In a study by Rutter (1977b) 13 different parameters were used to describe the components of speech patterns. Some of these parameters will shortly be described for a better understanding of our methods used later. These parameters may be subsumed under the heading of active and inactive aspects of speech.

Activity aspects of speech

Generally, parameters of time duration and frequency are used to cover activity aspects. A current parameter is the relative duration of vocalizations labelled also as "relative duration of speech activity", "relative amount of speech" or "percent time speaking" (Rutter, 1977b). The sum of vocalization intervals is divided by total time interval and given as a proportion (%) or the relative amount of speech. This measure which will be used in our longitudinal study too, describes an aspect of the magnitude or amount of verbal production.

A frequency aspect is covered by "speech rate" whereby the number of words or syllables per time unit (= duration of an utterance, a monologue or a one minute interval) is determined. This refers to velocity of speech and at the same time describes the magnitude of verbal production. The "speaking rate" measured by Starkweather (1967), however, refers to the relative duration of speech. These standards are not always defined in the same way by different authors. The use of various ratios impedes easy comparison of the reported figures.

Pauses as passive aspects of speech

Complementary to speech, silent periods without verbalization occur during monologues or dialogues. Again various parameters are used in the literature to describe the different aspects of these pauses: "latency" as the time interval between question and answer, "silent" or "unfilled" pauses with criteria of at least 0.2, 2, 3 or 5 seconds duration, "filled pauses" with expressions as "hm", "ehm", haw" etc. and other silent periods. Ratios like the "sound silence ratio" (Goldman-Eisler, 1968) are used to further process this information. Other measures refer to speech disturbances like stuttering, repetitions, etc. (Mahl, 1956), interruptions and simultaneous talk (Meltzer, Morris & Hayes, 1971; Ferguson, 1977).

Since some of these parameters are highly correlated, verbal productivity may according to Murray (1971) be assessed positively by a verbal quantity and speech rate as well as negatively by measures of silence periods. A systematic comparison of methods within this area would still be desirable in order to clarify which measures or ratios are best suited to different problems.

In our study, the relative amount of speech, i.e., percent time speaking, will be used as a parameter to describe the active part of verbal utterances.

6.2.1 Functional aspects of speech

Events that are fused into parameters as described above may well have different meanings. Different forms of simultaneous speech may have specific connotations (Ferguson, 1977) as different kinds of pauses are functionally not equivalent. Neither the functions of these behaviours have been sufficiently determined (Siegman, 1978b) nor have the related methodological problems been resolved up to now (Scherer, 1982, pp. 152-3).

As a (negative) contribution to verbal productivity, pauses have been shown to be related to personality traits like anxiety (Murray, 1971; Helfrich & Dahme, 1974; Siegman, 1978a). Extraversion, rated competence and amiability (Siegman & Pope, 1965; Addington, 1968; Lay & Burron, 1968; Scherer, 1979b) are associated with a higher amount of speech and fewer pauses.

Apart from this the function of pauses for the planning of speech has been investigated in various studies. While Goldman-Eisler (1968; Henderson, Goldman-Eisler & Skarbek, 1965; Henderson, 1975) regard pauses as essential for speech planning, Hänni (1974) and Beattie (1979) provide evidence that speech planning is accomplished during speech as well and pauses are not a necessary condition for this process. Filled pauses have been shown to be related to emotional disturbances (Boomer, 1963; Boomer & Dittman, 1964; Mahl & Schulze, 1964; Rochester, 1973).

Whereas pauses reflect amongst others processes of speech planning and instances of conflicting emotional events within the individual, simultaneous speech as their counterpart is a genuinely social event. Experimental evidence supports a dominance concept where at moments of simultaneous speech the louder person tended to win the floor (Meltzer, Morris & Hayes, 1971). However, a detailed analysis revealed that from the various forms of this simple event only one is related to dominance (Ferguson, 1977) whereas others are simple overlaps or injections, without the goal to take the floor.

Mutual influence
In most of the studies on mutual influence in speech it was found that speech-pause-behaviour in a dyad during a dialogue is dependent on both partners (Goldman-Eisler, 1952; Webb, 1970; Jaffe & Feldstein, 1970; Feldstein & Welkowitz, 1978). In his overview, Capella (1981) points out that compensatory as well as reciprocal tendencies between partners can be observed during the course of a dialogue. A tendency to react with longer utterances to short ones from the partner points to a compensatory process, whereas a tendency to react with short to short and with long to long utterances indicates a reciprocal process. Compensatory effects are mainly found in the duration of utterances whereas reciprocal effects prevail for duration of pauses and latencies. Which of these tendencies develops within a single dialogue seems, according to Capella, to be partly specific to the dyad.

6.2.2 *Speech activity in depression*

Up to now there are several inconsistent reports on the relation of depression and temporal aspects of speech. Nevertheless, prolonged pauses and a slowed and reduced amount of speech together with a monotonous voice are one of the few nonverbal features being mentioned as criteria for depression in DSM III (American Psychiatric Association, 1980, pp. 210-24).

Speech samples of 40 patients with affective disorders were characterized by psychiatrists as follows (Newman & Mather, 1938): For classical depression, lax articulatory movements, slowed speech rate, frequent hesitation pauses, short answers, prolonged reaction times was remarked. For some patients, however, raters observed firm articulation, short latencies, fast speech rate and long answers. This indicates substantial inter-individual variation. Aside from these clinical descriptions no quantitative data are prodvided by this study.

Other than for gaze, it is difficult to compare figures on speech activity across different studies since situations differ remarkably. So dialogues, interviews, monologues spoken on a tape and speech tests like counting from 1 to 10 were used.

Most of the studies refer to mood and motor retardation in depression with a retarding effect on temporal aspects of speech. Aronson & Weintraub (1967, 1972) found the "verbal energy output" of depressive patients to show reduced productivity and slowed speech rate with a low speech/silence ratio. The authors note, however without data, that agitated patients behaved in the other direction. Similarly, Hinchliffe, Lancashire & Roberts (1971b) found a reduced words/minute ratio for depressed patients.

According to Siegman (1978a, p. 215) the low energy and the reduced level of activation are the main influences leading to a low rate of verbalization in depression. According to Szabadi, Bradshaw & Besson (1976) a test for operationalizing motor retardation in depression is provided by a simple counting task counting the numbers from 1 to 10. Like Greden, Albala, Smohler, Gardner & Carroll (1981) they found a prolonged "speech pause time", i.e. longer silent intervals between phonations for depressed patients compared to controls. Greden et al. (1981) found no differences between monopolar and bipolar depression. There were shorter pauses with improvement of depression.

These findings have been replicated recently by various authors (Teasdale, Fogarty & Williams, 1980; Hardy, Jouvent & Wildlöcher, 1984; Godfrey & Knight, 1984, Bouhuys & Mulder-Hajonides van der Meulen, 1984; Hoffmann, Gonze & Mendlewicz, 1985) providing good evidence for a stable effect.

Not only with a counting task but also during interviews these prolonged pauses can be found. Especially the occurrence of pauses with >2sec duration turned out to be, according to Klos, Bildhauer, Ellgring & Scherer (in preparation), a sensitive indicator of changes during depression.

With regard to the active part of speech, Starkweather (1967) found that 3 out of 4 depressed patients in a longitudinal study increased their "speaking rate", i.e. the relative amount of speech during 10-15 minute interviews from 14%-18% to 45%-62%. For one agitated depressed patient the initial high rate of 60% remained quite stable during improvement of depression.

Thus, retardation and reduction in speech, as has been found during interviews and standardized speaking tasks, apparently indicate a psychomotor retardation in depression.

Comparison with schizophrenics

Speech behaviour of schizophrenic patients seems to be less homogeneous than that of depressives. Disintegrated conversation (Matarazzo & Saslow, 1961), irregular lengths of actions and less coordinated speech flow (Chapple, Chapple, Wood, Miklowitz, Kline & Saunders, 1960) but also a reduced speech activity with depressed mood (Truax, 1971; Glaister, Feldstein & Pollack, 1980) have been found in schizophrenics.

A significant higher proportion of pauses and "listening" in an interview situation was found by Rutter & Stephenson (1972b) in depressed patients compared to normals. In a later study, however, Rutter (1977b) reports that during a "natural conversation" (problem solving tasks) depressed patients showed no significantly different speech behaviour compared to controls and schizophrenics. This lack of differentiation in a "natural conversation" could be due to a higher variance induced by different contents. Differences which are accentuated by the homogeneous interview situation or a standardized task may have been blurred by the variation in content during the "natural conversation".

Anxiety and speech

Contrary to reduction tendencies during depression a higher speech production is reported to occur with anxiety. According to Siegman (1978a) most studies show that anxiety arousal is associated with reduced silent pauses and an increasing speech rate, thus having a facilitating effect on verbal behaviour. A reverse U-shaped relationship between anxiety and talk-silence measures has been postulated by Murray (1971), but this still lacks empirical support.

When inducing situational anxiety, Helfrich & Dahme (1974) found an increase in the less controlled short silent pauses. For longer pauses situational as well as personality factors played a role. Compared to low anxious subjects high anxious individuals increased the number of long pauses in those situations experienced as threatening whereas in positively evaluated situations no difference was found. According to the authors this behaviour is determined by self-presentation: High anxious subjects as "sensitizers" appeal to the environment by longer pauses whereas low anxious "repressors" avoid these pauses, thus giving the impression of self-confidence.

Repeated comparisons of speech samples with anxiety and depression ratings from psychosomatic patients revealed, according to Pope, Blass, Siegman & Raher (1970) a counter effect: on days with high anxiety or low depression ratings patients tended to have a higher speech rate and a lower silence quotient. Unfortunately it is not reported how confounding of anxiety and depression ratings was avoided. It can thus only be regarded as a hint to possible counteractive effects of these psychological states on speech.

Consequences

Anxiety seems to induce a higher speech production. This tendency is also observed for socially active, extraverted individuals who in turn are positively evaluated. In contrast, the expected retardation and reduction in verbal productivity in depression is opposite to a behaviour evaluated as being positively and socially competent.

This does not imply that anxiety and depression generally function as independent or counteracting factors with regard to speech behaviour. It could be that the extreme states of anxiety experienced during depression differ qualitatively from an experimentally induced anxiety. Possibly an inverse U-shaped relation between anxiety and reduced speech as postulated by Murray (1971) applies to these extreme states. But also when presenting oneself as socially introverted, low in dominance and emotionally unstable this could lead to a reduced verbal productivity as well. This kind of self-presentation would also be conceivable for depression.

Speech rate as a speed aspect is not to be equated with the relative amount of speech during a defined period. Both, however, are part of an active verbal production and it is not plausible to assume that one is increased and at the same time the other is decreased during depression. At any rate, from those studies where various parameters have been applied (Starkweather, 1967; Rutter, 1976, 1977a) they showed similar effects.

Even though the relation between speech parameters and depression appears clearer than with anxiety some questions remain. In some depressed patients (Starkweather, 1967) or groups of patients (Rutter, 1977a and b) speech activity turned out not to be reduced or different from controls or other groups of patients. Therefore, it will be assessed as to how this behaviour changes in the individual and how these changes are related to changes in the depressed state and in other nonverbal behaviours.

6.3 Summary and hypotheses

It can be gathered from the various group comparisons discussed above that depressive and schizophrenic patients cannot be reasonably differentiated on the basis of their gaze and speech behaviour. If, according to Rutter (1976) differences between schizophrenics and normals with regard to their gaze behaviour occur with neutral, impersonal contents only, this would imply an influence of the short term emotional involvement but not of the mood as a relatively enduring psychological state. The lack of major differences between various groups could also be due to the heterogeneity of populations as suggested by Jones & Pansa (1979). Except for comparisons of monopolar and bipolar depressed patients with the counting task (cf. Greden et al., 1981) various forms of depression have not been sufficiently differentiated when analysing their gaze and speech behaviour.

It is a question of principle whether a behavioural indicator of psychological processes must always differentiate between clinical groups or nosological entities. For various individuals in different groups the same psychological function may be disturbed or changed in a similar way. This may then be indicated by the same behavioural change.

Thus, a comparable negative emotional state may be present in subgroups of depressed and schizophrenic patients resulting in a similar nonverbal behaviour. As an example, anxiety may be a central part of the psychological disorder in depressed as well as in schizophrenic patients. Nevertheless, these psychological functions are not necessarily criteria for the differentiation between these groups. Comparing agitated and retarded depression according to their nonverbal behaviour as in the study of Bouhuys & Mulder-Hajonides van der Meulen (1984) aims at a differentiation which takes different psychological functions into account.

Furthermore, individuals may not react uniformly in their behaviour as a consequence of their psychological disorder. This, however, is assumed by group comparisons.

For the study of nonverbal communication, gaze and speech behaviour is to be analysed in natural or quasi-natural situations. The question is whether changes in mood are associated with individual changes in these behaviours. Both behaviours are closely linked and coordinated. Thus, according to the reduction hypothesis, both behaviours should be reduced given a lower level of psychological performance during depression. In addition it has to be asked with reference to a postulated breakdown of coordinated behaviour during psychosis whether the coordination of both behaviours is altered by depression.

6.4 Methods for the analysis of gaze and speech

Gaze and speech behaviour of patients and interviewers were registered continuously by observers as "on-off patterns" for five minute segments taken from the standardized and the free part of the SID. Altogether, data were available from about 500 standard resp. free parts of the interviews.

Since details of observation, registration, and processing of these data have been described elsewhere (Ellgring & Clarke, 1978; Clarke & Ellgring, 1983; Clarke, Wagner & Ellgring, 1984; Wagner, Ellgring & Clarke, 1981) only the parts of current interest will be presented here.

Continuous assessment of behaviour
In order to simultaneously observe and register gaze and speech of the two individuals – patient and interviewer – four observers were rating during one observational session, one for each behaviour of each individual.

An observer had to press a button as long as the observed individual

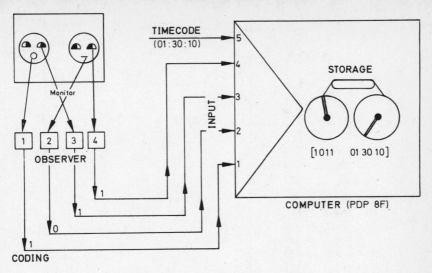

Fig. 6.3 Observation, coding and data storage of binary coded gaze and speech

spoke and release it when this was not the case. Correspondingly, another observer had to register whether there was gazing at the partner or gazing away. These on-off signals together with video-time code information (minutes – seconds – frames) were processed in 4 channels as binary coded states by a video computer system for PRocessing AudioVisual DAta (PRAVDA, Clarke & Ellgring, 1983). Fig. 6.3 schematically represents the processes of observation and data storage. The behavioural flow can be visualized pictographically as a sequence of a repertoire of 16 discrete states (see Fig. 6.4).

The maximum temporal resolution for coding this behavioural stream is $\frac{1}{25}$ sec (= 40 msec according to the synchronization of video frames). Depending on the liveliness of a dialogue, there are 200 to 500 discriminable states within a five minute sequence during the interview.

For data analysis a filter of 280 msecs (= 7 video frames with 40 msecs each) was chosen in order to obtain optimum error reduction (cf. Wagner, Ellgring & Clarke, 1980; 1981). This filter nearly corresponds to the filter of 300 msec used by Jaffe & Feldstein (1970) for speech. For the US standard of 30 video frames per second, 300 msec equals 9 video frames. In the European standard for synchronizing video to 25 frames per second, a filter can be chosen as a multitude of 40 msecs, i.e. either 320 msec (= 8 frames) or 280 msec (= 7 frames) as was used in our case.

Reliability
Observers were trained, tested, and selected according to their performance

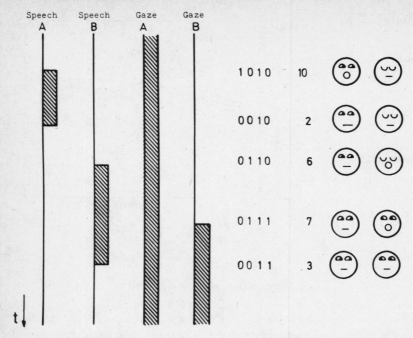

Fig. 6.4 Coding and pictographical representation of a behavioural flow in a dyad

on specific test video tapes. Before accepting an observer for observation, his accuracy had to be within a range of +/-2.5% deviance with reference to the thoroughly analysed test tape. If the observer deviated more, he or she was excluded.

Reliability of observation was about 95% for coding of speech and about 94.3% for gaze assessed by point-to-point correspondence. Reliability checks were repeated at irregular intervals by having unannounced replication tests. In short, reliability considerably exceeded the standards required in the literature (Wagner et al., 1980). An important precondition for these reliability figures was that each observer had to register only one behaviour of one individual at the time. Given the high reliability of the coding procedure a lack of association or poor association between these behaviours and the subjective state cannot be attributed to a weakness of the observation method.

"Eye contact"

Gaze behaviour can be reliably observed as gaze at or away from the other. It is, however, hardly possible to register "eye contact", i.e. a mutual looking into each other's eyes reliably (von Cranach & Ellgring, 1973) even though accuracy may be improved by giving feedback (Ellgring & von Cranach, 1972). In addition, accuracy decreases as the distance between observer and observed individual increases.

Because of these difficulties it seems appropriate to use the term "gazing at the other" or "gaze at the face" of another person. Even though it is probably the region around the eyes which is looked at most, this can be also true for the root of the nose or – as has been reported by deaf individuals – the mouth for lip reading. An observer or an interactant could gain the impression of being looked at. The term "gaze" or "gaze at the other" will be used in the following for looking at the other's face without specifying whether this is the eye region or not. Given this limitation gaze can be observed with a high degree of accuracy.

Data analysis

As main parameters relative amounts of time were assessed where gazing at the other (G%) and speech activity (S%) takes place. Like for the other behaviours these data were compared for extreme states of wellbeing. In addition, individual correlations could be determined to describe linear relationships of behavioural measures with subjective wellbeing on an individual basis. These correlations are based on 10 or more interviews for each of the endogenous and 5-7 (mostly 7) for each of the neurotic depressed patients (see Appendix Table B.8). For controls there were not enough observations available for a reasonable computation of individual correlations. The individual correlations can be regarded as descriptive statistics corresponding to cross-correlations with a lag of zero.

Coordination of gaze and speech was analysed by a method for the assessment of "local contingencies" in a behavioural flow, developed by Wagner et al. (1981).

6.5 Stability of data from controls

Both behavioural aspects are highly stable within a situation. This is verified by high correlations between values from the standardized (ST) and the free (FT) part of the interview. For gaze (G%) this correlation is $r = 0.86$ (n = 493 interviews), for speech (S%) it is somewhat lower, but still fairly high with $r = 0.71$ (n = 492 inverviews, both $p < 0.001$). Although the stability of behaviour is affected to a minor extent, speech activity seems to reflect more the situational differences between the two parts of the interview. Given these high correlations, it was decided to use the data from the standardized part of the interview for the following analyses. Especially for speech behaviour this ensured a higher homogeneity of the interviewer's behaviour.

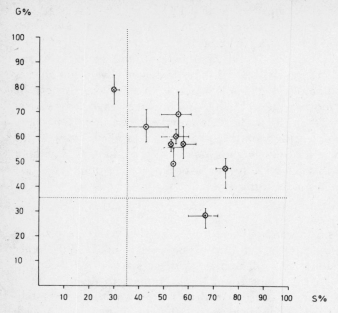

Fig. 6.5 Gaze and speech in controls. Relative duration of gaze (G%) and speech (S%) during interviews. Menus and ranges for each of the male (⊗) and female (⊙) control subjects. Criterion line (. . . .) separates "reduced" from "normal" values (for further explanation see Fig 4.5).

Control values

Across interviews, controls display a highly stable gaze and speech behaviour. Fig. 6.5 contains mean values and spreads (minimum and maximum) of the relative amount of gaze and speech for each of the control subjects.

As can be seen from this figure, values for an individual have a strikingly small range, showing a high intra-individual stability. Furthermore, for the mean values there is a clear negative correlation between gaze and speech activity ($r = -.87$) which shows that individuals have high or low values in either of the two channels only. This gives support to the hypothesis that a higher cognitive load by speech activity is associated with a lower amount of gaze.

Similar to the parameters of facial behaviour, limits for reduced values can be defined by excluding one individual with relatively low values for each behavioural aspect. By this, a level of 35% is defined as the lower limit. According to this limit, 6 out of 54 (= 11%) control values are below this limit. These values are from one male or one female subject. A relative amount of gaze or speech lower than 35% is thus regarded as "reduced" within this interview situation.

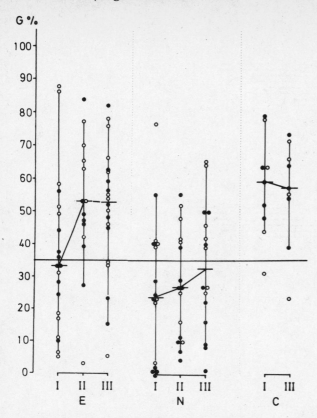

Fig. 6.6 Gaze. Individual values for the relative amount of gaze (G%) during a 5-minute interval. Criterion line separates "reduced" from "normal" values (for further explanation see Fig 4.5).

6.6 Results for gaze behaviour

A considerable part of neurotic and endogenous depressed patients, displayed reduced amounts of gaze during depression. For most of the patients the amount of gaze increased with improvement. For many patients, however, it remained below the "normal" limit (see Fig. 6.6; raw data see Table B.8 in the Appendix).

The median values of gaze significantly increased from 20% over 33% to 53% with improved subjective wellbeing for endogenous depressed patients (Wilcoxon-Test: p<.05), thus approaching median values of 58% for controls. For neurotic depressed patients, the amount of gaze increased to a minor extent from Mdn = 24% to 33% (Wilcoxon test p>.05), remaining below the medians of controls.

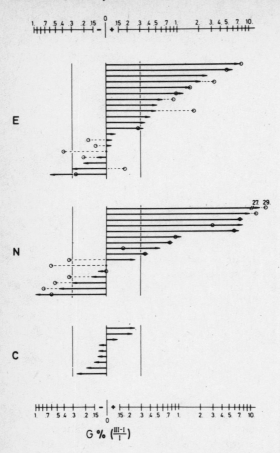

Fig. 6.7 Individual change ratios for gaze (G%) (for further explanation see Fig. 5.5).

Reduction

During their depressed state, 11 out of 20 (= 55%) of endogenous depressed patients had reduced values whereas with recovery, this holds for 8 (= 25%) patients only. The proportion of neurotic depressed patients showing reduced values decreased from 10 out of 16 (= 63%) to 8 (= 50%) patients. Stability of the behavioural measure for controls was evident with a median of 59% or 57% during both interviews.

Generally, neurotic and endogenous patients showed similar average initial values during depression. At the intermediate and the best state of wellbeing, however, neurotics showed a significantly lower average of gaze than endogenous depressed patients or controls (U-tests $p < .05$).

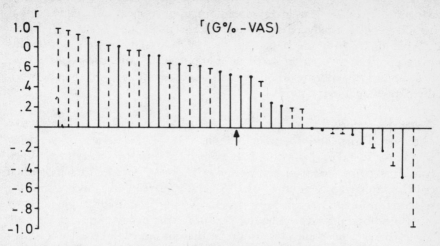

Fig. 6.8 Individual correlations between mood and gaze. Intra-individual correlations (r) between relative amount of gaze (G%) and subjective wellbeing (VAS) for endogenous (——) and neurotic (---) depressed patients. Arrow at median correlation.

Individual changes

More than half of the patients showed change ratios exceeding 30% of their initial values. For 21 of the 36 (= 58%) patients, gaze increases substantially with recovery (see Fig. 6.7). Given the change ratios of controls, a limit of CR = .30 was defined as the criterion for a substantial change.

In most of the cases (19 out of 20 = 95 %), where a substantial change occurred between the extreme states I to III, changes in the intermediate state II pointed to the same direction. *Consistency* of changes thus proved to be very high.

Initial values and substantial changes were correlated (r = − .55, p<.05) for patients, but not for controls (r = − .03). Substantial increases in gaze emerged out of reduced values for 16 out of the 21 (= 76 %) patients.

Individual correlations

Median of the individual correlations for patients was r = .58 for the relationship between gaze (G%) and subjective wellbeing (VAS). Fig. 6.8 shows the individual correlations computed from the available values of each patient (see also Table B.9 in the Appendix).

For a considerable proportion of patients quite high correlations describe the close association of gaze with subjective wellbeing over the course of depression. There was no clear difference between the subgroups. Only one patient showed a clear inverse relation. Improvement of wellbeing was associated with a reduced amount of gaze in this case.

After all, for 11 of the 36 patients (= 31%) correlations were r>.70. This corresponds to a common variance of about 50% and more between gaze and subjective wellbeing. There was, however, enormous variation between these individual correlations.

General description
The overall correlation between amount of gaze and subjective wellbeing was r = .55 taken from the data pool of about 500 interviews. When considering 90 values from states I and III, i.e. two values for each individual only, a similar correlation of r = .52 emerged. This also shows that the selection of interviews can be regarded as a representative sample not only for psychological data (cf. chapter 4), but for the behavioural data as well. These correlations come close to the median of individual correlations of r = .58. It should be reminded, however, that there was considerable variation between individual correlations pointing to different kinds of behavioural reactions to mood changes. General correlations between the amount of gaze and the Global Clinical Rating (GR) were somewhat lower; r = .44 for the total data pool and r = .40 for values from states I and III. Clinical impression does not seem to refer as closely to gaze as the correlation with self-rating of mood would suggest.

As has been described above, average amounts of gaze increased +20% for endogenous and less clearly +9% for neurotic depressed patients during recovery.

Sex differences
Generally there was a tendency for female individuals to show more gaze (Mdn = 45%) than males (Mdn = 37%) (U-tests p<.10 for the standard part, p<.05 for the free part of the interview). Since this comparison covers wide ranges between the subgroups and their different states of wellbeing, data need to be specified. At a closer look the difference between males and females was mainly due to the behaviour of neurotic depressed patients, whereby females tended to exhibit between 16% and 20% more gaze than males at the three states of wellbeing (see Table B.13 in the Appendix). For endogenous depressed patients and controls there was partly more, partly less gaze from females, values differing around Mdn +/−3%. From the low values given for neurotic depressed patients even at their state of relatively best wellbeing it is concluded that males in this subgroup deviated most from normal gaze behaviour in this situation.

Comparison with data from the literature
There was a tendency for lower values of gaze in this study than given by

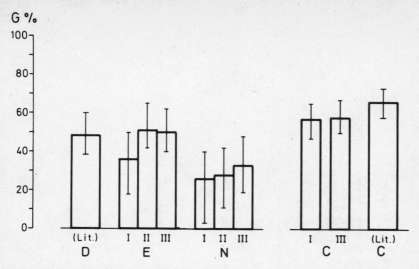

Fig. 6.9 Comparison of average data on gaze in depression. Average standard deviations (Lit) or quartile ranges of relative amounts of gaze (G%). D = depressed patients, E = endogenous, N = neurotic depressed patients, C = controls; Lit = data from literature. I, II, III = states of well-being (see Fig. 4.5).

averages reported in the literature (see Fig. 6.9).

With an average of G% = 58%, values of controls in our study were about 8% below those reported in the literature. Endogenous and even more so neurotic depressed patients on the average displayed 12% or 22% less gaze during depression than is suggested from averaging values of depression groups from the literature. With improvement, values of endogenous depressed patients came close to those of controls in our study and those of depressed patients reported in the literature. Neurotic depressed patients remained considerably below these averages. In all cases, however, variability between patients' data was generally high so that differences can hardly be statistically substantiated.

Lower values in our study could be due to observational procedures or situational influences. As an observational influence, the criterion for registering the event "gaze at the other" might have been more strict here than in other studies, thus yielding lower values. As a situational influence, the standardized interview as it was used here might have induced a higher cognitive demand than a general conversation. This could have led to less gaze at the other.

It has to be stressed, however, that the relations between average values of patients and controls closely resemble those taken from the literature.

To evaluate the results adequately it appears indispensable to take into

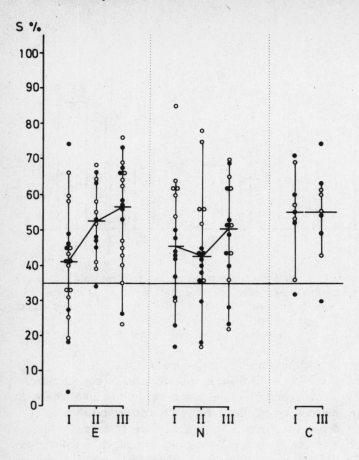

Fig. 6.10 Speech activity. Individual values for the relative amount of speech activity (5%) during a 5-minute interval.

account the extreme changes which have been observed within individuals. Especially the high individual correlations over the time course provide strong evidence for unequivocal behavioural reactions to mood changes. These close associations, however, hold for part of the individuals whereas in others, no clear relationship emerged.

6.7 Results on speech activity

Depressed patients exhibited reduced amounts of speech during depression and an increase with recovery less frequent than for gaze. Fig. 6.10 contains single values from interviews at different mood states.

Average values of normals and of neurotic depressed patients remained highly stable. For endogenous depressed patients, median values increased from 41% over 53% to 57% whereas for neurotic depressed patients no clear trend could be observed. All median values were above the critical level for "reduced" behaviour. For endogenous, but not for neurotic depressed patients, values were significantly lower during the depressed state compared to the intermediate and recovered state (Wilcoxon-test: p<.05) or compared to controls (U-test: p<.05).

Reduction

During depression, 8 out of 20 (= 40%) endogenous and 4 out of 16 (= 25%) neurotic depressed patients showed reduced values. While for neurotic depressed patients this proportion remained constant, only 2 (= 10%) of the endogenous still had reduced values when recovered at state III.

Individual changes

As is suggested by group comparison, more of the endogenous depressed patients showed a substantial increase in their speech activity with recovery from depression (see Fig. 6.11).

From the low variability of controls' behaviour a change ratio of CR>+/ -.20 could be regarded as "substantial". For endogenous depressed patients there were nine substantial increases and two decreases in behaviour according to this criterion whereas behaviour increased for three neurotic patients only contrasted to five substantial decreases.

Consistency of changes could be regarded as extremely high. Change ratios for the intermediate state pointed into the same direction for 15 out of 16 (= 94%) substantial changes from states I to III (see Fig. 6.11, comparing arrows and circles).

Although 12 patients substantially increased their speech activity, even for endogenous depressed patients this resulted in a median increase of 12% or 16% only. For part of the neurotic depressed patients, a reverse tendency of decreasing behaviour with improvement as for facial expression and gaze was present again.

Initial values and change ratios were negatively correlated for patients (r = -.52, p<.05) and less so for controls (r = -.33).Eight out of the 12 substantial increases evolved out of reduced values. Thus, an increase during improvement was dependent in part on low initial values.

Individual correlations

Individual correlations between the amount of speech (S%) and subjective wellbeing (VAS) over the time course were not as high as for gaze (see Fig. 6.12). For five patients these correlations exceeded r = .70, i.e. they repre-

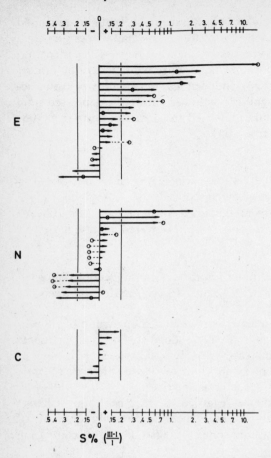

Fig. 6.11 Individual changes in speech activity. Change ratios for the relative amount of speech activity (5%) (for further explanation see Fig. 5.5).

sented a common variance of 50% and more between subjective wellbeing and behaviour. For these patients, at least, the correlation reflected a strong association between mood and speech activity. For the whole group, a median correlation of $r = .34$ described the average association. No significant differences were found with respect to sex and kind of depression for these correlations.

General description
The general correlation between mood and speech activity was $r = .42$, (n = 500 interviews p<.01), somewhat lower than for gaze. Taking interviews with extreme states of wellbeing only, this correlation remained $r = .41$ (n = 80 interviews, p<.05) (see Table B.11 in the Appendix). As for gaze,

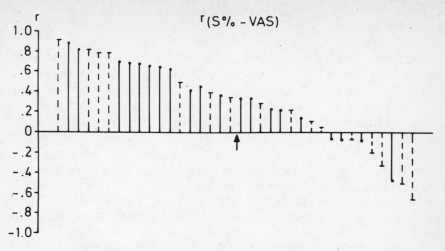

Fig. 6.12 Individual correlations of speech activity and mood. Intra-individual correlations (r) between relative amount of speech activity (S%) and subjective wellbeing (VAS) for endogenous (——) and neurotic (----) depressed patients. → at median correlation.

intra-individual comparisons, however, appeared to be more revealing for the association of mood and behaviour than these average descriptions.

Sex differences
There were no significant sex differences with regard to speech activity (cf. Fig. 6.10). For endogenous patients and controls average differences of +/−4% between males and females were nearly balanced (see Table B.13 in the Appendix). Female neurotic depressed patients tended to have a higher amount of speech than male patients during depressed state I (+ 19.5%) and intermediate state II (+ 15%). This nearly equalized during state III (+3%). This interaction effect of mood state and sex, however, would need further validation from larger samples.

6.8 Association of gaze and speech

Reduced behaviour during depressed states and substantial increases occurred with improvement independently as well as together in gaze and speech behaviour. There were minor correlations only between both behaviours with regard to the occurrence of reduced values (Cohen's Kappa k = .11, p>.05) as well as substantial changes (Cohen's Kappa k = .28, p>.05).

On a *general level* amount of gaze and speech activity were correlated to a negligible extent with r = .18 (p>.05, n = 90 values from interviews with extreme states of wellbeing). In contrast, average values for controls were negatively correlated (r = −.78). It is only for patients that both behaviours varied independently despite their considerable range.

For 26 (= 72%) of the patients one *or* the other behaviour was reduced during depression whereas for only 7 (= 19%) patients this was the case in both behaviours. Correspondingly, 24 (= 67%) of the patients substantially increased one *or* the other behaviour with improvement of subjective wellbeing, whereas only 9 (= 25%) showed an increase in both.

Individual correlations of gaze and of speech measures with wellbeing were correlated for their part to a negligible extent (r = −.07). This is further evidence that intra-individual associations of subjective wellbeing and behaviour occur independently over the time course of depression. Individual correlations of r>.70 with subjective wellbeing for at least one of the two behavioural measures were found for 11 (= 36%) of the patients.

In sum, reduced amount of gaze *or* speech occurred independently as was the case for their substantial increases and their individual correlations over the time course. Thus, in a "logical or-connection", i.e. for gaze *or* speech activity, most of the patients (about 3 out of 4) showed clear state dependent behavioural reductions during depression and increases with improvement. However, in only 25% this occurred for both behaviours together.

6.8.1 *Coordination of gaze and speech*

In order to determine the coordination of gaze and speech, a model of "local contingencies" developed by Wagner (Wagner, Clarke & Ellgring, 1980; Wagner, 1981) has been applied. This method is comparable to the evoked potential approach for EEG: During a behavioural flow, certain changes in one behaviour were defined as trigger points. At these points in time the respective states of another behaviour were averaged over a series of these events.

A speaker's turn during a dialogue is an obvious example for an external behavioural coordination where the end of an utterance elicits a subsequent utterance from the other. The end of the utterance is the trigger point. The average latency for answers is a parameter characterizing the coordination of respondent's behaviour. Contingency of speech and gaze is a known example of an internal coordination. Beginning and end of an utterance are the respective trigger points here. The probability for gazing at the other decreases at the beginning of one's utterance and reaches its maximum again at the end of the utterance (Kendon, 1967; Ellgring, 1981, cf. this chapter 6.1.2). Various contingency types can be considered depending on the kind of trigger points chosen.

For the internal and external coordination of patient's gaze with speech

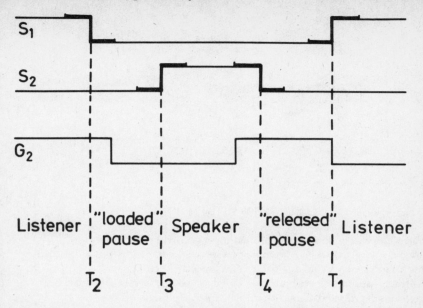

Fig. 6.13 Contingency of gaze and speech: Trigger points. Trigger points (T1-4) for contingencies of gaze (G) of the patient (Pt) on speech (S) of patient and of interviewer (I) (for further explanation see text).

four contingency types have been analysed. In Fig. 6.13 the four trigger points of speech activity are schematically represented. They were taken as the reference points for gaze states of the patient.

External coordination of patient's gaze (G2) is determined with regard to onset (T1) or offset (T2) of interviewer's speech (S1). Internal coordination is determined with regard to onset (T3) or offset (T4) of patients' speech (S2). The interval between T2 and T3 can be regarded as a "loaded pause" since an answer is required from the patient. During the "released" pause between T4 and T1, cognitive load for the patient is assumed to be lower since this is the interviewer's turn. Within the temporal neighbourhood of these trigger points, "on-states" of gaze, i.e. gazing at the other, are summed across events.

For this analysis two to four interviews were taken from the depressed or the recovered state from each of 14 endogenous depressed patients. Thus, data are based upon about 20 minutes of the interview for each patient representing extreme states of subjective wellbeing. Endogenous depressed patients were selected for this analysis for two reasons: First, a collapse of behavioural coordination was expected during psychosis of these patients. Second, each of these patients offered a sufficient number of interviews during depressed and recovered state.

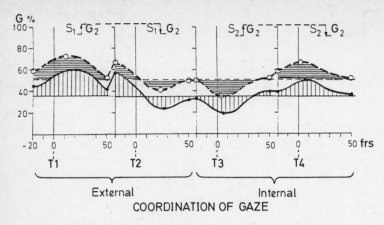

Fig. 6.14 External and internal coordination of gaze and speech. Average continguencies of gaze (G%) depending on speech events (T1 to T4). On and off points for interviewers (S1) and patients (S2) speech. Intervals from −20 to +50 video-frames around trigger points. —— = depression, ---- = remission, n = 14 endogenous depressed patients (for futher explanation see text).

The average relative duration of gaze (G%) during each of the two states is taken as a reference which defines a given behavioural level. This level would be constant if gaze was independent from internal or external factors. Amplitude and latency of phasic deviations from this level, on the other hand, describe the strength of the contingent relationship. The maximum of the amplitude defines the point in time with highest probability for a reaction. Latency refers to the difference between this point and the trigger point.

A delay of the temporal contingency is to be expected from the retardation hypothesis and a lack of phasic variation from the hypothesis of a behavioural coordination collapse during psychosis.

Results on coordination of gaze and speech

Given a reduced tonic level of gaze, latency of the phasic reaction was elongated during depression whereas amplitudes appeared to be unaffected.

In Fig. 6.14 average values of the four contingency types during depression and remission are presented together.

The four trigger points are depicted in sequence omitting variable intervals between them. From left to right this sequence represents a sequence of question and answer during the interview: the beginning (T1), then the end (T2) of interviewer's speech. This is followed by the beginning (T3) and the end (T4) of the patient's utterance. Changes in speech states are indicated by arrows. Trigger points are at 0-points on the x-axis, with an interval around the trigger point of 60 frames.

Table 6.1: *Amplitudes and latencies of gaze reactions.*

Trigger	Amplitude (%)		Latency (video frames =40 msec)	
	Depr	Rem	Depr	Rem
T1	−15.8	−15.6	6.4	3.6
	(8.9)	(7.6)	(9.3)	(10.8)
T2	15.1	16.0	6.4	1.4
	(10.5)	(8.3)	(13.9)	(11.7)
T3	25.1	21.1	20.0	11.4
	(10.9)	(9.7)	(14.7)	(14.1)
T4	−10.9	−9.8	25.7	22.9
	(9.4)	(10.9)	(12.8)	(12.7)

Note:
Average amplitudes (G%) and latencies (in video frames) and standard
deviations ( ) for internally (T3 and T4) and externally (T1 and T2) triggered
gaze reactions
Depr. = depression, Rem. = remission, n = 14 endogenous depressed patients.
Negative amplitudes indicate a level below the general average level.
(For further explanations see text.)

Thus, a period of about 10 seconds (4 x 60 frames = 9600 msecs) is represented in this graph. Gaze as the dependent variable is triggered externally in T1 and T2 by the interviewers' speech and internally in T3 and T4 by the patient's speech itself.

The average level of gaze (G%) during these interviews was 36% during depression and 50% during remission, corresponding to levels found for the total sample. Areas above and below these levels describe the extent of phasic deviations at a given point in time.

As can be seen from these deviations, speech of the interviewer elicited a gaze reaction of the patients whereas at the end of his utterance the patient tended to look away. This tendency is continued at the beginning of the patient's utterance. At the end of the patient's answer, the amplitude for gaze at the other is on a high level again.

Average maximum amplitudes and latencies of gaze reactions are given in Table 6.1.

There was no significant difference with regard to amplitudes of gaze reactions during depression and remission (t-test p>.05). With regard to latencies, a significantly later maximum of the gaze reaction elicited by the interviewer (T1) could be found (t-test p<.05) as was the case for the latency between question and answer. Thus, a retarded latency of the answer and of the externally triggered gaze reaction was found during depression.

Given different general levels during depression and recovery internal and

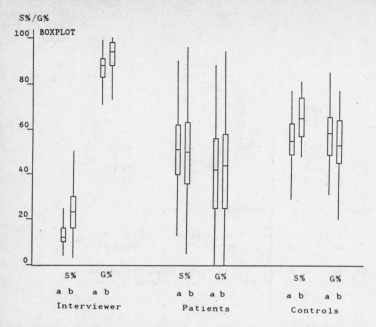

Fig. 6.15 Gaze and speech during interviews. Boxplots (except outlayers) for relative amounts (%) of speech (S%) and Gaze (G%) of interviewers and depressed patients during the standardized (a) and free (b) parts of interviews for the total of available interviews (n = 385).

external coordination of gaze reactions with speech patterns remained highly stable. A retardation, but contrary to expectation, no dissolution of the coordination between both behaviours could be observed during depression.

6.9 Characteristics of the situation

Patients and interviewers clearly differed with regard to their average amount of speech and gaze (see Fig. 6.15).

For the interviewer the average amount of speech activity is complementary to the proportion of gaze. During the standard part as well as during the free part of the interview, interviewers showed a high degree of gaze toward the patient (x = 85%, s = 9.1 resp. x = 90% or s = 8.5) and a low amount of speech activity (x = 14%, s = 5.7, or x = 26%, s = 11).

During the free part of the interview, the interviewer spoke slightly more (on the average +10%) which is, however, still far below average values for patients with x = 51%, s = 15 or, x = 49%, s = 17. There are only minor differences with regard to gaze of the patients between the two parts of the situation (x = 43% or 45%, s = 22 for both). Greater standard deviations for patients point to the range where state dependent behavioural changes can take place.

Bound to the situation, the considerable role asymmetry of patient and interviewer becomes manifest in both behaviours. This asymmetry more or less remains unaltered during the following free dialogue.

Because of bottom and ceiling effects for speech and gaze behaviour of the interviewer mutual influences can hardly be substantiated for statistical reasons. Therefore, this problem of behavioural interdependency will not be pursued here.

While role prescription has a homogenizing effect for the interviewer's behaviour in both parts of the interview, there is a much larger margin for the patients' behaviour. Within this margin, mood can become an active factor determining the amount of gaze and speech and their changes over time.

6.10 Discussion of results on gaze and speech

"The depressed state is associated with reduced amounts of gaze and speech". According to the present data, this statement is true and false at the same time. It fits for some of the individuals, whereas for others this association is not apparent. Each of the behaviours may reflect the depressed state independently from the other. Even for the single behaviour, its amount may be considerably reduced without changing substantially with improvement.

For about 75% of the patients, peculiarities in gaze *or* speech can be found. This may be an increase in the amount of gaze *or* speech when depression improves, or it may be a rather stable though continuously reduced amount of behaviour. These behavioural peculiarities occur in a "logical or connection". Changes in one of the behaviours do not necessarily imply changes in the other. Taking the single case analyses as a series of independent investigations, their results describe the behaviour of different populations with specific reaction properties.

There is no clear hierarchical order of gaze or speech with regard to their relationship to mood even though individuals react more often and more sensitively with gaze than with speech to changes in subjective wellbeing. From this it follows, that both parameters are to be regarded as independent indicators. They cannot sensibly be added into a measure of "expressive strength" or some other quantity. They rather reflect – often independently – changes of mood in an individual specific way. Since this is more often the case for gaze, clearer effects for this behaviour than for speech are obtained from group comparisons. These group effects, however, yield an equalized picture mixed from "reacting" and "non-reacting" individuals. Thus, correlations across the total data pool between subjective wellbeing and gaze (r = .55) or speech (r = .42) give a rather misleading impression. They suggest an admittedly highly significant though intermediate general association between these behaviours and mood.

Individual specificity

The individual specificity of the behaviours is implied when stressing the considerable inter-individual variability of speech (Starkweather, 1967) and gaze (Strongman & Champness, 1968; Rutter, 1973). According to Spence & Feinburg (1967) individuals can be differentiated as "lookers", "peekers" and "avoiders" when attending to slightly threatening stimuli. This classification assumes different individual dispositions for gaze behaviour. Furthermore, a dyadic specificity has to be taken into account according to Capella (1981) for speech, where reciprocal or compensatory adaptations can be observed.

In this sense, our data support the concept of individual specific relationships between behavioural measures and subjective data.

Gaze avoidance and social withdrawal

Patients showing less than 35% gaze (or speech), i.e. less than controls during the interview situation might avoid eye contact, mutual gaze or generally social contact and thus perform some kind of a social withdrawal during interaction. Rutter & Stephenson (1972a) favour this interpretation rather than assuming that looking away might cause a reduction in cortical arousal. The social withdrawal hypothesis is derived from the similar results obtained for gaze behaviour of depressives and schizophrenics. To our view, there is no contradiction in both interpretations. Gaze avoidance by autistic children (Hutt & Ounstedt, 1966; O'Connor & Hermelin, 1967) can be explained by a tendency to avoid excessive cortical arousal. This arousal can be reduced by social withdrawal as well as by very selectively looking at social or other stimuli. The relationship between gaze and mental, namely emotional load, is also stressed by Rutter (1976) when reporting abnormal gaze behaviour in schizophrenics during discussion of personal topics compared to neutral ones.

From the other person's point of view, gazing away during a considerable part of a dialogue obviously operates as a kind of social withdrawal. For the patients as senders in our case, this behaviour can regulate their cognitive and emotional load or arousal by actively selecting incoming visual information. This interpretation is in accordance with the experimental and ethological literature regarding gaze as an actively selecting attentional behaviour (Day, 1964; Chance, 1962; Ellgring, 1981). The increase of GSR arousal during eye gaze found by Nichols & Champness (1971) also supports this notion.

It is still open whether the reduced behaviour during depression is due to a general high arousal, a cognitive overload or a specifically emotional arousal. In any case, social information is produced by speech or received by gaze to a very limited degree for a considerable part of the patients during depression. Since these behaviours change with recovery, it is reasonable to assume that the reduced behaviour is part of an adaptive process whereby behaviour corresponds to the capacity of the mental state. On the other hand, an enduring by reduced speech or gaze behaviour as it occurred namely in neurotic depressed patients could point to deficits in social skills or to a still unstable mental state.

Coordination

Coordination of gaze and speech provides further evidence for the assumption that gaze has an internal regulatory function in which incoming visual information is selected according to the momentary mental load. This coordination, as described early on by Nielsen (1962) and Kendon (1967) and others remains unaffected even during depression. The coordination is operationalized by changing probabilities for gaze during interactional sequences. Gaze appears to be internally triggered by one's own utterances as well as externally triggered by the speech of the others. Even at a low level of gaze during depression, this coordinative performance continues.

The persisting coordination could explain why clinical descriptions rarely refer to abnormal gaze behaviour or gaze avoidance during depression in contrast to reports about abnormal gaze in schizophrenia. The coordination of gaze behaviour with speech could be a clue to the other that both social and internal releasers are still working in the patient. Gazing at and away from the other indicates a continuous processing of social information and cognitions apparent for an interactant. This coordination could communicate to the other that the patient remains capable of social contacts even during depression.

Mutual influence

The mutual influence of behaviours between interactants can be analysed on a micro level as a coordination of gaze with the beginning and end of the other's utterance, as a tendency to aim at or to avoid eye contact, as an adaptation of speech patterns, or for other events. Because of the comparatively constant behaviour of the interviewer adaptive or compensatory processes for speech as summarized by Capella (1981) could not become apparent in our study. This applies to gaze as well with its constantly high amount for the interviewer. Moreover, for gaze there has been no evidence from the literature for a seeking or an avoiding of eye contact in dyads (Wagner, Clarke & Ellgring, 1983). Instead of depending on the partner's gaze, looking behaviour appears to be regulated mainly by internal processes and a corresponding selection of information. This also holds for changes in gaze, externally triggered by the speech of the interviewer. The interviewer elicits mental processes which in turn control the gaze behaviour.

Given the comparatively constant gaze and speech behaviour of the interviewer in our case, the influence of internal psychological states of the patient becomes dominant. The internal state then can become manifest within the boundaries set by the situation.

Situation
Both gaze and speech very clearly reflect the asymmetry of roles during the interview. This asymmetry remains quite unchanged during the free part of the interview. In comparison to patients' behaviour interviewers exhibit considerably more speech and less gaze. Thus, both parts of the clinical dialogue are determined by the position of the interviewer as the one who receives maximum information. As has been mentioned above, this limits the range within which a mutual influence on these behaviours can take place between patient and interviewer.

Diagnostical valence of gaze and speech behaviour
The usefulness of gaze and speech parameters for diagnostics and clinical behaviour assessment can be appraised on the one hand with regard to their power to differentiate between various clinical groups. On the other hand, their sensitivity in reflecting a changing mood state has to be considered.

From our data as well as from those of the literature, it follows that both behaviours are valid to some degree for cross-sectional assessment. It is, however, not possible to differentiate validly between clinical groups, such as schizophrenics and depressives using either gaze or speech (cf. Rutter, 1984, pp. 19-30). Gaze behaviour seems to be suited in the first place as a valid criterion to a current mood state and its changes. In the second place this is the case for speech activity, the behaviour considered as the main nonverbal indicator for depression in DSM III (1980).

Speech activity, according to the present results, is reduced less clearly and less frequently than gaze. Therefore, more attention should be paid to gaze behaviour when objective indicators for mood changes are needed.

Since the active part of speech was investigated, pause behaviour has been excluded in our current analysis. The study of silent pauses within an utterance and speech velocity (Greden et al., 1985; Klos, Ellgring & Scherer, in preparation), however, appear to be promising measures which are easy to obtain. High correlations with depression have been reported. A high correlation of $r = 0.67$ between a pause factor with the degree of retardation in depression has been reported, e.g. by Bouhuys & Mulder-Hajonides van der Meulen (1984). During antidepressive drug treatment a triangle relationship between psychopathological states, speech/pause variables, and EEG measure have recently been reported by Renfordt & Ulrich (1986). According to this study correlational patterns changed differentially given various drug treatments. Behavioural combined with neurophysiological data may turn out as differentially valid criteria for treatment outcome. For a behavioural sample, even a simple counting task could be sufficient (Szabadi et al., 1976) to gain robust parameter estimates on speech rate or pause behaviour.

After all, one third of the patients in our study showed very high individual correlations between mood and their speech activity. On an individual basis, these data correspond to those of Starkweather (1967), and Aronson & Weintraub (1972). On a group level, however, they are close to those of Rutter (1977b) who on the basis of lacking group differences concludes that there is no definite relationship with mood.

As for gaze, reduction and mood dependent changes of speech activity can be shown unequivocally during the course of depression when analysing on an individual basis.

Diagnostical valence of gaze and speech can thus be derived from their intra-individual changes in different situations or in different psychological conditions. While speech primarily reflects the social aspect of a conversation (Dabbs, 1980), gaze indicates above all the attentional structure from moment to moment (Chance, 1962). The changing state of depression may become manifest in both behaviours, however independently, and specific to the individual. In comparison to speech, gaze appeared to be the more sensitive and more general indicator for mood changes over the course of depression.

7 Gestures

Gestures are part of the nonverbal behaviour which is most closely related to psychomotor retardation. Emotional, cognitive, and social functions are ascribed to gestures when regarding their function in nonverbal communication.

Considering the functions of gestures on the one hand and psychopathological changes on the other, an opposite behavioural tendency can be expected. A reduced gestural behaviour should follow from a general retardation and from social withdrawal during depression. In contrast, the impeded planning of speech resulting from cognitive retardation should promote increased gestural behaviour given its postulated speech facilitating function.

7.1 Classification and assessment of gestures

Two main classes of hand movements can be differentiated in systematic observation: gestures in a narrow sense on the one side and manipulations or adaptors on the other. Most of the functional classifications proposed so far very closely agree in their distinctions between various forms of gestures (Wallbott, 1981, 1982).

Firstly, *gestures* are hand or arm movements which are closely related to speech, illustrating or supplementing it. They are referred to as "non-social", "conventional" and "pseudo-conventional" hand movements by Krout (1935), as "communicative gestures" by Sainsbury (1954) and Mahl (1968); as "illustrators" and "emblems" by Ekman & Friesen (1969a, 1972; Friesen, Ekman & Wallbott, 1979), drawing from Efron (1941); gestures are referred to by Freedman, Blass, Rifkin & Quitkin, 1973) as "object-focussed" movements. They further differentiate between movements with motor primacy, which are mostly larger and are related to contents, and movements with speech primacy, which are mostly smaller and are associated with the act of speaking.

Hand or arm movements are labelled *"emblems"* if they contain information which can be expressed by one or few words. In most instances, these movements are consciously used, e.g. under conditions where verbal communication is difficult. They may, however, occur spontaneously and unconsciously during speech as well. Hand movements directly accompanying verbal output are classified as *illustrators*.

Secondly, *manipulations or adaptors* are hand movements which are focussed on one's own body or which iteratively handle objects. They appear as "centripetal" rather than "centrifugal" movements and a relationship to speech is not obvious. These movements are labelled "autistic gestures" by Krout (1935) and Sainsbury (1954), "autistic actions" by Mahl (1968), "adaptors" by Ekman & Friesen (1969a), "body focussed movements" by Freedman & Hoffman (1967) and "self-manipulations" by Rosenfeld (1966b).

Thus *adaptors* are hand movements without conscious intention to communicate. These are rubbing, itching or other hand activities as well as covering the eyes, holding one's head. Body focussed movements (Freedman & Hoffman, 1967) correspond to self-adaptors (Ekman & Friesen, 1969a).

There is to our knowledge no methodological study which empirically tested the concordance of the various labels and functional classes for hand and arm movements. It is, however, reasonable to assume a high agreement at least wih regard to the phenomena to be described. In our study, we mainly refer to the classifications and definitions given by Ekman & Friesen (1969a), Freedman (1972) and Wallbott (1982), concentrating our analysis on speech related gestures.

In addition to distinguishing between speech-related and illustrating gestures, Günthner (1982) proposed to differentiate gestures according to their spatial extension. Gestures may have large or small extensions. By this a specific function of gestures as regulating the relationship between interactants can be covered. It is assumed that by using gestures an individual enlarges his personal space for a short time. Personal space which otherwise manifests itself in body positions, body orientation, and interpersonal distance as well (Sommer, 1967; Hall, 1963, 1969, pp. 101-29; Hayduk, 1983) could thus be also more or less enlarged on a micro-level by using more or less extended gestures towards the other.

7.2 Functions of gestures

Differentiating between gestures and manipulations implies a functional distinction made in a number of studies. Manipulations (adaptors or body-focussed movements) are regarded as being mainly state-dependent and reflecting general arousal or negative affects. They are not, however, partner-oriented.

Gestures (illustrators and emblems or object-focussed hand movements) are directly related to language and speech production. They are part of the social nonverbal activity oriented towards the other. It is this social activity which will be analysed in the following.

There is no doubt that gestures as social signals can transmit information to others, express emotions and conflicts. In his "tenets of gestures" Quintilian (according to Bühler, 1933/1968, pp. 227-35) gives early instructions for using gestures in rhetoric. Moreover, gestural behaviour is seen as an indicator of personality traits, thus representing general behavioural tendencies. Aside from this general notion, however, the exact meaning of gestures in a given instance remains open in most of the cases. The specific functions of gestures are far from clear as well. Exceptions are emblems with culturally defined meanings which are explicitly used instead of words. The relationship of gestures with language and speech planning seems to be of special interest in this respect.

Coordination with speech

A large amount of gestural behaviour occurs during utterances of an individual, during speech or when being occupied with speech planning. According to Dittman (1962, Dittman & Llewellyn, 1969) hand movements and also head movements occur at the beginning of "phonemic clauses", i.e. at the beginning of units during the speech flow which are separated by changes in vocal elements, like phonemic stress, intonation contour, etc. These movements follow a temporal pattern "...early in encoding units or following hesitation in speech" (Dittman & Llewellyn, 1969, p. 105). An increased frequency of gestures can be observed in the middle of the "floor-time", i.e. during the utterance of a person encircled by utterances of another person (Hiebinger, 1981; Feyereisen, 1982).

Various theoretical considerations with regard to the function of gestures as well as methodological consequences follow from this association with speech. From a methodological point of view the amount of gestural behaviour is confounded with the amount of speech. The more a person speaks the more there are occasions for displaying gestures. When assessing their relationship with mood, the amount of speech has to be taken into account. A measure of the amount of gestures has to describe to what extent speech is accompanied by gestures, i.e. how many gestures occur within a defined period of verbal behaviour.

With regard to functional aspects the association of gestures with speech, specifically at phonemic clauses and in the middle of the floortime, points to their facilitating effect on speech planning and speech performance (Freedman, 1972, 1977; Butterworth & Beattie, 1978; Hiebinger, 1981). This is corroborated further by studies which show impeded speech performance when gestures are forestalled (Wolff & Gutstein, 1972; Graham & Heywood, 1975).

The close association of gestures with speech and speech planning is at variance with Luria's (1932) theory whereby during conflicts rising energy distributes randomly over various motor systems. Gestures appear not to be one of these randomly activated motor systems. Gestures rather seem to be active specifically to facilitate speech planning and pave the way for speaking.

Relationships with personality variables

Since the classical expression psychology, gestures are regarded as indicators of personality or character traits (Krout, 1937; Strehle, 1960; Kiener, 1962). Because of their mainly qualitative descriptions, validity of these impressions is difficult to evaluate (cf. Wallbott, 1982). Studies using detailed behavioural measurements, however, provide empirical evidence for stable individual differences in general motor and gestural behaviour (Frey, 1975) so that the search for related personality variables is still relevant. In a study of interaction between public servants and citizens, Scherer & Scherer (1979) found individual differences in gestures associated with a tendency to control others. Public servants high on a scale for Machiavellianism showed fewer gestures and consequently were rated as more cautious than those who were low on this scale. An extensive review on the personality aspect of gestures is given by Wallbott (1982). Generally some significant though low to medium effects characterize the results of these studies which will not be dealt with here since our main concern is the state dependency of behaviour.

Expression of emotions, mood, and conflicts

Stimulated by psychoanalytical ideas about conflict actualization, gestural behaviour has been analysed as a modality by which psychological processes are mediated in the clinical interview (Krout, 1935; Deutsch, 1951; Dittman, 1963; Mahl, 1968; Loeb, 1968). Gestures are regarded as indicators of conflicts. Mahl (1968) reports on single case analyses where idiosyncratic behaviours are related to the verbal content during the interview.

With regard to their function, specific gestures appear to express the experience of conflicts given certain emotions or moods. Thus, Sainsbury (1955) found an increase of gestural activity during anxiety-inducing situations. Similar observations are given in the detailed descriptions of Mahl (1968). However, these relationships as they emerge from the single case analysis appear to be highly idiosyncratic again.

On a more general level, Freedman, Blass, Rifkin & Quitkin (1973) found that hostility, overtly expressed during the interview and assessed by content analysis (Gottschalk, Wingert, & Gleser, 1970) was associated with object-focussed movements, whereas covertly expressed hostility was accompanied by body-focussed movements. During utterances with extreme hostility no hand movements occurred at all. These movements occurred, however, shortly before or after these utterances. According to these relationships, affects and moods can be expressed simultaneously by verbalization and nonverbal gestural behaviour.

Gestures as a social signal

Hand movements become effective as social signals on different levels. This can be seen in the sign language of the deaf but also in easy to understand gestures with a communicative intention – pointing to one's head, a hitch-hiker's thumb, etc. From the classical observations of Efron (1941) it became evident that these gestures are culturally dependent and are carried over within a subculture even over generations after immigration.

As has been shown by Cohen & Harrison (1973) the presence of another person is an important releaser for gestural behaviour. In comparable dialogues via microphones there were fewer gestures than during the presence of the other.

Except for emblems, i.e. gestures with a defined meaning which are used instead of words, it is still unclear in what way the other may profit from this information source. Apart from communication about form features (Graham & Argyle, 1975) there have been no indications as to detrimental effects on the listener if gestural information is lacking. Probably the main effect of gestures for a listener is given by a repeated stimulation which maintains a constant level of attention.

Just because gestures seemed to be used in an idiosyncratic way, as has been shown by Krout (1935), Dittman (1962) and Mahl (1968) no simple, general influences on the listener are to be expected. The positive effects on speech planning (see above) for the gesticulating individual appears to be clearer than the effects for the listener.

7.3 Gestures and depression

Systematic observation of gestures in depressed patients approximately confirm clinical impression. In a strikingly homogeneous way clinicians describe the speech related hand and arm movements of depressed patients as being reduced and retarded. Again, systematic observations give only weak support when compared to the strong impression these behavioural features elicit in the clinician.

Clinical descriptions

In accordance with psychomotor retardation, gestural behaviour during depression is described by psychiatric and classical expression psychology literature (Enke, 1930; Kretschmer, 1967, p. 181; Bleuler, 1969, p. 333; Strehle, 1960, p. 80; Kiener, 1962) as slow, laborious, and feeble. It is also described as retarded (Arieti, 1974; Redlich & Freedman, 1970, p. 323; Hoffmann, Schädrich & Schiller, 1976) and reduced (Fischer-Cornelssen &

Abt, 1980; Spiegel, 1959, p. 947). Together with other parts of the motor behaviour, gestures appear as a main indicator for depressive retardation. While movements of the depressed patient are described as mostly slow and without vigour (Kraepelin, 1883), agitation is characterized by a restless-anxious activity where mainly the hands are continuously in movement (Weitbrecht, 1968).

In his review on movement characteristics of schizophrenic and depressed patients, Wallbott (1982) resumes the variety of these descriptions according to spatio-temporal, spatial, energetic, categorial and Gestalt criteria. Gestures of depressed patients are characterized as follows:

by *spatio-temporal features* (speed, acceleration), such as slow, tired, oppressed, dragging;
by *energy and power aspects* (intensity, tension, etc.), such as powerless, retarded, faint, limp, without tension, ponderous;
by *categorial aspects* (frequency), such as scarce, little or decreased activity;
by *spatial aspects* (extension of movements, usage of space), such as narrow, with little radius;
by *Gestalt aspects* (behavioural flow, qualitative features), such as soft, rounded, disharmonic, unelastic, monotonous, without expression.

Gestural behaviour of manic patients is described according to Wallbott (1982) similar to that of schizophrenics: fast, hasty, short, abrupt, erratic, impulsive, intense, restless, but also as retarded, slow, laborious, stiff, awkward, clumsy, uncoordinated. For schizophrenic patients, these features frequently are summarized by terms like "bizarre" or "stereotypical". It should be noted that some of the features are attributed to depressive and schizophrenic patients likewise when describing their behaviour as slow, tired, retarded, stereotypical and monotonous.

In order to differentiate clinically between agitated and retarded depression, the IMPS (Lorr et al., 1962) uses the presence of motor retardation as a criterion. It seems highly probable that gestural behaviour contributes substantially to this evaluation. There is, however, no mention in the clinical literature as to whether neurotic and endogenous or psychotic depressed patients differ with regard to their gestural or motor behaviour.

According to general clinical descriptions the reduced, slow, limp gestures correspond to the motor retardation and reduced motivation during depression. This gestural behaviour seems to accompany and mediate the slowed and retarded cognitive processing in an adequate way.

Systematic observations
Generally, systematic observations found fewer gestures shown by depressed patients and a decrease of manipulations (adaptors or body-focussed

movements) with recovery from depression. This would be in accordance with clinical descriptions.

From a closer look at the data reported in the literature and also from our study, this statement, however, needs some clarification. From two case studies on a schizophrenic and a depressed patient, Freedman (1972; Freedman & Hoffman, 1967) reported an increase in object-focussed and a decrease in body-focussed movements with recovery from depression. Also, for behavioural ratings, hand movements turned out as differentiating features for evaluating depression (Waxer, 1974; Ulrich, Harms & Fleischhauer, 1976). According to Ulrich et al. (1976) "iterative manipulations" and restricted object-related and speech-related gestures are characteristic of depression. Since in their study retardation and agitation of the patients were closely correlated it is not astonishing that restricted speech-related gestures were significantly associated with retardation and – to a lesser extent – with agitation as well. In further studies by Ulrich (Ulrich, 1979, 1980, 1981; Ulrich & Harms, 1978) a decrease of continuous body-focussed hand movements (manipulations) and an increase in object-focussed movements (illustrators, gestures) was found with clinical improvement of depression. This is interpreted as reflecting a generally reduced vigilance during depression.

When analysing interactions of depressed patients with a partner, Hinchliffe, Hooper, Roberts & Vaughan (1975) found more object-focussed hand movements and also more congruent movements and body positions in both persons after therapy. In his doctoral dissertation, Kiritz (1971, reported by Ekman & Friesen, 1974) analysed gestural behaviour during a clinical interview of 9 psychotic, 8 neurotic depressive and 15 schizophrenic female patients. Generally, an increase of illustrators was found at the end of therapy, especially for improved psychotic depression. Frequency of illustrators was negatively correlated with rated degree of depressive mood on admission to the clinic ($r = -.51$) as well as at discharge ($r = -.39$). Similarly, negative correlations were obtained for ratings of motor retardation and emotional withdrawal. The fewer illustrators the more depressive, motorically retarded, and emotionally withdrawn the patient was rated. It is not possible to assess from these data to what extent these ratings included the behavioural information.

A re-analysis by Wallbott (1982) using the video tapes of a sub-sample of 20 patients from the original Kiritz study, also revealed a significant increase of illustrators at the end of the clinical stay. Statistical significance, however, was according to Wallbott mainly due to two patients with extreme values. From a single case comparison between admission and discharge it turned out that 11 patients had an increase of illustrators, but 8 patients had a decrease and one patient had a stable frequency. Statistical significance, thus, was given by few patients reacting strongly in the expected direction.

This study was discussed in some detail since it shows the importance of comparing individual cases. Moreover, gestural behaviour still needs to be analysed as a possible general indicator of improvement during depression.

7.4 Summary and hypotheses

Gestural behaviour appears mainly to reflect psychomotor retardation. Clinical judgements will probably make use, at least implicitly, of gestures as a source of information for this aspect of depression. Although clinical observations and systematic studies are in accord in reporting reduced speech-related gestures during depression, a closer look reveals that the effects are less clear than expected. Retardation and agitation cannot be differentiated according to ratings of gestural behaviour (Ulrich et al., 1976). Moreover, comparing single cases a substantial number of the patients increases but part of the patients also decreases their gestures with improvement (Wallbott, 1982).

Considering the various functions of gestures, one could theoretically assume two counteracting behavioural tendencies: as a social signal, gestures transmit information in addition to other verbal and nonverbal behaviour. Gestures may stress, punctuate or modulate what is said or even substitute verbal content. From clinical and general understanding one would expect such a socially active behaviour to be reduced during depression.

On the other hand, an opposite effect could be possible as well. Taking the function of gestures as a speech facilitating psychomotor activity, this behaviour should increase during utterances if cognitive processes are impeded and retarded. Retarded thinking and a psychomotor retardation are regarded as a central feature of depression. It seems impossible at the moment to clearly separate both tendencies, especially when observing during quasi-natural situations.

Therefore, on a more simple level the individual changes of gestural behaviour with reference to the subjective wellbeing of the patients and in comparison to normals will be described. From the analysis of Wallbott (1982) it follows that individual comparisons are necessary here. As a methodological aspect the amount of speech has to be taken into account since gestures as they are studied here are closely linked to the act of speaking.

Compared to the other behaviours analysed before, gestural behaviour has a less central place within our study. In addition, we restrict our analyses to social gestures, omitting manipulations. This does not imply that gestural behaviour is less important as an indicator of psychological processes. An adequate treatment of this whole area, however, would require a far more extensive presentation. This has been given by Ulrich (1981) and Wallbott (1982).

According to the general reduction hypothesis and according to results from studies reported in the literature it has to be expected that inhibiting tendencies are dominant during depression and thus gestural behaviour is reduced. Whereas speech production is required by the interview situation, gestural behaviour is a free running, deliberate, additional activity. According to the reduction hypothesis, this activity should be reduced in depressed patients compared to controls and it should increase with improvement.

7.5 Methodological aspects of gesture analysis

Gestural behaviour was analysed for the same 120 five-minute interview segments which were taken for facial analysis. As categories, incidents of large and small spatial gestures as well as of object-focussed gestures with motor primacy and speech primacy according to Freedman (1972) and Ulrich (1980) were assessed. Gestures with "motor-primacy" will be referred to in the following as "object-related gestures" and gestures with "speech-primacy" as "speech-related" gestures. Mainly because of the more unequivocal definition and because of higher inter-rater reliability results for small and large spatial gestures will be presented. Primarily, the total amount of speech- and object-related gestures will be dealt with.

7.5.1 *Small and large spatial gestures*

Both forms of gestural behaviour were differentiated on the basis of their theoretical interpersonal function. They were operationalized by Günthner (1982) as follows:

In *large spatial gestures* upper and lower arm contribute to the movement covering a distance clearly visible and active. By this, torsions of the arm, minimal movements or passive movements from position changes of trunk or shoulder are excluded.

In *small spatial gestures* single fingers or the hand contribute to the movement with resting lower and upper arm. Movement comes out of the hand or finger joint. All movements of the hand or fingers are included except manipulations.

This definition takes the physical dimension of distance as the basis. At the same time it differentiates between arm (large) and hand (small) gestures. In addition, gestures were classified according to the functional definitions of Ekman & Friesen (1972) and Freedman (1972) as speech related gestures and object-related gestures.

Reliability

Inter-observer reliability was high with regard to the total amount of gestures. Taking a sample of 9 interviews, two independent observers agreed in 81% of cases of coding the presence of gestures whereby a window of 15 video frames was the limit for agreement. Differentiating between large and small gestures (69% agreement) and between object-related and speech-related gestures (54% agreement) was much more difficult. Since inter-observer reliability was higher for the physically defined large and small differentiation, these were taken for further analysis, and both were combined into a total for gestural activity (GA). Since the total amount of gestures was of main concern in this study, the high inter-observer reliability for coding a gestural event is the relevant figure.

Correcting for the co-occurrence of gestures and speech

Gestures occur almost exclusively during utterances, and rarely while listening. Therefore the quantity or frequency of gestures is confounded with the amount of speech. In order to resolve this confounding, the number of gestures within a five minute period was corrected by the factor $1/p(S)$, where $p(S)$ is the relative amount of speech of the patient during the analysed period. The relative gestural activity is

GAR = number of gestures within a five minute period x $\frac{1}{p}$ (S).

For example, if 20 gestures occur within an analysed period and speech occurs during 50% of the time ($p(S) = 0.50$), GAR would be $20 \times \frac{1}{0.50} = 40$. The resulting relative gestural activity indicates the extent to which the patientıs speech is saturated with gestures. Since patients as well as controls speak for less than 100% of the time, these values are higher than the original frequencies. Although this correction does not take into account short pauses during utterances, it is in our view sufficient to overcome the confounding effect of the amount of speech.

Our results are reported in terms of the relative gestural activity excluding manipulations (adaptors). The parameter GAR indicates how many large or small gestures occur during a period of five minutes pure speech.

7.6 Results on gestures

Gestural behaviour as it has been assessed here, rarely revealed clear associations with mood. The relative gestural activity increased and decreased to similar degrees with changes of subjective wellbeing. The extent of gestural activity had a high intra- and inter-individual variability which appeared to be unrelated to the subjective wellbeing. Values for gestural activity are

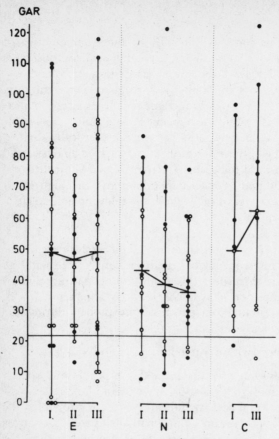

Fig. 7.1 Gestural activity. Individual values for gestural activity relative to amount of speech (GAR) during a 5-minute interval. Criterion line separates "reduced" from "normal" values (for further explanation see Fig. 4.5).

shown in Fig. 7.1. In both patients and controls there were strikingly large ranges in the amounts of gestural behaviour. The distributions overlapped to a great extent. For patients, gestures showed weighted frequencies with medians between GAR = 36 and GAR = 48. This means that during one minute of speech activity the median lies between 7 and 10 gestures. Values varied between percentiles C10 = 0 and C90 = 107. For the controls the medians lay between 10 – 13 gestures per minute of speech activity. The relative number of gestures varied between percentiles C10 = 15 (corresponding to 3 gestures per minute of speech activity) and C90 = 123 (corresponding to roughly 25 gestures per minute of speech activity). There are no statistically significant differences between groups or between different states of wellbeing.

Reduction

During depression 6 out of 20 (= 30%) of the endogenous depressed patients had reduced GAR values (GAR < 20). For neurotic depressed patients this was the case for only two patients (= 13%). The criterion of reduction was set at GAR = 20 which corresponds to 4 gestures per minute of speech activity. For less than a quarter of all the patients (8 out of 36 = 22%) gestural behaviour was reduced during the depressed state according to this criterion.

There was no apparent general increasing or decreasing tendency for reduced GAR values with increase in subjective wellbeing. For endogenous depressed patients the number of individuals showing reduced values decreased from 6 to 5 with recovery. For neurotic depressed patients the number of individuals showing reduced values increased from 2 to 3 with improvement of subjective wellbeing.

Individual changes

A substantial increase of gestural activity with increase in subjective wellbeing was found only in 5 of the 20 endogenous depressed patients. The direction and amount of individual changes for patients and controls is shown in Fig. 7.2.

The high intra-individual variability of gestural behaviour becomes apparent in the large range of change ratios within the three groups of patients and controls. According to values of the controls, the critical level for a "substantial" change is given by CR > 1.10, i.e. a change of more than 110% of the initial value.

According to this criterion, 5 (= 25%) of the endogenous depressed patients substantially increased their gestural behaviour with improvement in subjective wellbeing. Below this critical level, increases and decreases were quite balanced. The median of change ratios for patients and controls was about CR < 0.30.

The stability of the few substantial changes was high. For 4 patients with CR > 1.10 and three measures available, a consistent increase in the median state occurred. For the fifth patient with CR > 1.10 no measurement of the median state was available.

Initial values and substantial change Since few substantial changes occurred, one can only state that for the four of the five patients the substantial increase emerged out of reduced values. Change ratios correlated with the initial value for r = 0.51 (p<.01), i.e. higher change ratios tended to come from low initial values.

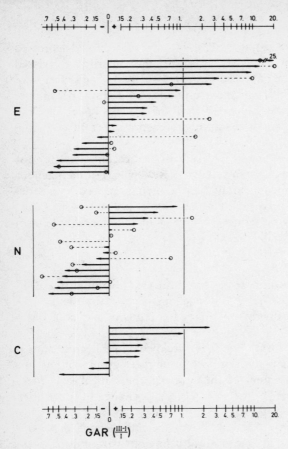

Fig. 7.2 Individual changes in gestural activity. Change ratios for general activity relative to the amount of speech (GAR) (for further explanation see Fig. 5.5).

General description

Taking the 90 interviews from states I and III, relative gestural activity (GAR) is only negligibly correlated with subjective wellbeing (VAS), (r = 0.08) and with Global Clinical Rating (GR) (r = 0.02). No statistically significant differences could be obtained between clinical subgroups or between males and females (U-tests and Wilcoxon test: p>0.10). There was only a slight tendency for male controls to have a higher median in gestural activity than females in both measurements (+29 for state I and +49 for state II). Higher and lower medians were irregular for patients during all states, (see Table B.13 in the Appendix).

Table 7.1: *Intercorrelations of gestural parameters*

Gestures		ORE	SRE	AMB	LA	SM	GA	LAR	SMR	GAR
Object-related (ORE)		–	.26	.54	.86	.38	.78	.79	.18	.61
Speech-related (SRE)			–	.38	.32	.87	.79	.24	.68	.68
Ambiguous relation (AMB)				–	.52	.51	.66	.49	.38	.60
Large movements (LA)					–	.20	.79	.93	–.01	.55
Small movements (SM)						–	.80	.12	.82	.72
Total gestural activity (GA)							–	.65	.55	.83
Gestural movements	Large (LAR)							–	.02	.62
relative to amount	Small (SMR)								–	.80
of speech	Total (GAR)									–

Note:
Dotted lines indicate correlations between object and speech-related versus large and small gestures.
Object-related (ORE), speech-related (SRE), ambivaleutly related (AMB), gestures, large (LA), small (SM) movements and total gestural activity (GA). n = 120 interviews.

Intercorrelations

In order to determine the influence of the correcting factor for speech on our results, correlations were computed for the unweighted and uncombined frequencies as well. Slight correlations between total gestural activity and subjective wellbeing (VAS) or Global Clinical Rating (GR) emerged (r = −0.17 to r = −0.29). The data pool from 120 interviews was taken (see Table 7.1) to determine these general relationships.

The highest correlation with subjective wellbeing turned out for the sum of small and large movements to be (r = −0.29). This correlation, however, vanished when one corrects for the amount of speech. Despite the wide range and variation of values, there was a significant correlation (r = 0.61, p<.05) between GAR measures of state I and state III for the patients. This means that the relative position of an individual patient within the group remained relatively stable with regard to the amount of gestural behaviour. This stability was independent from the state of subjective wellbeing.

Behavioural rating

Higher correlations with the depressed state appeared for the global rating of gestural activity on a nine-point scale, (see Table B.11 in the Appendix) compared to the behavioural assessment of gestures (r = 0.36 with VAS and r = 0.39 with GAR). Rating of the manipulations only correlated r = 0.20 with the depressed state and the Global Clinical Rating (see Table 7.2).

Rating of gestural behaviour was correlated with the measurements to a moderate degree (r = 0.40 for small movements and r = 0.62 for large movements). Again, correlations become considerably smaller when cor-

Table 7.2: *Intercorrelations of gestural behaviour and clinical state.*

		LAR	SMR	GAR	Rating Gest.	Manip	VAS	GR
Gestural movements	Large (LAR)	–	.02	.62	.52	.03	.06	.03
relative to amount	Small (SMR)		–	.80	.21	.09	.08	.01
of speech	Total (GAR)			–	.48	.09	.10	.03
Rating of gestures					–	.13	.36	.39
Rating of manipulations						–	.20	.18
Subjective wellbeing (VAS)							–	.85
Global Clinical Rating (GR)								–

Note:
Thicker lines separate parameters from ratings of gestures and from Global ratings.
Large, small gestural movements and total gestural activity related to the amount of speech.
VAS = Visual Analogue Scale, GR = Global Clinical Rating of depression.
Ratings of gestures and manipulation on 9-point scales. n = 120 interviews.

recting for speech activity ($r = -0.22$ to $r = -0.52$). This means that the measured gestural activity is reflected in the rating with a common variance of 36% maximum. Other behaviours like the amount of speech may additionally influence the rating. This may then contribute to the higher correlation of the depressed state with the behavioural rating compared to the systematic observation.

In summary, the gestural behaviour increased substantially with improvement of the depressed state for only five endogenous depressed patients. Reduced values during the depressed state were present for 6 of the 20 endogenous and for 2 of the 16 neurotic depressed patients. Differentiating between large and small gestures revealed no closer relationships with mood.

The greatest changes in the averages were shown by controls when comparing their two interviews. Generally there were no significant differences between groups and states of wellbeing with regard to the relative amount of gestural activity.

Surprisingly enough the relative position of an individual within the sample remained rather stable with respect to the number of gestures despite the great individual variability.

7.7 Discussion of results on gestures

Even though some patients clearly showed more gestural activity with improvement of subjective wellbeing, this behaviour appeared to be associated least of all with mood. Contrary to our hypothesis there were no clear general relationships between the amount of gestural activity and subjective wellbeing.

Patients and controls show very high inter- and intra-individual variations in this behaviour. Despite this intra-individual variability, according to the correlations between the two measurements, the amount of gestural activity for an individual in different situations is relatively stable in comparison to the variability between individuals. This points to individual characteristics in the usage of gestures.

It has to be concluded that variables besides mood are responsible for the variability of the behaviour. Individual differences, situational features, short-term phases of cognitive planning, or the amount of the current mental load may determine the extent of gestural behaviour from moment to moment. The higher frequency of gestures at the beginning and especially in the middle of the floor-time, i.e. when a person takes the speaker role (Hiebinger, 1982; Feyereisen, 1982) are in favour of the assumption that gestures are related to cognitive planning (cf. Dittman, 1962; Butterworth & Beattie, 1978; Kendon, 1980).

This association of gestures with cognitive planning is compatible with their function as "turn taking" or "turn yielding" signals assumed by Kendon (1970) and Duncan (1972). The absence of gestures prompts the partner to take the role of the speaker. Presence of gestures indicates still unfinished cognitive processes which should not be interrupted by the other. At the beginning of this chapter two contradictory expectations were discussed: In the state of depression the social communicative repertoire, including gestures should decrease. On the other hand, the presumed retarded thinking would predict and increase in gestural activity to facilitate speech planning. It may be that depending on the preponderance of one or the other function in the individual an increase or decrease of gestural activity follows.

But how can the inconsistency of our results with those reported by Freedman & Hoffman (1967), Kiritz (1973, from Ekman & Friesen, 1974) and Ulrich (1981) be resolved? These authors generally found an increase of illustrators or object-focussed movements with improvement of depression.

The kind of clinical samples may have played a role. Also, in our data there was an increase in gestural activity with improvement of subjective wellbeing for some of the endogenous depressed patients. This was not the case for neurotic depressed patients. According to Wallbott (1982) differences in the Kiritz study which were tested parametrically yielded statistically significant results because of a few extreme values. This is plausible considering the high variability of values found in our study. The time sample of five minutes may also have been too short to ensure stable measures of gestures.

Other qualitative aspects of gestures which were not covered here could be more influenced by mood. Dynamic aspects of gestures like amount of energy, velocity etc. are such features which could represent the low energy and the retardation of thought during depression more clearly than the frequency parameter used here. A collapsed body position and slow body movements may be indicative as well. Clinical descriptions of retardation during depression stress these dynamic aspects which might influence clinical impression more than the amount of gestural behaviour.

Manipulations (adaptors) were not assessed here, except through a behavioural rating scale. From the low correlations of the ratings with subjective wellbeing clear effects are hardly to be expected from measurements either. In addition, Hiebinger (1982) found from longitudinal observations on six endogenous depressed patients that four of them decreased and two increased their frequency of manipulations with improvement of subjective wellbeing. Here, also substantial intra- and inter-individual variation of behaviour has to be taken into account.

The possibility cannot be excluded that our results on gestures are due to the definition of behavioural categories or due to low reliability of observation. However, several reasons argue against this. Checking inter-observer reliability revealed a high agreement when considering the presence of gestures without differentiating them. In addition, by setting a critical level of change ratios as a criterion for substantial change, an allowance was made for possible errors in observation as well.

Thus, we have to consider that the number of gestures reflects subjective wellbeing for comparatively few individuals. For patients as well as for controls this behaviour shows great intra- and inter-individual variability which cannot be attributed to changing state of mood in most cases. Short term processes associated with cognitive planning or short term interactional conditions, like a momentary stressing of an utterance and also individual differences are probably more responsible for the variation in the amount of gestural behaviour than mood.

8 Exemplary single cases

The intra-individual character of changes and associations between mood and behaviour will be presented here through the description of four prototypical patient's. Firstly, gaze and speech together with subjective wellbeing will be described for each patient followed by a survey of their nonverbal reaction patterns.

For the four endogenous depressed patients, 19 to 41 interviews were available. The patient's subjective wellbeing changed greatly over the time course. These changes were more pronounced than those of neurotic depressed patients. Marked behavioural changes are thus expected.

8.1 Time course of subjective wellbeing, gaze and speech

Different reaction patterns of relative amount of gaze and speech are shown by the four patients. For the first patient, both behaviours are closely correlated with mood changes. For the second patient both behaviours are only negligibly correlated with the changing state despite an abnormal gaze behaviour. The third patient mainly reacts with changes in gaze behaviour, the fourth mainly with changes in speech activity.

(a) Description of the case EM5
For this patient, nonverbal behaviour and subjective wellbeing changed in the expected way. Both behaviours, speech and gaze increased substantially with improvement.

The 46 year old, married, male patient had been working as a clerk for 28 years for the same insurance company and was head of a group of 10 employees. Months before his clinical stay, the patient recognized problems with concentration and shortness of memory. The patient's demotion within the company elicited vehement and angry responses. His state was worsened by sleep disturbances, heart troubles and problems at work. Finally his wife arranged for his treatment at the institute.

On admission, the patient stated that he had changed completely. He had loss of appetite, had lost 5 kg of weight during five weeks and his libido was markedly decreased. He complained about sleep disorders and early awakening, heart troubles, sensations of numbness in his hands and feet, and pressure on the head. His mood changed considerably during the day with a clear low in the morning. The patient felt restless and depressed but said he could not weep. Because of his feelings of guilt he claimed to have considered suicide. He had delusions of guilt and impoverishment and was in permanent fear of being murdered. His state was diagnosed as the first phase of an endogenous depression (ICD 296.0). The patient participated in the project and was medically treated from the twelfth day on with amitriptylin. There was no indication of depression three months after his clinical stay, during post control. The patient worked in his company again without complications.

Time course of subjective wellbeing, gaze, and speech

About 32 days after admission, 20 days after medical treatment, a clear improvement of subjective wellbeing began which continued according to the Visual Analogue Scale even during follow-up. Both behaviours change accordingly (see Fig. 8.1). Relative durations of gaze as well as speech essentially follow the course of wellbeing. Taking the 25 interviews together, mood is correlated with gaze $r = 0.80$ ($p<.05$) and with speech $r = 0.84$ ($p<0.05$).

For both behaviours there are reduced ($<35\%$) values at the beginning and values higher than the critical level later during the time course. With regard to speech, the patient has stable values above the critical level from about the 10th interview on. For gaze this is the case later, from the 14th interview on. Given some major variations, these changes are indicated early in both behaviours. Even minor changes in the VAS (see arrows) are reflected in considerable behavioural changes.

The Global Clinical Rating (GR) is also highly correlated with gaze ($r = 0.73$) and speech ($r = 0.83$, both $p<.05$). Thus, for this patient both behaviours appear to react in the expected way – they are reduced during depression and substantially increase up to the normal range with improvement, being closely correlated with mood changes.

(b) Description of case EW11

Despite an extremely reduced amount of gaze no behavioural changes occur with improvement of this patient's mood. Speech activity also varies independently from changes in subjective wellbeing.

The 52-year-old, single, female worker came to the clinic with her second depressive phase. Two months before, feelings of anxiety and joylessness started in addition to irritations already present. Up to admission, considerable mood changes with lows in the morning, reduced appetite, feelings of pressure in the throat and a decrease in efficiency intensified. Her religious beliefs prevented her from committing suicide. The patient was unable to work. She can be described as shy, desperate and extremely melancholic.

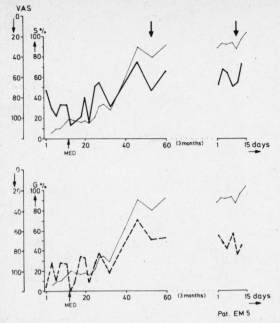

Fig. 8.1 Individual time course of mood, speech, and gaze (a). Patient EM5. Subjective wellbeing (VAS) (——), relative amount of speech activity (S% = ——) and gaze (G% = ----) during depression and follow up. Beginning of medication (MED) and disruptions in the course of subjective wellbeing indicated by arrows.

Her state was diagnosed as the second phase of a monopolar depression (ICD 296.2).

Time course of subjective wellbeing, gaze, and speech

Subjective wellbeing of the patient improves slowly with relapses during the time course. Not before follow-up do the values in the upper half of the Visual Analogue Scale point towards better wellbeing (see Fig. 8.2).

It should be noted that there is an almost total lack of gaze over the whole time course. A relationship between gaze or speech with mood is not apparent.

Correlations of gaze (r = 0.02) and speech (r = 0.20) with subjective wellbeing are similarly low as are those with the Global Clinical Rating (r = 0.32 or r = 0.09). For gaze, these correlations have to be expected due to the constantly low values. Compared to normals, gaze remains reduced during depression as well as during remission whereas speech varies independently of the depressed state.

(c) Description of the case EW10

For this patient, gaze behaviour most strongly reacts to changes of mood.

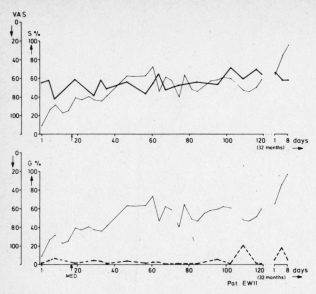

Fig. 8.2 Individual time course of mood, speech, and gaze (b). Patient EW8 (for furhter explanation see Fig 8.1).

These changes appear to be even more obvious in the behaviour than in the subjective scales. Speech activity, however, turned out to be less affected.

For this 57-year-old married housewife it was the third clinical stay having previously had 6 phases of depression. Months before admission her state got worse proceeding into a long phase of depression. This was combined with changing somatic symptoms, mainly head, neck, and back aches, and over-sensitivity of the extremities. She developed strong feelings of guilt and insufficiency, showed marked changes and lability in affect and expressed ideas of suicide.

On admission, a mask-like face, monotonous speech with an increased, thematically narrow flow of speech is recorded. Abrupt weeping, unmotivated anxiety and delusions occured. The patient complained about sleeping disorders, early awakening, loss of appetite and obstipation. The state of the patient was diagnosed as an agitated depressive phase of a monopolar depression (ICD-296.2).

Time course of subjective wellbeing, gaze, and speech

During her clinical stay, the patient improved with some relapses (e.g. between 18th and 25th interview). During follow-up, nine months later, slight symptoms of depression were still present which increased and lead to renewed medication with subsequent improvement. The considerable

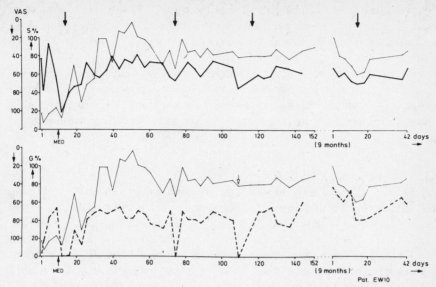

Fig. 8.3 Individual time course of mood, speech, and gaze (c). Patient EW10 (for further explanation see Fig 8.1).

changes in subjective wellbeing at the beginning appear to stabilize from the 26th interview on. During post control, the deterioration is apparent from the 42nd interview (see Fig. 8.3). Gaze varies considerably over time and corresponds to subjective wellbeing especially during post control.

Various points of disrupture should be noted where relatively small changes in mood correspond to extreme changes in gaze (see arrows). There are four incidents from the 4th to the 5th, from 6th to 7th, from 23rd to 24th, and from 31st to 32nd interview where these disruptures are clearly present.

At one instance during the 32nd interview, there is a discrepancy between the Global Clinical Rating, stating considerable depression (a 7 on the scale) and the Visual Analogue Scales showing a slight decrease only. During this interview, the patient admitted having faked a better state at the beginning of the interview when answering the Visual Analogue Scale because of her despair about an experienced change for the worse. During the interview, this was cleared up. There was no further evidence that this patient or other patients deliberately indicated a totally different subjective wellbeing (cf. correlations between VAS and GR in chapter 4).

From the ruptures in subjective wellbeing it could clearly be seen that gaze behaviour repeatedly reacted to changes in mood with considerable variations. Speech activity seems to reflect changes in mood less clearly. Only a higher variability during the more negative states compared to the positive ones appears to be present. For the total of 42 interviews subjective wellbeing correlated with gaze for r = 0.58 and with speech for r = 0.34. In a similar way Global Clinical Rating correlated with gaze for r = 0.69 and with speech for r = 0.35 (all p<.05).

In sum this patient reacts to changes of mood mainly in her gaze behaviour and to a much lesser extent with her speech activity. The extreme deflections in the amount of gaze, given minor changes in subjective wellbeing, point to the sensitive and clear behavioural indication of the internal state.

(d) Description of case EW41

Behavioural changes depending on different phases of subjective wellbeing are remarkable for this patient. Mood changes seem to be more sensitively reflected in speech activity whereas gaze reacts to extreme changes only.

This 57-year-old female patient was a married housewife whose children had left home. The patient had experienced depressive and slight to marked manic phases with progressively shorter intervals for eight years. During her depressed states the patient was unable to manage the household. She suffered from sleep disorders and self-accusations. During her manic phases the patient was extremely active and restless, worked during the night, started many activities without finishing them and had difficulty with her daily obligations. Despite treatment by a psychiatrist, depression-free intervals became shorter so that the patient was admitted to the clinic on the advice of her daughter.

On admission, the patient was in a good mood, active, busy, though not in a clearly manic state. Through her clinical stay the patient wanted to gain more information about her condition. At the beginning she was anxious for her good state of wellbeing to persist. The diagnosis was a bipolar depression (ICD Nr. 296.3).

Time course of subjective wellbeing, gaze, and speech

The good state of wellbeing on admission with a slight improvement up to the 25th day abruptly fell into a deep depression. After medical treatment, an improvement can be seen with a climax on the 80th day. A slight relapse occurred between the 100th and 120th day of her clinical stay. After repeated medical treatment her subjective wellbeing improves again and remains stable during post control (see Fig. 8.4).

Generally the changes in the behaviours observed correspond to those of wellbeing. Gaze decreased from initially 50% to 20% during depression, but then soon rose to 60% again. The relative amount of speech decreases from 70% to 19% during depression and then slowly increases again.

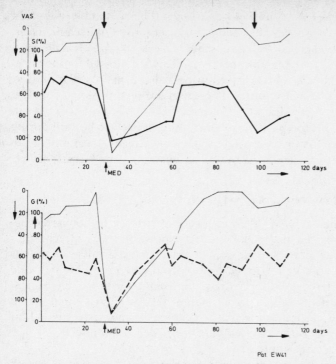

Fig. 8.4 Individual time course of mood, speech, and gaze (d). Patient EW41 (for further explanation see Fig 8.1).

During the slight relapse in subjective wellbeing, speech activity was reduced to 30%.

Given the total of 21 interviews, subjective wellbeing correlates with gaze for $r = 0.55$ and with speech for $r = 0.65$ (both $p < .05$). It should be noted that two extreme values for gaze during depression mainly contribute to the correlation. During the time course mainly two levels of gaze, high and low amounts are present whereas for speech values they are distributed equally over the whole range.

Interestingly enough, Global Clinical Rating is correlated with speech for $r = 0.90$ ($p < .05$) whereas for gaze this is only $r = 0.44$ (n.s.). It can be concluded that clinical judgement in this case relies on speech more than on gaze.

Some points of this case are remarkable. Firstly, it shows that during severe depression, both behaviours decrease considerably. This supports the reduction hypothesis. However, for this patient, speech activity represents changes in mood for a longer period of time than gaze. Gaze in turn, only reacts to the extreme change for the worse. Clinical impression seems to account for these behavioural differences.

Secondly, from the time course of subjective wellbeing and behaviours, a prototypical course of endogenous depression seems to have been manifest. After a period of good mood with a subsequent elevated state of wellbeing a sudden fall into a deep depression occurred. This is followed by improvement with slight relapses, similar in form to a dampened oscillation. Extreme deflections in the behaviour still occurred during this phase. Finally a stabilized state was reached.

Such a marked, prototypical time course will, however, be rare during clinical observations. Patients come to clinical treatment when already in the depressed state and they leave the clinic when the state has improved.

8.2 Comparison of nonverbal reaction patterns

Each of the patients showed different reaction patterns of nonverbal behaviour which have been analysed, i.e. facial expression, gaze, speech activity and gestures. This holds for the occurrence of reduced values as well as for substantial changes. Values for each of the four patients are summarized in Fig. 8.5. The different reaction patterns for each patient become evident from the marked fields of the figure. Only patient EW41 reacts in all parameters in accordance with the general reduction hypothesis whereas for the other patients this is the case for part of the behaviours only.

Correspondingly, the number of patients reacting with a specific behaviour varies: more patients react with facial activity and gaze than with speech activity, gestures and facial repertoire. In this, these single cases represent the general behavioural patterns to be discussed in chapter 9.

8.3 Summary of single case descriptions

Each of the four patients described has particularities in his or her nonverbal behaviour. The kind of relationship between subjective wellbeing and the behaviour has characteristic qualities for each individual. While patients EM5, EW10 and EW41 change their gaze behaviour and their speech activity in accordance with subjective wellbeing, the extremely low amount of gaze for patient EW11 remains unchanged, like her rather normal speech activity. Patient EW11 has, however, reduced gestures and facial expression which increase with improvement.

The individual correlations and the analysis of the time course give further evidence that behaviours differ with regard to their sensitivity to mood changes. Moreover, in the case of EW41, it turned out that one behaviour (speech) was a more sensitive indicator for a broader range of mood states than another (gaze). It can already be seen from these cases that the various behavioural parameters differ with regard to their generality as an indicator of mood. All patients react in the expected way in their

Pt	MIAK	AU 12	REP 2	G %	S %	GAR	m
Values during depressed state (I)							
EM 5	16	1	1	28	27	42	5
EW11	18	1	3	5	58	2	4
EW10	44	1	7	18	43	63	2
EW41	3	0	1	6	19	0	6
(Crit.<)	23	4	3	35	35	20	
n	3	4	2	4	2	2	
Change ratios							
EM 5	.44	5.00	5.00	.61	1.70	.46	5
EW11	.67	13.00	.33	.00	.01	3.40	3
EW10	- .34	2.00	- .29	2.10	.54	- .23	4
EW41	3.70	10.00	1.00	7.30	2.60	13.30	6
(Crit.>)	.33	.60	.50	.30	.20	1.10	
n	4	4	2	3	3	2	

Fig. 8.5 Nonverbal reaction patterns of four depressed patients. Values on nonverbal parameters (MIAK to GAR, abbreviations see Appendix A1) and change ratios for endogenous depressed (E), male (M) and female (W) patients. Reduced values or substantial changes marked according to critical (Crit) limits. m = number of reduced or substantially changed nonverbal parameters, n = number of marked patients for each parameter.

frequency of smiles. But in the general facial activity this is the case for three patients only. One of the patients reduces her initial high frequency in facial activity with improvement. Amazingly for this patient the statement on admission reports a "mask-like, frozen" facial expression. This judgement could have been based on a lack of the "normal" smile as a conversational signal whereas other facial activity was not regarded.

Even though gestures and facial repertoire are less frequently changed, they can be regarded as clearly reduced and substantially increasing in two cases. For these patients they are specific indicators of mood.

In all of the single cases described here, individual specific reactions to mood changes have been obtained. Different aspects of nonverbal behaviour are reduced during depression and substantially increase with improvement.

9 Nonverbal reaction patterns

When regarding the behavioural aspects for all patients, a variety of reaction patterns emerge. In general, patients react to improvement of subjective wellbeing in different ways. Correlations and group comparisons, to be presented later insufficiently reflect the behavioural reactions. They combine strong association of mood and behaviour shown by some patients with weak associations shown by others. Sex differences which will be mentioned shortly in the following turned out to be of minor importance. As a methodological aspect behavioural rating and measurement will be compared.

9.1 Individual reactions

Individual reactions can be described with regard to the defined criteria of reduced values and substantial changes. Moreover, an attempt is made to group the patterns of nonverbal behaviour by use of a cluster analysis.

9.1.1 Reduced values and substantial changes

All patients except three showed reduced values and substantial changes in one *or* more behavioural aspects. As can be seen from the accumulative frequency distributions in Figs. 9.1 and 9.2, very few patients show no reduction or substantial change in any of the behavioural aspects. But there are also only a few patients with reduction or substantial increase in five or six of the behavioural parameters.

When comparing the different states it can be seen that for endogenous depressed patients the average amount of reduced nonverbal aspects (50% level) decreases from 4 to 2 (Wilcoxon-test $p < .05$). For neurotic depressed patients, however, this amount decreases less from 3.3 to 2.5, a difference which is not statistically significant. However, even during the relatively best state of wellbeing, 2 to 2.5 aspects are still reduced for half of the patients. This shows that there are still deficits in part of the nonverbal behaviours. During recovery, normal behaviour (as defined by control values) in all of the analysed aspects is shown by about 20% of the patients only. As for the reduced values, few patients show substantial increases in 4, 5 or 6 behavioural aspects with improvement (see Fig 9.2).

150

REDUCED BEHAVIOUR

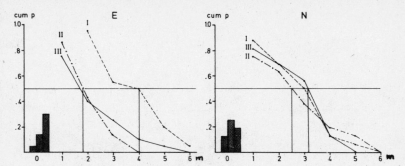

Fig. 9.1 Reduced nonverbal parameters. Cumulated proportions (cum p) of endogenous (E) and neurotic (N) depressed patients showing 1 to 6 reduced nonverbal parameters (m) at depressed state (I = ---), intermediate state (II = -·-) and recovered state (III = ——). Vertical lines at cum p = .50 indicate the median number of reduced parameters on the x-axis. Bars = proportion of patients with 0 reduced parameters at the three states.

With improvement of subjective wellbeing significantly more nonverbal parameters increase in endogenous (Mdn = 3) than in neurotic depressed patients (Mdn = 2), (U-Test: p<.05). Again, only some of the nonverbal parameters increase for an individual. There are four endogenous depressed patients who show increases in five or six nonverbal parameters. For 9 of the 16 neurotic depressed patients, however, one or more nonverbal parameters even decrease with improvement.

Generally there is a positive correlation of r = 0.70 (p<.05) between the number of reduced nonverbal parameters and the number of substantial increases. The more parameters reduced within an individual then the more will substantially increase.

Sex differences were neither found with regard to reduced values nor with regard to substantial changes (U-tests: p>.05). This is surprising since a tendency for stronger nonverbal reactions would be expected for females (cf. Vrugt & Kerkstra, 1982; Hall, 1984).

The depressive illness could have a stronger effect here than sex differences. The tendency of a higher frequency of smiling and more facial activity in female controls would be in accordance with this interpretation. However, the control group is too small for statistical comparison. Sex differences in the behaviour may also have been diminished by the interview. The interview was meant to homogenize the situation. This, however, put high demands on the patient. In such a situation the influence of mood on the behaviour may become dominant.

For the occurrence of reduced values during depression and their substan-

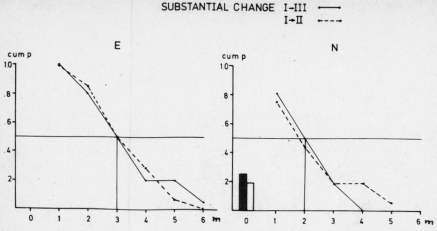

Fig. 9.2 Substantial increases in nonverbal parameters. Cumulated proportion (cum p) of endogenous (E) and neurotic (N) depressed patients showing substantial increases in 1 and 6 nonverbal parameters (M) with improvement of subjective wellbeing in the intermediate (I → II, = ---) or recovered (I → III = ——) state. Vertical line at cum p = .50 indicates the median number of substantially increased parameters on the x-axis. Bars = proportion of patients with 0 substantial increases in intermediate and recovered state.

tial increase with improvement the main finding is that nearly all patients react in at least some of the nonverbal aspects. Although few patients react in more than three of the six nonverbal parameters, there are also few whose nonverbal behaviour is totally unaffected by a change in mood.

9.1.2 *Patterns of nonverbal reactions*

For the 36 patients there are 22 different patterns of reduced values during the depressed state. There are still 17 during the recovered state. With regard to substantial changes there are 28 different patterns, often characteristic of one or two patients. In contrast, patterns of controls are nearly identical.

In order to combine similar reaction patterns and to structure this variety, a cluster analysis was performed similar to that for the facial patterns. Because of its complexity the procedure will be described step by step.

1   The parameters used for the analysis were: (a) presence of reduced values during state I as a dichotomized variable. It was recorded if a specific behaviour was either reduced or not. (b) Presence of substantial changes as a three level variable. A substantial decrease, unchanged, or a substantial increase were recorded. Each individual is

thus characterized by a vector with six nonverbal parameters either 0 = non-reduced or 1 = reduced plus these six parameters either decreased $= -1$, unchanged $= 0$ or increased $= +1$ with improvement of subjective wellbeing.

2   As in the procedure for facial patterns (cf. chapter 5), similarity of nonverbal reaction patterns was defined by the Euclidean distance between these vectors.

3   Individuals were grouped according to similarity of patterns by means of the Ward procedure with a consecutive optimizing by a minimal distance procedure ("Hill climbing", SPSS-X, 1986). Given an optimum of the F-criterion and the goal function value, a solution with six clusters was accepted.

4   Reaction patterns of the individuals within a cluster are given by the corresponding centroid values for each behavioural aspect. A centroid value gives the proportion of individuals showing reduced values or substantial changes for a specific behaviour. These proportions are taken as the reaction pattern characteristic for the respective cluster.

Results
Reaction patterns differ considerably between patients. Moreover, clusters appear to differentiate between endogenous and neurotic depressed patients. In Figure 9.3 these reaction patterns for the six clusters are presented.

The content of the various clusters will be characterized in the following.

Cluster I: Generally strong nonverbal reactions
The five endogenous depressed patients in this cluster showed reduced values and substantially increased values in nearly all of the nonverbal features. All of the patients showed reduced values in general and specific facial activity (MIAK and AU12) as well as for speech; in four patients reduced values for gaze were found. Correspondingly substantial increases occurred with increased state of well-being. For gestural behaviour this was the case for only two of the five patients. With regard to the other behaviours four to five patients showed a substantial increase.

Cluster II: Smile, speech and gaze reactions
For the five endogenous and two neurotic depressed patients within this cluster, reduction in the frequency of smiles (AU12), speech activity (S%) and amount of gaze (G%) during depression and their substantial increase with recovery appeared to be characteristic.

Cluster III: Reduction of facial behaviour
This group is composed of nine patients (three endogenous, six neurotic depressed) and one control. They mainly showed reduced amount of smiles and of general facial activity which increased only in some of them with

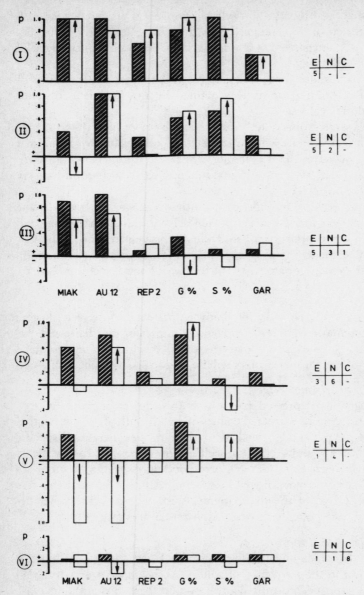

Fig. 9.3 Nonverbal reaction patterns. Proportion of patients (p) with reduced values (shaded bars) or substantial changes (open bars) in nonverbal parameters within each cluster (I to VI). Arrows indicate an amount > .20 and direction of substantial changes, either increase (+) or decrease (−) with improvement of subjective wellbeing. Abbreviation for nonverbal parameters (MIAK to GAR) see Appendix A1). Number of individuals of each subgroup (E, N, C) within each cluster are given besides each graph.

increased wellbeing (six or five of the nine individuals). The other behavioural aspects appeared nearly unaffected.

Cluster IV: Gaze reaction with reduced facial behaviour
For this group with three endogenous and six neurotic depressed patients, clear increases of the initially reduced gaze behaviour are present. The amount of smiles and of general facial activity, which were also frequently reduced, increased to a lesser extent. Speech activity even decreased substantially for four patients.

Cluster V: Decrease of facial behaviour
The remarkable substantial decrease of facial behaviour (MIAK and AU12) with improvement is characteristic of the four neurotic depressed patients and for one endogenous depressed patient within this group. Three patients showed reduced gaze which, however, like speech, rarely increased with improvement.

Cluster VI: Unaffected nonverbal behaviour
In this cluster of ten individuals, including eight controls, one endogenous and one neurotic depressed patient, reduced or substantially changed behaviours were quite sparse. This pattern reflects a stable nonverbal repertoire which for the two patients is unaffected by mood changes.

Assignment of individuals to clusters
As can be seen from Fig. 9.3 controls and patients can be clearly assigned to separate clusters.

For controls this assignment is partly due to the definition of critical levels. However, the distinction between subgroups of depression would not follow from that.

Mainly endogenous depressed patients are grouped into Clusters I and II whereas Clusters IV and V with their unexpected behavioural decreases mainly contain neurotic depressed patients.

Cluster III with reduced facial activity contains endogenous and neurotic depressed patients according to their proportion in the total sample. Included was one control. Male and female individuals are distributed with similar proportions over all clusters.

This cluster analysis reveals that when grouping individuals according to their nonverbal behaviour, a variety of nonverbal reaction patterns characterize depressed patients. Moreover, there is evidence that different subgroups of patients show characteristic nonverbal patterns: endogenous depressed patients appear to react in more behavioural aspects and in accordance with the general Reduction Hypothesis whereas for neurotic depressed patients this is less the case. In addition, unexpected decreases of behaviour occur with improvement.

These nonverbal reaction patterns of depressed patients are clearly dis-

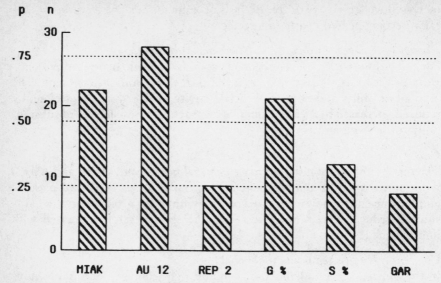

Fig. 9.4 Reduction for nonverbal parameters during depression. Number (n) and proportion (p) of patients showing reduced values for different nonverbal parameters (MIAK to GAR) during depressed state. (For abbreviations for nonverbal parameters see Appendix A1.)

tinct from controls. The patterns of patients represent a variety of behavioural reactions to changes of mood during depression.

9.2 Characteristics of behavioural features

When comparing the behavioural parameters it turned out that the frequency of smiles and the amount of gaze most frequently increase substantially. Together with general facial activity, they are the most often reduced during depression (see Figs. 9.4 and 9.5).

As can be seen from Fig. 9.4, fewer patients show reduced values in their speech activity. Even fewer show reduced values in their facial repertoire and in gestural activity than is the case for facial activity and gaze. This result suggests that behaviour can be rank ordered according to probability of deficits during depression.

For substantial changes, there is a slightly different rank order (see Fig. 9.5).

Sensitivity to changes of mood is similarly high for the frequency of smiles and for the amount of gaze. This is less so for general facial activity. Nevertheless, the number of increases in general facial activity surpasses that of decreases as is the case for speech activity.

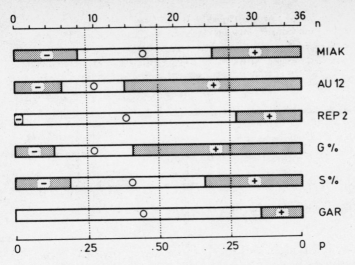

Fig. 9.5 Changes in nonverbal parameters with improvement of subjective wellbeing. Substantial increases (+), decreases (−) and minor variations (0) of nonverbal parameters (MIAK to GAR): number (n) and proportion (p) of patients. (For abbreviations for nonverbal parameters see Appendix A1.)

For most of the patients changes occurred in agreement with the hypothesis that behaviours increase with improvement of the depressed state. It should be noted, however, that for six out of sixteen (= 38%) neurotic and two out of twenty (= 10%) endogenous depressed patients more parameters decrease substantially than increase. For behaviours that were rarely reduced or changed one has to keep in mind that corresponding values clearly deviated from those of normals. According to the criteria set, these behaviours are valid indicators of mood, though only for fewer patients.

The parameters analysed here as indicators of mood thus differ considerably with regard to their specificity or generality.

9.3 Intercorrelations

Intercorrelations show an intermediate general association between subjective wellbeing and behavioural parameters (see Table 9.1).

The parameters associated with mood most frequently are highly significantly correlated on a general level. Correlations with subjective wellbeing and the Global Clinical Rating are similar in size. For gaze, these correlations are $r = 0.52$ resp. $r = 0.40$. For the frequency of smile the correlation coefficients are $r = 0.49$ or $r = 0.60$. Speech activity correlates with subjective wellbeing and Global Clinical Rating at $r = 0.41$ $p < 0.1$. For general facial activity the correlation coefficients are somewhat lower: $r =$

Table 9.1: *Intercorrelations of nonverbal parameters*

90 interviews from n = 45 individuals; two values for each. Significance for n = 45.

	MIAK	AU12	REP2	G%	S%	GAR	VAS	GR
Facial activity (MIAK)	—	.60**	.66**	.16	.09	.11	.17	.26
Smile (AU12)		—	.33*	.33*	.26	-.09	.49**	.60**
Repertoire (REP2)			—	.12	.06	.12	.08	.17
Gaze (G%)				—	.18	.21	.52**	.40**
Speech (S%)					—	.16	.41**	.41**
Gestures (GAR)						—	.08	.02
Subjective wellbeing (VAS)							—	.86**
Global Clinical Rating (GR)								—

Note:
Thicker lines separate bahavioural parameters from Global Ratings
* = p<.05
** = p<.01

0.17 or r = 0.26 and for gestures they are not higher than r = 0.08. The intercorrelations of the various behavioural parameters are less than 0.33, except for facial parameters.

The current correlations for gaze, speech and smiles exceed the characteristic upper limit of r = 0.30 assumed by Mischel (1968) for correlations in personality research. However, correlations in our study did not describe relationships between stable personality characteristics but rather between states and behavioural changes. In addition, the considerable variation in mood states which is not usually found in normal populations and the homogeneous interview situation might have contributed to the size of correlations in our study.

Nevertheless, when expressed as a coefficient of determination these correlations describe common variances between 17% and 30% only. Taking into account the individual associations during the time course it becomes evident that the general correlations yield an insufficient picture of individual associations.

Correlations with specific aspects of depression

From the psychological variables assessed, the Visual Analogue Scale (VAS) and the Global Clinical Rating (GR) were most significantly correlated with the behavioural measures (see Table B.11 in the Appendix). Correlations with the specific aspects of depression, including variables like "activity and social contact" or "positive emotions and future expectations" are usually lower. Since these aspects are highly correlated with each other, this could reflect a psychological homogeneity in depression which is represented best in the two global measures. It cannot be excluded, however, that specifically selected subgroups, for example, with independently assessed deficits in social skills, would reveal other associations with nonverbal behaviours.

Table 9.2: *Critical limits and correlations with initial values for nonverbal parameters*

		Change		x(I)vs. CR		Correlations x(I)vs.x(III)	
	Reduct	Subst	Consist	Pt	Contr	Pt	Contr
Facial activity (MIAK)	f<23	> .33	82%	−.50**	−.48	.47**	.61
Smile (AU12)	f<4	> .60	82%	−.53**	−.16	−.03	.73
Repertoire (REP2)	m<3	> .50	75%	−.59**	−.52	.25	.51
Gaze (G%)	<35%	> .30	95%	−.55**	−.03	.50**	.83
Speech (S%)	<35%	> .20	94%	−.52**	−.33	.20	.87
Gestures (GAR)	<22	>1.10	(100%)	−.51**	−.33	.61**	.72
Subjective wellbeing (VAS)				−.31	+.22	.01	.99
Global Clinical Rating (GR)				−.61	(−)	.20	(−)
(n) of samples				(36)	(9)	(36)	(9)

Note:
Correlations of initial values [x(I)] with change ratios(CR) respectively with values at relatively best state of subjective wellbeing. [x(III)] for patients (PT) and controls (Contr). No indications of significance for controls because of low sample size.
** = p <.01

9.4 Methodological aspects

The methodological aspects discussed will refer to the criteria by which critical levels were defined, to the problem of initial values and their effect on change ratios, and to the comparison of rating and measurement of behaviour.

Criteria for reduced values and substantial change

Since behavioural parameters are defined on different dimensions, only critical levels of change ratios can be immediately compared. The change ratios give the amount of change relative to the initial value. The initial value was taken from the relatively worst state of wellbeing (I). This can be done without any problem for normals since their reports on mood show little variation compared to patients. Patients' initial values could also be taken from a relatively good state of wellbeing, similar to a rest condition in psychophysiological measurements. Since according to our hypothesis, an increase of behaviour was postulated with improvement, the earlier point of time, i.e. the depressed state, appeared to be a better reference for determining changes in behaviour.

Critical levels for reduced values and substantial changes are summarized in Table 9.2 together with correlations between initial values and change ratios and figures for consistency of changes.

Behaviour	Subjective Wellbeing Measure vs. Rating		Clinical Impression Measure vs. Rating		Measure vs. Rating
	Measure	Rating	Measure	Rating	
Facial Activity	.11		.20		.33
Smile	.47		.57		.41
Facial *) Repertoire	.05	.45	.15	.57	.23
Gaze	.55	.47	.44	.45	.71
Gestures	.10	.36	.03	.38	.48
Speech	.42	.29	.42	.28	.60

*) Rating of "Facial Variability"

Fig. 9.6 Correlations between behavioural measures and ratings. Marked correlations specially referred to in the text.

Critical levels for change ratios of gaze (.33) and speech (.20) in controls indicate a low variability of values. This means that less than 33% and 20% deviation from the initial value can be regarded as a normal variation on repeated measurement of these behaviours within the given situation. This variation is greater for the facial parameters and yet greater for gestural activity. Here the normal variation from the initial value can be 110%.

For patients, change ratios are negatively correlated with initial values to a medium degree (r = – .50). For controls, this is the case for general facial activity only. Thus, high change ratios tend to emerge from low initial values. However this does not permit predictions in each single case.

Consistency is a relevant criterion to evaluate the stability of change effects. As can be seen from Table 9.3, consistency of changes is between .75 and 1.00. For at least 75% of the substantial changes between extreme states of wellbeing (I-III) there is a change in the intermediate state (II) pointing in the same direction in these cases. The consistency of change is further evidence that the influence of mood on specific nonverbal behaviours in the individual is not a random effect.

Measurement vs. rating of behaviour
Since behavioural measurement is a more costly undertaking than ratings the question arises whether similar results can be obtained from both methods. Does a rating validly represent the measured behaviours?

Behavioural ratings on nine-point scales (see Appendix A3) were made immediately after the interview using parts of the videotape. The correlations between these ratings and measurements of behavioural aspects and their relationship with subjective wellbeing and the Global Clinical Rating are given in Fig. 9.6.

Only the measurement and rating of gaze behaviour are highly correlated ($r = 0.71$; $p < .01$). The corresponding correlation for speech activity is $r = 0.60$ ($p < .05$), whereas the other correlations are significant but below $r < 0.50$.

Correlations of rated and measured behaviours with subjective wellbeing and Global Clinical Rating are similar in magnitude. It should be noted that the rating of "facial variability" is obviously primarily based on the frequency of smiles (AU12, see marked correlations of measurement and rating).

Rating of gestures correlates better than measurement with subjective wellbeing. It could be that in this case the rating also accounts for qualitative aspects of gestures not covered by the measurement. The rating of gestures could also be influenced by other contextual information yielding a higher correlation with subjective wellbeing. For speech activity the correlation between measurement and subjective wellbeing is significantly greater than the correlation with the rating. This finding supports the use of automated speech analysis which is now easily available.

Although rating and measurement for gaze and facial behaviour both correlate to a similar extent with data on subjective wellbeing this does not imply that the easier method should be favoured in all cases. Measurement guarantees a higher resolution and differentiation of the behaviour. This is especially evident in facial behaviour and in the individual correlations with mood, as described for the individual cases. Moreover, it cannot be excluded that behavioural rating implicitly includes additional information and is influenced by the general knowledge of the rater.

In sum, behavioural ratings can validly represent behavioural measurement. Waxer (1976, 1979), Renfordt & Busch (1976), Jones & Pansa (1979), Pansa-Henderson & Jones (1982) and others have shown that behavioural ratings can be used as valid indicators for the changes of psychopathological states. Objective measurements, however, are advantageous when (a) the observer's influence has to be minimized, (b) when confounding effects from different sources of information have to be avoided, and (c) when differentiated behavioural information is needed.

9.5 Summary

In response to the question which of the nonverbal behaviour differentiates the best, at least four answers can be given.

The first answer is closest to the phenomena observed. It proposes that each of the assessable behaviours which are reduced during depression and increase with the improvement of subjective wellbeing can be a valid indicator of mood.

The second answer applies to the relative weights of single nonverbal aspects as indicators of the depressed mood. Here, a rank order can be given with the frequency of smiles at the top followed by general facial activity, gaze, and speech. The facial repertoire and the number of gestures appears to be less valid in this sense.

A third answer refers to change. Here, gaze and frequency of smiles proved to be the most sensitive indicators.

A fourth answer refers to the differentiation between endogenous/ psychotic and neurotic depressed patients. In neurotic depressed patients general facial activity most frequently changes in the counter direction, i.e. it decreases with improvement. Also, their gaze behaviour often remains reduced in an improved state. This pattern is rarely to be found in endogenous depressed patients.

When comparing the individuals, a variety of nonverbal reaction patterns emerged. In a few cases all behavioural aspects are affected. Usually only some of the nonverbal behaviours react to changes in mood without a clear hierarchical order between them. A few patients show no reduction or subsequent changes in any of the nonverbal behaviours.

Correlations insufficiently represent the individual associations of mood with nonverbal behaviour. Different individual reaction patterns with the smile, amount of gaze and speech as the most salient features seem to reflect this association more adequately.

10 Nonverbal expression of mood – General discussion and conclusions

The following considerations on the expression of affective states, which in our view follow from the results presented so far definitely need further validation. From the longitudinal data there is evidence for the individual specificity of nonverbal reaction patterns. This touches our concepts of behavioural diagnostics and nonverbal communication. The crucial question is how does the variety of behavioural patterns express the psychological changes during depression and how are they to be recognized and understood.

10.1 Nonverbal expression of the depressed state

The comparatively homogeneous state of depression is expressed in a variety of behaviours and behavioural patterns. The receiver integrates this information into a homogeneous impression. If depression is considered a "final common pathway" resulting from different dispositional, social, cognitive, biochemical, and physiological, etc. factors (Akiskal & McKinney, 1975; Akiskal, 1979) this state unfolds again into the various nonverbal behaviours.

The Lens Model (cf. chapter 2) describes how a state or trait is expressed by various behavioural effectors. According to this model an observer combines a variety of behavioural indicators as is the case in the Global Clinical Rating. The clear changes during depression, although recognized in the global rating, seem to disappear when systematically assessing the single behaviours and comparing them across individuals.

On the average, only moderate correlations describe the general relationship of depressed mood states with nonverbal behaviour. If, on the other hand, individual associations are determined clear changes in nonverbal behaviour indicate the improvement of the depressed state for most patients. Behaviours contribute to the expression of a state in a way which can be characterized by a model of "logical or-connections".

Specific associations between mood and behaviour
According to the present results it cannot be assumed that the depth or severity of depression is associated generally with the lack of facial expression, for example. There is no general linear or monotonous relationship

163

between the extent of depression and the amount of behavioural reduction. This relationship, however, exists in individual cases.

The reduction hypothesis described earlier thus applies only in an individual specific way, i.e. not for all individuals and all behaviours at the same time. If it applies more frequently to smile and gaze this indicates that behaviours vary with regard to their generality or specificity as an indicator of mood.

Even from our high individual correlations, no cause-effect relationships can be deduced. Nevertheless, it is plausible to assume that the nonverbal behaviour is primarily dependent on the psychological state of depression and not vice versa.

Individual activation of independent behavioural domains

It was initially expected that the psychological state could be expressed by various nonverbal behaviours. According to our results, these have to be specified. For an individual the expression occurs through some nonverbal behaviours and not through the total repertoire. Usually, only part of the available behavioural repertoire varies depending on the mood state. For one individual this can be the smile or the general facial activity, for another it can be gaze or speech, etc. As an expression of the depressed state, the potential indicators enter the picture only partially and independently from each other.

The two elements − intra-individual association and the "logical or-connection" of the single nonverbal behaviours are important for the expression of mood and state of wellbeing. Associations of mood with a specific behaviour can be ascertained intra-individually. Combining data of differentially reacting individuals may lead to the inappropriate conclusion that there is an overall weak association. This points to a reaction specificity for individuals.

10.2 Specificity of nonverbal reaction patterns

The specificity of nonverbal reactions resemble psychophysiological reactions. Various aspects have been worked out for these reactions in the 1960s (Lacey & Lacey, 1958; Lacey, 1967; Engel, 1960; Engel & Bickford, 1961; Fahrenberg, Walschburger, Förster, Myrtek & Müller, 1979).

According to Lacey (1967) situational stereotypy can explain only part of the variance of physiological stress reactions. Individuals show different physiological reactions to an identical stimulus. In some cases an increase in heart rate occurs, in others an increase in skin conductance appears, in still other cases both increase in response to the same stressor. According to Lacey, intra-stressor stereotypy accounts for individual differences in reactions. Inter-stressor stereotypy means that an individual reacts with similar physiological changes independent of the stressor type.

Considering the "stimulus-response" and "individual-response" specificity, the question whether there are more and less relevant features cannot be reasonably answered according to Engel (1960). Each of the physiological features *can* be relevant for certain individuals or for certain stimuli. Also in our study, where speech activity and gestures appeared less frequently as state dependent indicators of wellbeing, these behaviours cannot be considered as less meaningful. They appear as relevant indicators for only a few individuals.

Degrees of specificity Modes of expression are obviously used in different ways and to different extents by individuals. Some behaviours have a higher degree of generality as indicators of mood than others. General indicators are those behavioural aspects which vary with psychological processes for most individuals and which thus are generally understood. Specific indicators are those behavioural aspects which vary with psychological processes in a few individuals only, but still validly reflect the changing state. As has been mentioned before, smile and gaze are more general, speech and gestures are more specific indicators. Thus, it has to be assumed that there exists a continuum of specificity to generality where different behaviours can be located according to their relationship to psychological states.

These individual specific reactions probably hold for certain ranges of mood states. Given extreme conditions of depression or stress, the whole behavioural and communication system will break down. Then a condition arises where no movement at all can be seen, where the person does not say a word, does not look at the other and activates almost no part of the behaviourial repertoire. Not until some improvement in the state occurs, the specific parts of the behavioural repertoire become important again. An example of this extreme condition is the catatonic state during psychosis where no movement is apparent. Another is the appalic syndrome which occurs after a severe head injury. When this syndrome diminishes emotions reappear in a certain order. At the beginning of remission, anxious expressions and displeasure reappear, followed by anger and affection. Later during remission joy is expressed and finally sadness or grief (Gerstenbrand, 1967). Our analyses were taken during a less extreme range of psychological conditions although our patients had suffered from severe states of depression. Under these conditions the specificity of nonverbal reactions becomes relevant and can adequately represent the depressed state and its changes.

Stability It cannot be ascertained from our data nor from the literature whether specific reaction patterns are constant over longer periods of time. There are, however, various indications for stability within the temporal range of our observations. The patient's individual changes in all behavioural aspects were highly consistent. With the exception of gestures, control values on repeated measurements, compared to those of the patients were very stable. Repeated mood dependent changes could be shown for gaze and speech in the single case analysis. Only longitudinal observations could determine if this stability also holds over longer periods.

10.3 Characteristics of the different nonverbal components

When comparing the various nonverbal components they appear to differ in their sensitivity to changes in mood states. Pathological states are obviously differentially expressed by these nonverbal components as was also shown by Jones & Pansa (1979) and Waxer (1974). Since our analyses of the different nonverbal behaviours have already been discussed, only some general features will be mentioned in the following.

10.3.1 *Facial expression*

As an expression of psychological processes facial behaviour points to affective events which manifest themselves given a general mood state. Contrary to our expectations a variety of facial patterns can be observed during depression. The depressed mood obviously allows short-term facial reactions which can be understood as the expression of affects or as general conversational signals. It cannot be decided to what extent these behaviours actually reflect affective phenomena or conflicts. They may also be consciously used as regulating signals or affect displays, controlled by "display rules". From observations in nearly natural situations as was the case in our study it is difficult to determine which of these mechanisms was active at a given moment and if indeed the facial behaviour represented the emotions or affects.

In any case, there is a variety of facial activities during depression. In accordance with the observations of Grinker et al. (1961) there was no total lack of facial expression.

If a patient avoids social interaction and withdraws on the ward or at home this could lead to the observation of a total absence of facial expression. The reason for this is that there is little opportunity other than during communicative interaction to show facial expression. In our study, however, the interview situation forced the patient to actively report about his actions, feelings and thoughts. In this case, a facial expression is stimulated.

Yet another reason for the impression of lacking facial activity could be a low number of smiles during depression. The correlation of rated facial variability with frequency of smiles would support this view. Thus, this impression could be mainly based on one facial aspect, the normally frequent smile, which is considerably reduced during depression. Other facial elements would be more or less ignored.

Clues to emotions can be derived from the patterns of facial activity. It is interesting to note that facial elements that appear in the patients' behaviour are those that can be associated with the emotions of anger, anxiety, and disgust (cf. Ekman & Friesen, 1978). These emotions are seen as central processes of the psychodynamics in depression (Abraham, 1912; Rado, 1928). Anger and inward-directed aggression during depression could be culturally specific elements (Kendell, 1970). From the appraisal of "depressive situations" Izard (1972) concludes that depression has to be regarded as a combination of fundamental emotions including inward and outward directed aggression.

In our study it turned out that indications of positive affects were reduced during depression which corresponds to the observations by Jones & Pansa (1979) and Matsumoto et al. (1983). Since such a reduction has also been found in stutterers it could be concluded that any psychological suffering is associated with less indications of positive affects (Krause, 1983).

Except for the smile, facial elements cannot be associated with depression or recovery in a comparatively unequivocal way. The more frequent occurrence of the Veraguth fold with a habitual AU4 (contracting the brows) in female endogenous depressed patients needs to be treated separately and should be analysed together with EMG measures (Greden et al., 1985). According to our observations the baseline potential of the EMG should be an interesting parameter. From our observations it could be increased mainly in subgroups of depressed female patients.

An active expression of sadness or grief was hardly observed in the patients. This could be explained by the principle of antithesis (Darwin, 1872; Leyhausen, 1967) where the minor motivation develops into an expression and the major motivation leads to the corresponding action. In our case, the depression is the major motivation present in the general depressed and sad mood state. It would determine the general behaviour, like social withdrawal and inactivity. The facial indications of anger and fear, on the other hand, could be seen as the expression of minor motivations also present during depression.

It seems worthwile to pursue the method of facial analysis where facial actions can provide access to momentary "minor motivations" and parts of affects present during depression.

10.3.2. *Gaze and speech*

Observations of gaze and speech over the time course clearly showed that for the individual the specific behavioural effectors are independently associated with the state of mood.

In accordance with Rutter (1977b) it can be stated that during depression gaze is not greatly reduced when regarding group averages. On an individual level, however, gaze and, less frequently, speech clearly change in a state dependent way. This is in accordance with Starkweather's (1967) observations of speech for single cases.

Moreover, from the individual time courses it became evident, that for single cases behaviours were more precise and sensitive indicators of change in mood than patients' self-rating. These infrequent but clearly identifiable events may contribute to the credibility of nonverbal information. Nonverbal information should be trusted over verbal content if the two are inconsistent.

Coordination of gaze with speech remains unaffected by depression in its form, although it appears to be partially retarded. The internal and external coordination of gaze and speech provide signals to the partner which repeatedly indicate that the patient is continuously in tune with the other. The general level of gaze is reduced during depression and retardation is present in the form of a prolonged latency. A de-coupling, i.e. a collapse of the coordination, as described for psychotic communication could not be observed for these behaviours.

The individual associations of mood and behaviours and the stable coordination of gaze and speech are the main results derived from this part of the analysis.

10.3.3 *Gestures*

The relative amount of gestures turned out to be the parameter analysed here which was least associated with subjective wellbeing. Only some of the endogenous depressed patients substantially increased their gestural behaviour with mood. Since for three of these five patients neither gaze nor speech reacted in this way, gestural behaviour can be regarded as their specific indicator of wellbeing.

The remarkably large inter- and intra-individual variability in the number of gestures in patients and controls is probably influenced by short term factors rather than by the mood state which is comparatively stable within a situation. On the other hand, high correlations between the measurements within subjects point to stable individual differences or personality traits which have an influence on the number of gestures (cf. Wallbott, 1982).

Here, the amount of gestural activity relative to the amount of speech was assessed whereas qualitative aspects like speed, amount of vigour, etc. of gestures were to a large extent omitted. The only distinction made in our analyses was between large and small movements. It did not make the relationship to mood clearer. Possibly qualitative aspects are influenced more by the depressed state than the quantitative aspects of gestures.

Yet another approach, presented by Mahl (1980) and Kendon (1970, 1980) for some single cases could contribute to clarify the meaning and function of gestures in a clinical context. The relationship between gestures and aggressive verbal content reported by Freedman et al. (1979) points to an association with momentary cognitive or emotional events rather than with general wellbeing.

In sum each of the behaviours can be seen to vary according to the changing mood state at least to some degree. There are, however, specific conditions for behaviours depending on the mechanisms which presumably control them. Therefore it cannot be expected that each of the behaviours reacts to mood changes, to a similar degree, for all individuals. Moreover, differential expressive functions have to be taken into account. Facial expression can indicate short term negative affects, gaze the social reactivity, etc. In order to study these specific functions, independent information about incidents of various subjective experiences have to be obtained and have to be specified under experimental control.

10.4 Dispositional factors and state dependency of behaviour

The meaning of a behaviour and its indicative functions results from consistent occurrence or change of the behaviour as a function of different situations or of different states of the individual. We studied the influence of a slowly and continuously changing subjective state of wellbeing during depression on the amount of nonverbal behaviour. Personality traits obviously also have to be considered as factors influencing these behaviours. It can be assumed that the behavioural changes occur on a dispositional level, which is characteristic of the individual. Such levels were marked, e.g. by the low intra-individual variation in speech and gaze behaviours for controls.

Behavioural differences of individuals with a stable psychological state in a comparable situation are attributed to personality factors. Despite the large individual variations of gestural behaviour high correlations between the repeated observations in our study indicated that personality factors play a role and partially account for the results.

Coordination of gaze with speech, however, is neither influenced by personality traits, by mood states, nor by variable situational elements. Here a stable behavioural mechanism appeared where gaze behaviour reacts according to short term internal and external events.

By defining critical levels for "reduced" behaviour and "substantial" changes an attempt was made to account for normal inter- and intra-individual variations. Individuals who react clearly and/or in many behavioural aspects according to these criteria could be labelled as "expressors".

On the other hand, even during recovery reduced values especially for gaze and general facial activity were still present. In these cases a disposition for a low rate of behaviour can be assumed whereby traits like "depressive tendency", "lack of social skills" or a tendency for "social withdrawal" are manifest. A general over-arousal in depression (Byrne, 1976) could also underlie the reduced amount of gaze. This explanation, which stresses the influence of internal factors, does not exclude the others where the social influence is accentuated.

Yet two other explanations for the continuously reduced behaviour are plausible: Wellbeing or mood could still be latently disturbed and remain in a labile state. This would not be evident in subjective data but rather be reflected in the behavioural measures.

The other explanation refers to the situation. The same place, the interview and the general setting could remind the former patient of his depression. This would not allow him to experience or display an "elated mood" or exhibit "normal" conversational patterns. The same situation, although superficially similar for normals and patients in a good mood state could still be different for both groups. In this respect personality factors need not necessarily be responsible for the enduring deviant behaviour but rather a still labile state or a specific perceptions of the situation.

Sex differences

Few significant sex differences were obtained with regard to the various behavioural parameters. The more frequent smiles of female controls correspond to the findings of Rosenfeld (1966), Duncan & Fiske (1977, p. 55), MacKey, (1976) (cf. Henley & LaFrance, 1984; Vrugt, 1987). However, for patients this was not the case. During the state of depression significantly more gaze and speech was found only in female compared to male neurotic depressed patients. A generally higher amount of gaze for females was not found, which is at variance with other studies (Exline, 1963; Argyle & Dean, 1965; Coutts & Schneider, 1975; Russo, 1975; Duncan & Fiske, 1977, p. 56).

As has previously been mentioned, the interview situation could have had a balancing effect. Additionally, the small sample of controls makes it difficult to obtain statistical significance. Above all, for patients the influence of the state of subjective wellbeing on the behaviour probably exceeds the possible effects of gender. Given the relatively homogeneous conditions of the clinical interview, effects of the changing states of mood on the behaviour became much more evident.

10.5 Relevance of specific nonverbal reactions for behavioural diagnostics

What are the consequences for the inferences about states of mood given the individual specific nonverbal reactions? Can these nonverbal behaviours validly indicate the state of an individual? These questions are also relevant for understanding the meaning of nonverbal behaviours during communication. Like a trained observer perceives and interprets this behaviour a normal interactant has to decode nonverbal signals during interaction and has to respond to them.

10.5.1. *Validity of nonverbal behaviour*

The diagnostic use of nonverbal behaviours depends on their validity as indicators of psychological phenomena. According to the Lens Model, validity is deduced from the relationship between a criterion, which in our case is the subjective wellbeing, and the distal cues, i.e. the observable behaviours. Furthermore, it has to be determined how these behaviours are perceived by an observer and integrated into a valid inference. For clinical inferences proximal percepts of the distal cues are relevant. These percepts are main influences for the attributions made by the clinician. A precondition for a valid inference is a close relationship between behaviours and the criterion, whereby the criterion itself has to be validly assessed.

Validity of the criterion
In addition to psychiatric diagnosis, the main criteria for determining the depressed state were the subjective wellbeing, assessed by a Visual Analogue Scale and a Global Clinical Rating of depression. Both integrate a number of quite different aspects: mood, bodily symptoms and cognitive distortions etc. without explicitly adding up single items to make a total score. The assumption is that both measures validly reflect the subjective state of the patient as well as the clinical picture perceived by the interviewer.

These global measures have been found to correlate highly with more complex depression or mood measures (cf. Prusoff, Klerman & Paykel, 1972; Schwarz & Strian, 1972; Shapiro & Post, 1974). Since self-rating of wellbeing and rating by the interviewer were highly correlated in our case, it is reasonable to assume that patient and interviewer have a similar understanding about the state. Behavioural measures were compared with reference to these ratings and the associations found can only be interpreted with this qualification.

It cannot be determined whether the subjective statements really represent the state of depression and validly reflect the more or less depressed mood. With regard to this it should be recalled that various proposals to describe the depressed state by independent dimensions (Klerman et al., 1979, DSM iii) have still not replaced unidimensional scales.

Here, too, a differentiation of depression had been attempted through assessment of various aspects of the interview. These aspects did not show closer links with the behavioural parameters than with the general measures of depression and mood. Given the different reaction patterns of nonverbal parameters and specifically for facial activity it could be argued that these patterns represent different structures of affect. For some individuals, e.g. anger or fear could be dominant whereas other aspects of affective disorders may be relevant for other patients.

Independent criteria on affective experience like those provided by content analysis (cf. Gottschalk, Wingert & Gleser, 1970) or physiological measures are necessary to obtain differential information on the subjective state. Generally this would require continuous assessment of affects and emotions independent of behavioural information.

Group Differences

Attempts to differentiate between different clinical groups by using nonverbal indicators were only partially successful. As has been stressed by Rutter (1976), even schizophrenic patients could not be differentiated from depressive patients according to their gaze behaviour. However, from the variety of nonverbal criteria compared by Jones & Pansa (1979) some criteria differentiated these two groups of patients. However, a diagnostic decision will be difficult to obtain given these differences. A tendency for different emotional expressions of psychotic and neurotic depressed patients has been reported by Matsumoto et al. (1983). However, a low amount of "felt happy" and "unfelt happy" expression on admission correlated with improvement on release in a similar way for both groups.

Comparisons between neurotic and endogenous depressed patients in our study revealed some interesting differences. These are to be taken as preliminary findings, since our study was not designed for group comparisons, but rather stressed the individual time course. In general, endogenous depressed patients showed reduction in nonverbal parameters more frequently during depression and had more marked changes with improvement than neurotic depressed patients. In contrast, neurotic depressed patients more frequently remained stable in their nonverbal behaviour or contrary to expectation it was even reduced with improvement of subjective wellbeing.

These opposite trends are hard to account for by the different treatments of endogenous and neurotic depressed patients. Given the primarily medical treatment of endogenous depressed patients and the behaviour therapy of neurotic depressed patients one would rather expect the contrary: attenuating the nonverbal behaviour by medication and activating it by behavioural treatment.

A somewhat speculative explanation would involve possible differential experienced changes of subjective wellbeing between groups. Although a comparison of data from the Visual Analogue Scale is somewhat problematic, one could infer from this measure that subjective wellbeing of the endogenous depressed patients improved more rapidly and more intensely. This becomes apparent in the corresponding nonverbal behaviour. On the other hand, the change is much slower and not as extreme for the neurotic depressed patients. It is possible that in the patients' self-presentation their slow and minimal progress was made apparent by constantly reduced amounts of nonverbal behaviour. Verbally they could behave according to the expectations of the therapist.

This explanation is tentative but could give some clues about clinical observations. Occasionally, discrepancies between the statement of the patient and the clinically assumed psychological state seem to be present. It would be expected from our data that neurotic depressed patients tend nonverbally to aggravate their state.

Without overrating these group differences they nevertheless suggest a need to differentiate and specify the type of depression. This is in accordance with Miller (1975) who proposed this with regard to psychological deficits in depression. Independent information on affective processes and mood would be required to clarify this picture. Further studies on nonverbal behaviour should at least differentiate the seemingly homogeneous picture of depression, be it according to the neurotic components, severeness or dominating affects like anger or anxiety.

10.5.2 *Nonverbal behaviour as a cue for predicting subjective wellbeing*

It cannot be the goal to use each behavioural aspect for each individual in order to predict his or her psychological state or traits. This follows from the individual specific associations of behaviours and wellbeing. A behaviour *can* express the mood of an individual but does not necessarily do so. Display rules for affective expression give an additional frame within which behaviour may occur. The question then is which model may be appropriate for predicting a state from indicators, which are differentially relevant for parts of the population.

Models for prediction
Additive models whereby the degree of a state or trait is given by the sum of items, as in a depression scale seem to be inappropriate for these nonverbal behaviours. Models using regression analyses in order to relate complex information to a criterion are at this stage not applicable.

Generally linear regression between a criterion and an indicator, multiple correlation or similar weighted linear combinations of indicators have been used, mainly for predicting personality traits (Hursch, Hammond & Hursch, 1964; Sawyer, 1966; Castellan, 1973). It was found that criteria were predicted less exactly when using test information like MMPI data in a "clinical intuitive" way compared to combining the same information within an algebraical model (Hammond, Hursch & Todd, 1964; Goldberg, 1970; Dawes, 1979; Szucko & Kleinmutz, 1981). Other models make use of subjective weightings of information (Anderson, 1979), Bayes-statistics and subjective probabilities (Slovic & Lichtenstein, 1971) or introduce adaptive components (Einhorn & Horgarth, 1978, 1981) in order to represent human decision making under conditions of uncertainty. The assumption that there exists a *similar relationship* between criterion and indicator across individuals is common to all of these approaches. The relationship between the behaviour as an indicator and the criterion, in our case the subjective wellbeing, would thus be best described by a population statistic.

It was evident, however, that this general relationship included data from individuals with a strong association between behaviour and criterion and others for whom this association was very weak. Not all the behaviours were equally suitable as an indicator of wellbeing for all individuals. This would be a precondition for applying regression-analytical models.

Moreover, no clear hierarchical relationship between behaviours could be seen which in turn would be required for models using linear combinations of predictors. Such a model in principle can be applied for single case analysis if a sufficient number of measurements for an individual is available. An example is given by Roessler & Lester (1976) who analysed voice parameters from a number of interviews of a female depressed patient.

Aside from using complex algebraic models it appears appropriate to regard the relationships between subjective and behavioural variables on a more elementary level. The clustering of individuals according to their individual reactions (cf. chapters 5 and 9) is one way to determine different groups of nonverbal reaction patterns. Algebraic models may then be tested for subgroups found in this way. For such models to be applied, it has to be borne in mind that the variety of reaction patterns would require large populations.

Asynchrony of changes

The asynchrony of the changes observed in the behaviours of single cases may further complicate the search for generally valid indicators. During an extremely depressed mood, behaviours may be reduced which return to normal degrees again given only a slight improvement and which remain stable during the following course (cf. single cases, chapter 8). Einhorn & Hogarth (1981) stress the importance of such extreme reactions.

. In fact, given a changing process, regressive predictions are suboptimal. The problem is that extreme responses can occur at random or they can signal changes in the underlying process. (p. 56)

In such a way, nonverbal reactions, which are significant at one point in time, can reflect a qualitative rupture of the state. Later they are not qualified as indicators any more.

Independent from a typological approach one has to make allowances for individual specific reactions. Thus, approaches have to be pursued which take the individual time course of behavioural changes into consideration.

10.5.3 *Idiographic behavioural diagnostics*

At this point the discussion on idiographic approaches within psychology as a nomothetical science (Allport, 1937; Bem & Allen, 1974; Lamiell, 1981) is relevant. Contrary to empirical research, our intuition works mainly idiographically and less nomothetically.

When we are asked to characterize a friend, we do not invoke some a priori set of fixed dimensions which we apply to everyone. Rather, we permit ourselves to select a small subset of traits which strikes us as pertinent and to discard as irrelevant the other 17.993 trait terms in the lexicon. (Bem & Allen, 1974, p. 410).

This appears to hold not only for our perception of nonverbal behaviours but also for their production.

Person and Situation
Idiographical descriptions of individuals are emphasized, by "Social behaviour theory" proposed by Mischel (1968, 1973, 1983) or the "psychology of personal constructs" proposed by Kelly (1955). With the "grid technique", e.g. (Kelly, 1955) the individual generates his own traits by which he characterizes himself and his social environment. The interaction of person and situation variables is, according to Mischel (1968) the important factor for predicting behaviour.

The individual, according to Bem (Bem & Allen, 1974; Bem & Funder, 1978; Bem, 1983) is a determining factor explaining a large part of the psychologically interesting variance of the behaviour. For certain individuals only certain behaviours can be predicted across various situations.

Person and situation variables also play a role in our case. The kind of relevant behavioural aspects with which an individual reacts appeared to be individual specific. This remained constant over time as could be shown for speech and gaze in individual cases. The situation, on the other hand, can make a behaviour more or less salient. The interview, in this way, was a releaser for the patient, for example, to display facial behaviour.

Given these conditions, the mood or motivation in an ethological sense, i.e. the subjective wellbeing during depression was the main underlying process that determined the occurrence and the formation of the specific behaviours.

Nomothetical and idiographical concepts can both be justified in an individual-centered approach. Assessment in behaviour therapy is clearly idiographical although building upon nomothetical concepts of learning theory (Kanfer & Saslow, 1969; Goldfried, 1976). From the behavioural assessment approach, at least two aspects can be brought forward with regard to our problem. One is initially to select a critical behaviour out of the total repertoire which is relevant for the individual. The other is to observe an individual over a time course under varying conditions to test behaviour as a state dependent variable.

Observing individual behaviour under various conditions
The validity of a specific behavioural indicator, although closely associated with psychological processes in the individual, can hardly be determined in group analysis. A behaviour has to be observed in the individual under different conditions in order to assess whether these conditions determine the behaviour. This was attempted by the longitudinal observations. From a methodological point of view (a) repeated observations which (b) are taken over longer periods of time would be desirable in order to test the stability of nonverbal reactions. It is still unknown how much information is needed in order to predict nonverbal behaviour intra-individually. This will depend in part on the general stability of the specific behaviour. According to the present data, this stability was higher for gaze and speech than for gestural behaviour. Thus, for the analysis of gestural behaviour time samples of longer duration than the ones chosen here could yield more stable results. For gaze and speech, however, five minute segments appeared to be sufficient.

10.5.4 *Clinical inference*

Specific nonverbal reactions do not imply that an inference of the psychological state is impossible for an observer, a rater, or an interactant who is confronted with this information. Since the inference aspect has not been studied explicitly in this study, only a few remarks will be made. It has repeatedly been shown that nonverbal information can be used to differentially rate the depressed state.

Moreover, from studies of Pattay (1982) and Avarello (1983) it follows that the patient's and also the interviewer's behaviour provide indirect nonverbal information from which the state of the patient can be validly inferred. An immediate comparison of the same interviewer with the same patient in different states of depression was a precondition for such a discriminatory performance. This was technically provided by video editing. Using this method, it can be shown that discriminatory performance on judging emotional states considerably increases when presenting behavioural information of an individual in succession (Vanger & Ellgring, in preparation). The behavioural information of an individual may be intuitively registered. The idiosyncratic information will be processed depending on one's experience with the individual in different states or situations.

Sequence and amount of information

It is yet unknown how much information or what amount of time is needed to notice these associations. From judgement studies it can be derived that very short behavioural samples are sufficient to detect subtle differences validly. Being presented with complex stimuli in a natural setting, experts need only a few cues to make their judgements (Phelps & Shanteau, 1978). Within the first three minutes of a 25 minute interview, psychiatrists recognize half of the symptoms assessed during the whole interview (Sandifer, Hordorn & Green, 1970). During the first 30 to 60 seconds of an interview the first diagnostic hypotheses are formed (Gauron & Dickinson, 1969). Nevertheless, there is little agreement between assumed importance and the factual contribution of this information in making a later diagnosis. Temporal aspects and consecutive processing of information appear to play an important role in reaching a judgement given complex behavioural information.

Problems of validity which arise from these judgements can only be pointed to (cf. Einhorn & Hogarth, 1981). Yet another aspect is the different weights of nonverbal elements (Waxer, 1974; Dzida & Kiener, 1978; Ekman et al., 1980) which have to be considered in the forming of an impression. Moreover, there seem to be individual differences with regard to the ability for decoding nonverbal information (Zuckerman & Larrane, 1979; Buck, 1979; Rosenthal, Hall, DiMatteo, Rogers & Archer, 1979; Hall, 1984).

Whether a behaviour can be used as a specific indicator for the inference of affective states probably depends on the different conditions under which the clinician (or a relative) was able to observe. The clinician and the relative know the person, experience him during different moods and can observe specific changes. They would thus have access to subtle behavioural changes as a basis for their inferences. In contrast, an incidental rater in a judgement study does not.

Applying idiographic elements for diagnostic purposes, at least when nonverbal behaviour is used as a source of information, would make allowance for the individual relationships between mood and behaviours found in this study.

Process of judgement

The individual associations should also be taken into account by admitting "or-connections" for behavioural ratings instead of "and-connections" as suggested by a questionnaire approach. Such a rating could assess whether an individual shows reduced facial expression *or* gaze *or* posture as independent and possible expressions of mood.

The meaning of some behaviours can be specific for the dyad. Some of the behaviours will be available as a source of information for only those persons who are acquainted with the individual. This may not always be the case for somebody who has to make a diagnostic decision in one session.

In the processing of nonverbal information various elements contribute differently to the impression. It is possible that nonverbal elements are not perceived analytically in a clinical judgement, i.e. they are not consciously recognized as single elements. It seems probable that nonverbal information is processed holistically and that it is impossible for the observer to name all the elements which determined the impression (cf. Gauron & Dickinson, 1969, Phelps & Shanteau, 1978).

Further critical investigations are necessary with regard to the indicative functions of nonverbal behaviour as well as to its observability. These studies should not require absolute judgements from observers about unknown individuals. Current mood of an individual can be inferred to a very limited degree only when being confronted with an isolated behavioural segment of short duration. According to the current findings and the discussion above, an immediate intra-individual comparison is essential for valid clinical judgements. This immediacy contingency can be facilitated also by the technical means of video editing. Under these conditions, nonverbal behavioural information can be used in an optimal way.

10.6 Communication with specifically used signals

The implications of specific associations between mood states and behaviour – for the indicative functions of nonverbal behaviour and for clinical inference – apply also to the problem of communication. The question is how is communication possible if signals are used in an individual-specific way. Yet the existence of a common code is regarded as the most important precondition to denote a behaviour as communicative.

At a closer look, behaviour which is used as a signal in a specific way appears to have certain advantages for communication. These advantages are: (a) information can be transmitted differentially, (b) communication in part is a partner-adaptive process and (c) the behavioural repertoire is used economically with a maximum amount of information.

(a) Differential transmission of information
Given an individual-specific usage of nonverbal behaviour, information can be transmitted with different degrees of differentiation depending on how acquainted the interactants are. The acquaintance can make use of more

cues and more subtle ones for his/her inference than a stranger. The stranger initially has to rely on generally used signals. In a similar way a behavioural researcher when studying an animal recognizes more behaviours in a more differentiated way than a lay person.

Intensity and amount of signals certainly play a role for the recognition and the inference of internal states. Nearly everybody will recognize that a man who sits totally collapsed, staring in front of him is not in good shape. The more subtle shades, however, the ill humor or the slight disgust will more probably be perceived by acquaintances who have got to know the specific signals and their meaning, i.e. their specific usage.

The validity of inferences, i.e. the correctness of decoding is not easily assessed. The same individual has to be observed in different situations or under different internal conditions to infer the specific meaning of behaviours. In the longitudinal study these internal conditions were given by the changing states of wellbeing over time. In such a way, an ethological approach infers from the situations where a behaviour occurs and from the reactions of other members of the species on the meaning of these signals for intra-species communication.

Generally and specifically used signals appear to be both necessary parts of human communication since they allow transmission of information and inferences on different levels and with different degrees of gradation.

(b) Communication as a partner-adaptive process

From the individual specific usage of nonverbal signals it follows that communication is to be regarded as a partner-adaptive process. The usage of signals and their meaning develops out of interaction and the relationship between individuals. Semantic (content), syntactic (grammar) and pragmatic (usage) aspects of nonverbal signals thus are to be understood as individual-specific as well as dyad-specific. Only when knowing the other long enough and having observed him in different situations may the brief twitch of the mouth corners show that a person is aroused.

From an ethological perspective dyad-specific signals have been demonstrated by Wickler (1980; Wickler & Seibt, 1980) for duetting in birds. This example might be unusual in the context of human behaviour. Nevertheless, the concept of a dyad-specific adaptation of communicative behaviour appears to be relevant for the present findings as well.

Out of a generally available repertoire, pairs of Symplectes bicolor, an African bird species, develop their specific duet songs. If one partner dies the remaining one develops a new specific duet song with another bird during the next season. According to Wickler (1980) these specific signalling systems function to promote stronger pair bonding. By using different signals which are not in tune individuals of different pairs do not understand each other as well as individuals within a pair. The low effort of communication with known signals maintains the bond between the pair. For a new pairing it is required that the signals which are latently present adapt to each other again.

It is important to note for our present considerations that signals which are used in an individual-specific way enable communication on different levels of intimacy or social closeness. Communication thus cannot be regarded as a uniform process whereby individuals as a homogeneous group use the available signals in the same way. On a dyadic level signals may become important which generally have no shared meaning. The notion of a dyadic level of information exchange includes the case where a decoder is given the opportunity to observe the individual sender under at least two different internal or external conditions and to compare the behaviour.

At the beginning, an unacquainted person probably can decode only generally used signs. These may be either very strong signals or their meaning may be given by an average association of behaviour and psychological states. Consequently one cannot expect to detect all the signals and their meaning at the first encounter. From a first confrontation with an individual the generally used part of the communicative behaviour will initially be recognized. This, by the way, is in most cases all that is observed by subjects taking part in psychological experiments on decoding.

More and subtler signals will be recognized from each other when one engages intensely and for a longer period of time with an individual.

Disorders in communication

The question whether disorders in communication can be derived from changes of the nonverbal behaviour has to be differentiated. One way of evaluating a behaviour as disordered refers to a deviance from the norm. Another is via the adequate transmission of information.

(a) Deviance from the norm

For at least part of the nonverbal behaviours nearly each of the depressed patients had values which were clearly below those of controls. These reduced values point to a behavioural disorder during depression. As these reduced values persist with improvement they also indicate deficits in the nonverbal components of social skills (Trower et al., 1978). This was mainly the case for part of the neurotic depressed patients. It held, however, for specific parameters from an individual whereby gaze and general facial activity turned out to remain reduced most frequently. Active emotional attention seems to be disturbed, i.e. reduced compared to controls, in these cases.

A deviance from normal behaviour does not necessarily imply a disorder in communication. An experienced emotion or a depressed mood represent a deviance from a homeostatic normal psychological state. Likewise, a corresponding change in the behaviour would be a deviance from the norm but by no means a disorder with regard to encoding. With regard to a disorder in encoding it has to be asked whether the psychological state is adequately expressed.

(b) Adequate expression of a state

A low amount of active nonverbal behaviour obviously expresses the depressed state in an adequate way. Accordingly, facial behaviour is not disturbed when being reduced during depression and when increasing with recovery. Also those patients whose gaze and speech behaviour is closely correlated with the changing wellbeing over the time course clearly communicate their state in an expected way. If somebody is asked to express a depressed mood voluntarily he will speak less (Feldstein, 1964) and probably look less at the other. Reduced behaviour during depression and mood dependent increase of behaviour are thus not to be regarded as a disorder in communication. There is a disorder of the subjective state of wellbeing during depression but not a disorder of nonverbal encoding. In various ways, the behaviours validly reflect and thus adequately express the mood state.

If, according to Prkachin et al. (1977) observers cannot differentiate between depressed individuals' reactions to positive and negative stimuli, patients still could adequately express their state. In this case their mood would dominate the influence of external stimuli. Given this notion, few of the endogenous but some of the neurotic depressed patients show disorders in their communication. For these patients, behaviour decreases with improvement or remains at a reduced state during recovery.

Also, if no behavioural changes can be recognized, one would assume an encoding disorder since the state cannot be inferred from the behaviour.

According to the cluster analysis of nonverbal reaction patterns (cf. chapter 9) an encoding disorder can also be stated for the patients grouped into the "normal" cluster and those in the "reduced" cluster v. The cases of substantial behavioural decrease with improvement cannot be explained by an agitated state since for neurotic depressed patients, "agitation" does not apply.

It is possible that patients who were not reacting with nonverbal behaviours observed here express their state by means of other indicators like voice, or their state indeed does not become apparent in the nonverbal behaviour.

Generally, however, most of the patients, i.e. the 29 being represented in the nonverbal reaction patterns I to IV, show mood adequate changes in various nonverbal behaviours. The variety of nonverbal reaction patterns in no way points to a disorder in communication as well as the fact that patients react on mood changes with only part of the repertoire. It is probably sufficient to use few behavioural "effectors" to express one's mood in an individual specific way.

Availability and usage of a behavioural repertoire

Both economizing of behavioural efforts as well as maximizing the amount of information can be achieved by using only parts of the available behavioural repertoire for communication.

The same behavioural repertoire may be available for all individuals, for example the innate potential for facial behaviour. Almost everyone frowns when asked to make an angry face and gazes away when being asked to look depressed. Nevertheless, only some of the depressed patients showed a clearly reduced gaze behaviour. Although the repertoire is available, an individual will obviously activate or "use" only parts of it in a state dependent way. The general availability of the repertoire is a precondition for the understanding of signals. As has been shown for facial expression, this behaviour can be decoded in various cultures (Frijda, 1968; Izard, 1971; Ekman, 1972). Furthermore, facial reactions in early infancy show that at least parts of this behavioural repertoire are universal and innate (Steiner, 1974; Oster, 1978; Ploog, 1980; Eibl-Eibesfeldt, 1984, pp. 558-600). The common code (von Cranach & Vine, 1973) refers to this potential repertoire. However, a current mood is obviously expressed by only part of the available nonverbal repertoire.

It is easy to understand that using part of the available repertoire implies behavioural economy. As a counter-example, one just has to imagine that an individual would activate all of the possible indicators: a facial expression of sadness, no gaze at the other, no speech and no gestures, when in a bad mood. This could be the case given an extreme state. For less extreme states, however, it would be less economical to react slightly in all of the nonverbal features instead of activating few behavioural effectors when small changes of wellbeing occur.

This behavioural economy has been postulated by Zipf (1965) for the usage of words. According to Zipf (1949/1965) writers can be identified from the respective frequency distributions of their word usage. His *principle of least effort* states that a few elements are used frequently and most of the elements are rarely used. In our view this also applies to nonverbal parts of our communication system.

It is a behavioural economy when an individual activates only a part of the facial repertoire or a limited number of other nonverbal elements. Some of these elements such as lifting the eyebrows or the smile are used frequently by most individuals. Others, such as the inward pulling of the mouth corners are activated by few individuals only. Similar to the specific usage of behavioural elements is their specific association with psychological states.

It remains unknown to what extent the specific usage of nonverbal elements is due to cultural conditions. For language, the influence of cultural conditions has repeatedly been shown (cf. contributions in Giles, Robinson & Smith, 1980). It would also be conceivable that during ontogenesis parts of the repertoire are reinforced by incidental activation and others are extinguished.

From information theory, it follows that specific signals contribute a good deal to the amount of information within a message. The different forms of nonverbal reactions of the depressed patients alone represent a greater variety than would be given by a hierarchical structure or strongly dependent behaviours. The nonverbal reaction patterns provide information about the state and about characteristics of the person.

The root of the word "communication" means to have something in common, to achieve understanding by using common signals. If this use of signals is also individual specific, the repertoire enables a variety of forms in communication. The meaning of the behavioural elements additionally develops out of the relationship between interactants. Aside from the general meaning the specific meaning of nonverbal behaviours and their function for the individuals in interaction with others seems to be a central part of the mutual understanding.

Appendix A1
Standardized Interview For
Depression (SID)

Heiner Ellgring, Jakob Derbolowsky, Anima von Dewitz and Silvia Hieke

Summary

The Standardized Interview for Depression (SID) has 28 questions and covers psychological, social, emotional and psychopathological aspects of depression. The questions are related to the current state of wellbeing, the period of the preceding two or three days, and the near future. They touch on matters which are likely to change within a few days. Certain aspects of the interviewer's behaviour, such as pauses and looking behaviour, are kept constant during the interview and additional questions are prescribed. The answers are evaluated on nine-point scales. The interview lasts between 5 and 15 minutes. It is used as the introduction to a free conversation in which diagnostic questions or therapeutic problems are further dealt with.

Content	Questions & rating scales
General wellbeing	2, 5, 9, 18
Activity and social contact	21, 22, 27, 28, 1
Emotionality and future expectations	25, 29, 30
Concentration and efficiency	14, 15, 16, 17
Somatic complaints and sleep	6, 7, 8, 10, 12

1 Introduction

In order to describe the course of an illness, methods to assess changes in various parameters affected by the illness are required. In the fields of psychopathology are psychotherapy these parameters mainly concern verbal and nonverbal behaviour. Our task is concerned primarily with an analysis of the course of depression, secondly with a prognostic assessment. In addition to this, the method presented here should serve as an aid to therapeutic procedures.

There are, at present, several self-rating methods of characterizing the depressive state (Beck, Ward, Mendelson, Mock & Erbaugh, 1961; Lubin, 1965; Zung, 1965; von Zerssen, Köller & Rey, 1970). Here the degree of the depression is defined by the sum total of depression indicating answers given to the items.

On the other hand, evaluations by the therapist are used. The IMPS by Lorr, McNair, Klett and Lasky (1962) and the Hamilton Scale (Hamilton, 1960) are especially well-known methods of this kind. Others are the Depression Status Inventory of Zung (1974) or the Present State Examination of Wing, Cooper & Sartorius (1974). Here the clinician assesses the patient's condition by means of a more or less structured interview.

Depression is generally not considered in terms of a one-dimensional concept but should be seen as composed of multi-factorial aspects, whereby the various components show differing degrees of severity. The fact that these components change at different times, appears to yield important keys to the understanding of the phenomenon of depression. This is the case, for instance, with the attempt to ascertain the relationship between depressive states and pleasant events (cf. Lewinsohn & Libet, 1972). To our knowledge, no standardized investigation procedure or interview exists in which observation of the various components in comparable situations can be made throughout the course of the illness.

2 Instrument and Procedure

The Standardized Interview for Depression (SID) was designed to enable registration and documentation of verbal and nonverbal behaviour in comparable situations over a longer period of time. Psychosocial, emotional and psychopathological features are touched on which (a) are characteristic of depression and which (b) may change during the course of the illness.

The interview should fulfill two functions: 1. The degree of the specific disorder can be assessed according to the answers given to the standardized questions. 2. Systematic observations of verbal and nonverbal behaviour during the interview can be made.

The method should allow the patient to answer freely. There is evidence that categorizing free answers yields more differentiated information than can be obtained from statements on a standard questionnaire. According to Kohnen and Lienert (1976), a psychopharmacon showed distinct effectiveness when the subjects could describe its effects in their own words (the description being classified by experts afterwards), whereas no difference could be seen between a placebo and the verum when a questionnaire was used. Similarly, the possibility for the patient to answer freely may yield a better basis for describing his condition. Like the questionnaire, the standardized form of the interview is designed to achieve a comparable stimulus situation for the patient. This means, of course, that significant aspects of the interviewer's behaviour can also be controlled. The possibility should be given of repeating the interview at regular intervals, so that intra-individual comparisons of the course of the depression can be made.

Formulation of the questions in the SID:

The Standardized Interview for Depression consists of 28 questions. The answers to these questions are rated on 30 nine-point scales.

The questions in the SID are formulated in such a manner that they can be repeated word for word. If, in the interviewer's opinion, the answer given to a question cannot be assessed satisfactorily, he may ask supplementary questions which are stipulated beforehand.

Explication and consent

Before the initial interview, the entire procedure is explained to the patient. The form the interview takes, the fact that the interview is being videotaped and the further course of events are pointed out to him. He is told that at the beginning of each conversation he will be asked a list of specifically formulated questions and, following this, topics chosen by himself will be discussed. Furthermore, the patient is told that all documents, recordings and conversational contents are covered by the professional code of conduct. Later on in his clinical stay, he is requested to give his written agreement to take part in the project and to consent to scientific evaluation of the data obtained.

The SID takes between 5-15 minutes, the duration of the following free conversation is not laid down. At the conclusion of each interview the patient is asked about his main concerns at present. This is followed by a free conversation which may touch on therapeutic or other matters.

Interviewer's behaviour

In addition to the prescribed verbal behaviour while asking the standardized questions, there are also several specifications regarding the interviewer's nonverbal behaviour.

Throughout the entire dialogue the interviewer should look at the patient as often as possible. If the patient has a very quiet voice the interviewer should be careful that his own voice does not become quieter or change in intonation as a reaction. To avoid monotony he should raise the pitch of his voice as seldom as possible at the end of each question.

After questions 1 ("How are you today?") and 17 ("What have you been doing in the last two days?"), the interviewer remains silent for at least 15 seconds. This is necessary to assess the patient's spontaneous speech activity. During this time, the interviewer looks at the patient. After 15 seconds, one of the supplementary questions may be asked.

These behaviour specifications apply to the standardized section only. However, the interviewer should keep the effects of his own behaviour, his voice and the way he looks at the patient in mind during the free conversation also.

Assessment of the interview answers and of behaviour

The answers given by the patient are rated on nine-point scales. In various scales not all points are specifically defined, but to ensure uniformity, nine-points have been taken through-out. The intermediate points may also be chosen in the assessment.

Similarly, several aspects of the patient's verbal and nonverbal behaviour in the interview situation can also be rated by means of nine-point scales. These include: quantitative aspects of speech activity, looking behaviour, facial expression, gesticulations, and bodily posture. Moreover, a global assessment is made of the degree of the depression by means of a scale designed by Schwarz & Strian (1972). For a condensed presentation, sub-scores may be formed.

3. Use of the SID

Interviewer's behaviour and recording situation: It is most important that the interviewer has conscious control over his own behaviour. This can only be achieved by observing and criticizing his behaviour himself in the interview situation at least in the initial stages, and when possible by receiving feedback from uninvolved observers. The time during which the interviewer should remain silent should be even longer than he himself feels necessary and he should remember to look at the patient during this time.

It appeared that the problems the interviewer usually has with the standardized form of questioning can be overcome quite easily. Objective observers do not seem to find the situation as strange as the interviewer does himself, so it may be presumed that the patient doesn't either. To sum up, several controlled practice interviews are considered necessary before a series of interviews begins.

It is difficult to judge how stressful the fact of being videotaped is for the patient, but presumably this situation causes no more stress for him than any other type of psychological or medical examination.

Variation of the interviewer Each patient was interviewed by two to four different interviewers. The standard part of the interview seemed to be only minimally affected by this variation of interviewers. However, because each interviewer had his own preference of topics, the free conversation was affected more significantly.

Necessary time and personnel Assessment, for which at least parts of the video recording are used, should be done as immediately after the actual interview as possible. It takes about 15 minutes. All in all, each interview together with the assessment takes about 30-60 minutes to perform. Apart from the interviewer, a technical assistant is of the utmost importance to run the video-recording and manage the documents and, perhaps, with the appropriate training, to assist in the assessment as well.

Rating Scales Apart from questions 4 and 13, the rating scales are graded from 1 to 9. Although some grades of the scale are not specifically named, they may still be taken as intermediate grades.

The appropriateness of such intermediate grades should be checked for each special case and for the representation of its course of progress.

In cases where no classification is possible 0 is given.

The interviewer should note:

Interviewer's behaviour

The interviewer looks at the patient most of the time and looks down only to read the questions.

The voice should frequently be dropped at the end of each question.

After questions 1 (!) and 19 (!) the interviewer should remain silent for at least 15 seconds.

Questions in brackets are those which depend on the type of answer given to the question before.

Questions in the Standardized Interview for Depression.

1. How are you today (15 seconds)
Speaks spontaneously:

hardly stops speaking	very much	a lot	rather a lot		rather little	little	very little	says nothing at all
1	2	3	4	5	6	7	8	9

2. What kind of mood are you in?

extremely good	very good	good	rather good	neither good nor bad	rather bad	bad	very bad	extremely bad
1	2	3	4	5	6	7	8	9

3. Was your mood changeable?

not at all		hardly		somewhat		noticeable		extremeley so
1	2	3	4	5	6	7	8	9

4. Were you in a different mood in the morning than in the evening?

distinctly worse in	slightly morning	distinctly worse in	slightly evening	distinctly worse at time	slightly another of day	change without a special pattern		
1	2	3	4	5	6	7	8	9

5. Have you been feeling tense?

completely relaxed		relaxed		neither re-laxed or tense		tense		very tense
1	2	3	4	5	6	7	8	9

6. How did you sleep?

very well		well		middling		badly		very badly
1	2	3	4	5	6	7	8	9

7. Were you able to fall asleep without difficulty?

very easily		easily		middling		without difficulty		with great difficulty
1	2	3	4	5	6	7	8	9

8. Did you sleep all night long (without waking up)?

(yes) very well		well		middling		badly		(no) very badly
1	2	3	4	5	6	7	8	9

9. How did you feel when you awoke?

very well		well		middling		bad		very bad
1	2	3	4	5	6	7	8	9

10. How is your appetite?

very good		good		middling		poor		very poor
1	2	3	4	5	6	7	8	9

11. How is your digestion?

diarrhoea				normal				constipa-tion
1	2	3	4	5	6	7	8	9

12. Did you feel physically unfit or unwell in any (other) way?

no com-plaints at all		very fit		neither fit nor unwell		very un-well		extremely unfit
1	2	3	4	5	6	7	8	9

13. In which way?

head	throat	chest	heart	stomach	sensitive sensory changes	vegetative changes	any other	no in-formation
1	2	3	4	5	6	7	8	9

14. How do you see your efficiency?

very good		good		middling		bad		very bad
1	2	3	4	5	6	7	8	9

15. Do you tire easily?

not at all		hardly at all		middling		rather easily		very easily
1	2	3	4	5	6	7	8	9

16. Do you find even the smallest thing troublesome?

not at all		hardly		somewhat		rather		very much so
1	2	3	4	5	6	7	8	9

7. Can you concentrate (on things)?

very well		well		middling		poorly		very poorly
1	2	3	4	5	6	7	8	9

8. Do you spend a lot of time worrying?

not at all	very little		little	middling	a lot		very much	nearly the whole time
1	2	3	4	5	6	7	8	9

9. What have you been doing in the last two days? (30 seconds)
speaks spontaneously

hardly stops speaking	very much	much	rather a lot		rather little	little	very little	says nothing at all
1	2	3	4	5	6	7	8	9

20. Informs about

extreme	very much	a lot	rather a lot	middling	rather little	little	very little	nothing at all
1	2	3	4	5	6	7	8	9

21. Activity

extensive activity		rather active		participation		rather passive		no activity whatsoever
1	2	3	4	5	6	7	8	9

22. Did you initiate any conversation?

very often		often		sometimes		seldom		not at all
1	2	3	4	5	6	7	8	9

23. How did you respond when someone spoke to you?

intensive participation		responding		formal response		no response, indifferently		rejecting
1	2	3	4	5	6	7	8	9

24. What made you angry yesterday?

a great many things		a lot of things		quite a few things		not much		nothing at all
1	2	3	4	5	6	7	8	9

25. What pleased you yesterday?

a great many things		a lot of things		quite a few things		not much		nothing at all
1	2	3	4	5	6	7	8	9

6. Have you had any difficulties or problems with other people?

none at all		hardly any		a few		quite a lot		a lot
1	2	3	4	5	6	7	8	9

7. Would you like to meet with friends or relations today?

enthusias-tic		greatly in-terested		quite in-terested		indifferent		rejecting
1	2	3	4	5	6	7	8	9

8. What have you planned to do today?

a great many things		a lot of things		something		hardly anything		nothing at all
1	2	3	4	5	6	7	8	9

9. Is there anything today you are looking forward to?

a great many things		a lot of things		something		hardly anything		nothing at all
1	2	3	4	5	6	7	8	9

0. How do you think things are going to turn out for you?

full of plans		optimistic		ambiva-lent		pessimistic		hopelessly pessimistic
1	2	3	4	5	6	7	8	9

Appendix A2
Rating Scales for Quantitative Aspects ofNonverbal Behaviour

(The scales are poled so that values are assumed to increase with depression)

1. Speech activity	continuously	1
2. Interrupts partner	very much	2
		3
3. Amount of time spent looking at partner	much	4
		5
4. Variability of facial expression	seldom	6
		7
5. Illustrative hand movements (Speech-related gesticulation)	very seldom	8
	not at all	9
	not at all	1
6. Adaptive hand movements, figdeting	very seldom	2
		3
7. Foot and leg movements	seldom	4
		5
8. Changes of body position	much	6
		7
	very much	8
	Continuously	9

Appendix A3
Global Clinical Rating of Depression

mania (inability to make a self-rating	1
hypomania – mania	2
normal – good tempered	3
normal – low-spirited	4
slightly depressed	5
clearly depressed	6
considerably depressed	7
severely depressed	8
most severe depression (inability to make a self-rating)	9

Appendix A4
"Current State Barometer"

Interview No. _____   Date: _____

Name: _____

Please indicate with a cross on the vertical line your *current state of wellbeing*. The highest point for an extremely good state, the lowest for an extremely bad state. A cross in the middle would mean that your current mood is neither especially good nor especially bad.

extremely good

extremely bad

Appendix A5
Glossary and Abbreviations

Glossary

Nonverbal behaviour The total of gaze, facial expression, speech activity, etc. These are *nonverbal aspects*.

Elements of behavioural aspect are, e.g. single Action Units in the facial expression, large and small movements in gesture.

Variables of nonverbal behaviour (or nonverbal variables) refer to specific features within a behaviour. As an example, variables of gaze could be: direction of gaze, duration of looking at the other, etc.

Parameters of nonverbal behaviour (or nonverbal parameters) specify the way in which measures of frequency, intensity, or duration are used. For gaze, the parameter chosen was relative duration of gaze at the other within the observational period. Another parameter could have been the average duration of single looks. For gestural activity, the parameter GAR included a correcting factor for speech activity.

Affect An emotion of shorter duration and/or greater intensity.

Affective state A comparatively lasting state of an intense mood. Also mood state.

Mood A shifting yet pervasive emotional feeling state of varying duration. Also a motivational state.

Emotion Psychological reaction to and evaluation of outer or inner stimuli.

Gestures Illustrators and emblems (according to Ekman & Friesen, 1972); object-focussed hand movements (according to Freedman & Hoffman, 1967)

Speech-related gestures Object-focussed hand movements with speech primacy (according to Freedman, 1972).

Object-related gestures Object-focussed hand movements with motor primacy (according to Freedman, 1972).

Manipulations Adaptors (according to Ekman & Friesen, 1969); body-focussed hand movements (according to Freedman, 1972).

Abbreviations

VAS	Visual Analogue Scale
SID	Standardized Interview for Depression
GR	Global Clinical Rating of Depression (see Rating Scales)
E	Endogenous
N	Neurotic
C	Controls
AU	Action Unit

G%	Relative amount of gaze
S%	Relative amount of speech activity
GAR	Gestural activity relative to the amount of speech
MIAK	General facial activity
AU12	Action Unit 12 = smile
REP2	Facial repertoire 2

Appendix B

Table B.1 *Levels of significance for correlations with different numbers of subjects*

n	p = .05	p = .01	Group
9	–	–	Controls
16	.54	.71	Neurotic depressed
18	.51	.67	Control values I-III
20	.48	.62	Endogenous depressed
36	.34	.45	Depressed patients
45	.30	.40	Total sample

Table B.2: *Patient's characteristics*

Patient number (Pt), age, period of observation, ICD classification, and number of interviews

Pt	Age	Period of observation (days) Main study	Post control	ICD classification	Number of interviews
Male endogenous depressed patients (EM)					
5	46	60	15	296.2	25
6	33	92	11	296.3	39
7	33	47	15	296.2	21
8	30	43	13	296.3	20
13	43	46	–	296.3	20
14	33	47	18	296.3	18
16	48	38	–	296.3	11
17	29	25	15	296.2	13
22	45	68	5	296.2	20
Female endogenous depressed patients (EW)					
9	45	98	14	296.2	38
10	57	152	42	296.2	49
11	53	120	8	296.2	34
15	47	66	13	296.2	18
18	57	46	13	296.2	17
19	59	78	–	296.2	23
20	70	44	13	296.2	17
23	67	106	–	296.3	20
41	57	113	5	296.3	21
42	56	111	–	296.2	24
43	57	38	–	296.0	11

Table B.2: *Continued*

Pt	Age	Main study	Post control	ICD classification	Number of interviews
		Period of observation (days)			
Male neurotic depressed patients (NM)					
2	30	119	6	300.4	6
3	34	103	6	300.4	6
6	34	66	8	300.4	7
7	31	85	7	300.4	7
9	29	117	6	300.4	6
11	26	95	6	300.4	7
13	40	57	6	300.4	7
14	43	107	6	300.4	7
17	27	94	6	300.4	6
Female neurotic depressed patients (NW)					
4	44	112	1	300.4	6
5	42	79	3	300.4	7
8	30	64	8	300.4	7
10	24	129	7	300.4	7
18	31	74	5	300.4	6
19	32	69	6	300.4	6
20	49	85	2	300.4	7
Male controls (KM)					
32	38	8			3
33	32	6			3
35	24	11			4
39	52	11			4
40	39	6			3
Female controls (KW)					
34	66	11			4
36	63	8			4
37	65	12			4
38	60	4			2

Table B.3 *Psychological parameters at different states during the course of depression.*

Pers = Person, E = endogenous, N = neurotic depressed patients, M = male, W = female; number refers to individual patients
INR = Interview number. Days of clinical stay. For follow up (either II or III), days count from the first day of re-admission at the clinic
Subjective Wellbeing indicated on VAS = Visual Analogue Scale
State of depression = I, intermediate = II, and recovery or relatively best state of wellbeing = III
GR = Global Clinical Rating of depression
SID components: A = General wellbeing, B = Concentration and efficiency, C = Activity and social contact, D = Positive emotions and future expectations, E = Somatic complaints and sleep.
Note: (also for the following tables) missing data = −1.

Pers	INR	Days	VAS	State	GR	A	B	C	D	E
EM 5	2	4	112	I	8	9.0	9.0	7.5	9.0	6.0
EM 5	18	60	25	II	3	4.3	4.5	3.5	4.3	3.4
EM 5	24	12	20	III	3	4.3	2.3	4.0	4.3	4.4
EM 6	6	15	55	I	3	6.0	5.5	3.5	6.3	3.8
EM 6	32	78	44	II	3	3.7	3.5	2.0	4.3	3.4
EM 6	37	6	25	III	3	1.7	1.0	2.5	4.3	1.6
EM 7	1	1	104	I	8	9.0	9.0	9.0	9.0	9.0
EM 7	14	47	25	II	3	4.3	2.8	2.5	3.7	3.4
EM 7	16	4	12	III	3	1.3	2.3	3.5	4.0	2.0
EM 8	13	43	72	I	5	3.3	6.5	5.0	6.3	3.0
EM 8	2	3	69	II	5	5.0	4.5	4.0	6.3	3.8
EM 8	19	10	39	III	4	3.3	2.5	3.5	5.0	1.8
EM13	2	4	71	I	6	6.0	8.3	6.8	6.3	2.6
EM13	11	35	49	III	4	3.5	4.3	3.8	3.7	2.6
EM14	2	5	90	I	6	7.3	7.5	6.3	6.0	5.2
EM14	14	47	16	II	3	1.8	1.5	4.3	3.7	3.6
EM14	16	5	0	III	3	2.8	1.8	3.8	3.3	3.2
EM16	2	5	111	I	8	8.5	8.3	5.3	5.0	3.8
EM16	5	17	12	III	4	3.8	3.8	3.8	3.5	3.0
EM17	2	4	63	I	6	6.5	3.8	6.8	7.0	3.8
EM17	8	25	32	II	3	1.8	2.8	3.3	3.3	2.8
EM17	12	12	15	III	3	2.5	2.5	5.0	4.7	2.4
EM22	1	1	94	I	8	6.8	6.8	6.5	8.3	6.4
EM22	19	1	12	II	3	2.3	2.8	3.5	4.0	2.6
EM22	17	65	1	III	4	2.5	2.5	3.5	4.0	2.4
EW 9	3	7	110	I	7	7.0	7.5	6.0	7.0	4.0
EW 9	27	74	19	II	5	5.3	5.5	3.8	7.0	4.2
EW 9	36	7	13	III	3	3.3	3.0	4.0	4.0	4.0
EW10	2	2	113	I	8	7.3	7.0	6.8	8.7	5.8
EW10	41	1	19	II	3	4.5	4.3	3.3	3.0	5.8
EW10	15	44	12	III	5	4.3	4.8	3.8	3.7	2.2
EW11	2	5	93	I	6	6.3	5.0	6.0	6.7	5.0
EW11	15	61	48	II	6	4.8	4.5	3.5	6.7	4.0
EW11	34	8	25	III	3	4.5	3.5	6.0	4.7	3.2
EW15	3	8	92	I	6	6.3	8.5	4.8	7.0	6.0
EW15	13	66	22	II	3	4.0	4.0	4.0	3.0	3.8
EW15	15	3	12	III	3	3.3	2.8	4.5	4.0	2.2
EW18	2	4	50	I	6	5.0	4.3	6.8	7.3	5.2
EW18	13	46	33	II	4	2.8	2.8	4.5	3.3	3.2
EW18	15	6	24	III	3	2.3	2.0	4.3	4.0	2.4

Table B.3: *Continued*

Pers	INR	Days	VAS	State	GR	A	B	C	D	E
EW19	2	4	89	I	7	6.5	3.5	5.8	5.7	4.6
EW19	22	74	18	III	4	3.0	3.8	5.0	5.7	2.8
EW20	2	5	77	I	5	5.3	7.5	6.3	6.3	3.8
EW20	12	40	2	II	3	2.8	4.3	5.3	4.0	3.4
EW20	16	10	1	III	4	3.8	3.5	4.3	4.0	2.6
EW23	2	4	64	I	7	6.5	6.5	7.0	6.0	5.8
EW23	19	99	18	III	5	4.8	3.8	4.3	4.7	3.4
EW41	8	32	113	I	7	7.3	7.5	6.5	5.0	5.8
EW41	21	5	8	II	5	2.5	3.8	4.8	4.0	2.6
EW41	6	25	0	III	2	2.5	2.8	3.5	3.3	3.0
EW42	2	3	108	I	8	6.7	7.5	7.0	7.0	7.8
EW42	24	108	15	III	3	3.7	4.5	3.5	4.3	3.0
EW43	2	3	110	I	7	7.8	6.8	7.3	8.0	4.0
EW43	11	38	12	III	4	3.8	2.5	3.5	3.0	3.6
KM32	3	8	27	I	3	3.0	2.3	3.3	3.7	3.0
KM32	2	5	24	III	3	2.8	2.5	3.0	4.0	2.8
KM33	3	6	24	I	3	4.0	2.3	4.3	3.7	3.8
KM33	2	3	17	III	3	2.5	2.5	3.8	3.0	5.0
KM35	2	4	20	I	3	3.3	2.5	4.3	3.7	1.0
KM35	3	7	18	III	3	2.5	2.5	2.5	3.0	1.8
KM39	2	4	9	I	3	2.5	2.5	4.3	4.0	2.4
KM39	3	7	6	III	3	1.5	1.8	5.5	5.7	2.4
KM40	2	3	49	I	4	3.0	2.8	3.8	5.7	2.6
KM40	1	1	45	III	4	3.8	4.0	4.8	6.3	3.0
KW34	2	4	7	I	3	2.3	2.8	4.5	3.3	3.4
KW34	4	11	6	III	3	2.5	2.5	3.3	3.0	3.8
KW36	2	5	7	I	3	2.3	2.3	3.5	2.3	2.0
KW36	3	8	6	III	3	3.0	2.8	4.0	3.7	4.6
KW37	2	5	13	I	3	4.3	2.8	4.3	4.3	2.0
KW37	3	8	13	III	3	3.8	2.8	4.0	4.0	2.6
KW38	2	1	20	I	3	2.8	2.5	3.5	4.0	3.6
KW38	3	4	18	III	3	2.5	2.0	3.8	4.7	3.4
NM 2	3	29	75	I	5	4.5	3.5	4.0	4.3	2.6
NM 2	5	119	55	II	4	3.5	3.5	4.0	3.7	3.0
NM 2	6	−1	40	III	3	3.3	2.5	3.8	4.3	2.2
NM 3	3	27	78	I	6	6.3	6.8	7.3	4.7	4.4
NM 3	5	103	29	II	3	1.5	1.5	2.8	2.7	3.2
NM 3	6	−1	25	III	3	4.5	2.8	2.5	4.3	3.2
NM 6	4	66	108	I	6	6.8	6.5	6.3	6.7	6.2
NM 6	1	1	75	II	7	6.3	6.3	6.5	7.3	6.2
NM 6	6	−1	68	III	5	6.5	5.3	7.5	6.7	4.6
NM 7	3	28	111	I	8	7.0	6.8	7.0	8.0	5.8
NM 7	6	−1	83	II	6	5.5	6.5	5.5	6.3	5.4
NM 7	5	85	23	III	3	4.5	3.8	4.8	3.7	4.4
NM 9	2	7	107	I	7	6.5	7.0	7.0	5.3	3.6
NM 9	6	−1	63	II	4	4.5	4.8	3.8	4.0	2.0
NM 9	5	117	58	III	3	3.0	4.5	4.0	5.0	1.4
NM11	3	29	85	I	4	6.8	5.8	4.0	5.0	4.4
NM11	6	−1	68	II	6	6.8	3.5	4.5	6.0	4.8
NM11	5	95	66	III	4	7.3	6.3	3.5	4.7	4.6
NM13	1	1	81	I	8	5.3	4.8	5.3	5.0	3.4
NM13	7	−1	73	II	3	4.5	1.8	3.5	3.3	2.4
NM13	5	57	33	III	5	4.3	6.5	5.5	3.0	5.6

Table B.3: *Continued*

Pers	INR	Days	VAS	State	GR	A	B	C	D	E
NM14	1	1	99	I	8	6.3	6.0	6.5	4.0	6.6
NM14	6	−1	68	II	6	6.8	6.0	4.3	4.7	6.2
NM14	4	64	53	III	5	5.5	7.3	3.5	3.7	5.6
NM17	2	7	113	I	7	4.8	7.8	5.5	3.7	4.6
NM17	6	−1	78	II	3	6.0	3.5	4.8	4.7	4.4
NM17	5	94	47	III	5	6.0	3.3	3.8	3.3	4.2
NW 4	6	−1	103	I	6	7.0	7.8	6.3	7.3	4.8
NW 4	4	62	102	II	7	7.8	7.3	7.3	6.3	6.2
NW 4	3	40	40	III	7	7.5	7.5	6.0	6.0	4.8
NW 5	1	1	60	I	3	4.5	3.3	5.3	5.0	4.4
NW 5	3	18	19	II	3	5.3	4.0	3.0	3.0	5.8
NW 5	6	−1	19	III	3	4.3	4.0	3.3	3.0	5.8
NW 8	2	7	67	I	5	5.8	5.8	3.5	4.0	3.2
NW 8	7	−1	36	II	3	4.5	3.5	4.3	4.0	2.4
NW 8	5	64	18	III	3	4.3	2.3	3.3	2.7	3.2
NW10	1	1	91	I	7	7.3	5.8	7.0	7.3	6.2
NW10	7	−1	68	II	7	6.8	5.8	5.8	7.7	5.0
NW10	2	7	66	III	6	6.5	5.5	5.3	5.0	5.0
NW18	2	7	113	I	7	5.0	3.8	6.0	5.0	3.8
NW18	5	74	74	II	4	5.5	4.3	4.0	3.0	3.6
NW18	6	−1	38	III	5	5.3	3.0	4.5	4.3	4.2
NW19	3	20	102	I	6	5.5	6.3	5.0	4.3	3.0
NW19	4	42	61	II	4	5.0	5.3	5.0	3.0	2.8
NW19	6	−1	17	III	3	2.5	3.8	4.8	5.3	2.6
NW20	3	22	88	I	6	4.3	4.5	3.5	3.7	4.8
NW20	5	85	43	II	3	4.5	4.0	3.0	3.0	4.0
NW20	6	−1	43	III	3	5.5	2.3	3.3	3.0	3.2

Table B.4: *Nonverbal parameters*

MIAK = General facial activity
AU12 = Frequency of smile
REP2 = Facial repertoire 2
G% = Relative amount of gaze at the other
S% = Relative amount of speech
GAR = Gestural activity related to amount of speech
Ratings
Mi = Facial variability
Ga = Amount of gaze
Spe = Amount of speech activity
Ges = Amount of gestural activity
Man = Amount of manipulations
(Other abbreviations see table B.3)
Values arranged according to groups and states of subjective wellbeing

Pers	INR	State	VAS	GR	MIAK	AU12	REP2	G%	S%	GAR	Rating Mi	Ga	Sp	Ges	Man
EM 5	2	I	112	8	16	1	1	28	27	41.7	9	7	7	5	9
EM 6	6	I	55	3	20	2	5	10	45	18.9	5	5	5	9	7
EM 7	1	I	104	8	10	0	3	24	4	.0	9	5	7	9	7

Table B.4: *Continued*

Pers	INR	State	VAS	GR	MIAK	AU12	REP2	G%	S%	GAR	Mi	Ga	Sp	Ges	Man
EM 8	13	I	72	5	6	2	2	33	41	50.0	7	7	5	7	3
EM13	2	I	71	6	41	8	4	37	74	83.1	5	5	3	5	4
EM14	2	I	90	6	14	1	5	56	41	47.7	6	5	4	5	6
EM16	2	I	111	8	25	2	6	44	18	109.7	5	5	4	4	4
EM17	2	I	63	6	18	6	4	33	49	107.0	8	5	5	5	8
EM22	1	I	94	8	18	0	1	36	46	19.1	8	6	5	8	3
EW 9	3	I	110	7	16	0	3	51	40	25.0	7	3	4	7	1
EW10	2	I	113	8	44	1	7	18	43	62.5	6	6	2	7	7
EW11	2	I	93	6	18	1	3	5	58	2.3	5	8	4	9	7
EW15	3	I	92	6	14	3	3	11	31	25.0	8	5	5	8	2
EW18	2	I	50	6	26	2	5	88	33	75.0	6	3	6	5	5
EW19	2	I	89	7	18	1	2	49	33	67.9	6	5	5	7	6
EW20	2	I	77	5	15	0	4	86	57	83.9	6	4	4	4	5
EW23	2	I	64	7	12	0	2	58	58	.0	8	7	5	9	1
EW41	8	I	113	7	3	0	1	6	19	.0	8	7	7	8	7
EW42	2	I	108	8	20	0	4	31	45	51.7	7	7	5	5	7
EW43	2	I	110	7	24	0	3	17	66	80.3	2	5	2	2	8
KM32	3	I	27	3	30	11	5	59	52	58.9	2	2	3	3	6
KM33	3	I	24	3	25	12	4	79	32	18.8	3	2	4	4	5
KM35	2	I	20	3	25	12	5	52	55	97.3	5	5	5	5	2
KM39	2	I	9	3	13	4	4	48	71	93.7	6	4	5	4	2
KM40	2	I	49	4	35	12	4	63	60	50.6	4	4	4	4	4
KW34	2	I	7	3	42	19	4	31	69	50.0	3	7	4	6	7
KW36	2	I	7	3	36	18	4	78	57	27.9	3	3	2	3	4
KW37	2	I	13	3	68	23	9	63	36	24.5	4	2	5	6	6
KW38	2	I	20	3	51	12	5	44	53	32.3	4	4	4	4	5
NM 2	3	I	75	5	14	12	1	24	37	42.3	6	6	5	7	8
NM 3	3	I	78	6	26	3	3	55	43	75.4	1	6	6	4	7
NM 6	4	I	108	6	32	0	4	1	31	71.4	5	6	4	5	5
NM 7	3	I	111	8	12	0	2	0	23	67.5	6	9	6	4	4
NM 9	2	I	107	7	29	0	4	2	17	80.0	7	7	6	7	9
NM11	3	I	85	4	29	11	4	23	44	29.8	4	4	4	6	5
NM13	1	I	81	8	7	0	2	29	48	87.2	6	5	5	5	4
NM14	1	I	99	8	22	2	6	40	50	44.8	7	5	4	7	7
NM17	2	I	113	7	34	6	5	1	42	8.0	3	7	5	7	8
NW 4	6	I	103	6	24	12	5	39	60	62.9	5	4	4	3	3
NW 5	1	I	60	3	25	15	4	77	64	61.3	4	4	3	3	5
NW 8	2	I	67	5	19	3	3	41	62	24.0	5	5	4	6	6
NW10	1	I	91	7	22	3	4	40	30	38.5	5	6	6	7	8
NW18	2	I	113	7	32	2	6	3	62	16.4	6	7	4	7	5
NW19	3	I	102	6	31	5	7	23	54	41.0	5	4	5	5	7
NW20	3	I	88	6	16	2	4	22	85	36.4	4	6	2	6	7
EM 5	18	II	25	3	21	5	5	53	66	40.0	3	1	3	5	3
EM 6	32	II	44	3	23	7	4	27	47	49.1	5	5	5	7	5
EM 7	14	II	25	3	13	5	3	47	68	13.2	5	5	7	5	5
EM 8	2	II	69	5	25	1	4	39	34	23.1	5	5	9	5	3
EM14	14	II	16	3	6	2	2	49	53	60.0	6	4	5	6	7
EM17	8	II	32	3	29	9	5	84	45	55.4	5	4	4	5	8
EM22	19	II	12	3	37	10	8	46	48	67.2	4	2	4	4	1
EW 9	27	II	19	5	19	4	2	42	52	43.9	5	6	4	5	7
EW10	41	II	19	3	21	9	3	77	68	64.1	5	4	2	3	5
EW11	15	II	48	6	25	0	4	3	55	25.4	6	8	4	8	4

Table B.4: *Continued*

Pers	INR	State	VAS	GR	MIAK	AU12	REP2	G%	S%	GAR	Mi	Ga	Sp	Ges	Man
EW15	13	ii	22	3	13	5	4	65	39	24.5	4	2	2	6	6
EW18	13	ii	33	4	31	2	6	70	58	74.3	4	4	4	6	6
EW20	12	ii	2	3	15	5	3	63	64	89.9	3	3	2	2	6
EW41	21	ii	8	5	9	8	1	53	41	19.6	5	4	4	6	3
NM 2	5	ii	55	4	10	7	1	10	40	45.2	5	6	5	6	8
NM 3	5	ii	29	3	31	14	4	55	38	76.9	4	4	3	4	6
NM 6	1	ii	75	7	36	1	5	7	18	122.2	6	7	7	8	6
NM 7	6	ii	83	6	8	0	2	29	36	10.0	6	5	5	5	7
NM 9	6	ii	63	4	46	14	7	27	30	69.4	5	5	5	6	5
NM11	6	ii	68	6	23	4	5	11	45	15.9	5	4	5	6	5
NM13	7	ii	73	3	12	1	4	39	44	58.5	4	3	5	3	3
NM14	6	ii	68	6	23	4	4	27	44	32.1	6	4	4	8	7
NM17	6	ii	78	3	19	3	3	4	42	6.1	2	8	4	7	6
NW 4	4	ii	102	7	22	6	3	16	52	42.3	6	6	4	6	5
NW 5	3	ii	19	3	30	13	5	52	75	41.5	5	4	4	4	5
NW 8	7	ii	36	3	18	7	3	48	56	57.3	5	3	4	4	4
NW10	7	ii	68	7	19	2	6	10	17	16.7	5	7	7	8	8
NW18	5	ii	74	4	35	6	5	25	36	20.0	5	5	5	7	6
NW19	4	ii	61	4	27	5	7	41	56	34.8	4	4	4	5	7
NW20	5	ii	43	3	34	6	6	42	78	36.8	5	4	3	5	5
EM 5	24	iii	20	3	23	6	6	45	73	60.8	3	5	3	5	5
EM 6	37	iii	25	3	26	10	3	15	57	16.5	3	5	5	5	5
EM 7	16	iii	12	3	15	6	4	52	67	25.0	5	5	5	6	5
EM 8	19	iii	39	4	26	3	4	23	26	100.0	5	5	5	5	6
EM13	11	iii	49	4	42	1	4	56	56	112.3	5	4	4	4	5
EM14	16	iii	0	3	3	0	1	59	66	86.4	4	4	3	3	5
EM16	5	iii	12	4	26	5	3	62	58	117.5	3	4	3	3	6
EM17	12	iii	15	3	21	7	6	82	45	46.8	4	5	4	5	5
EM22	17	iii	1	4	21	0	3	48	53	24.0	5	4	4	4	5
EW 9	36	iii	13	3	32	4	4	54	47	92.5	3	5	4	5	6
EW10	15	iii	12	5	29	3	5	55	66	48.4	5	5	2	6	6
EW11	34	iii	25	3	30	14	4	5	59	10.3	3	7	4	6	6
EW15	15	iii	12	3	24	4	5	76	35	7.7	5	4	4	4	5
EW18	15	iii	24	3	29	4	3	78	46	51.6	5	3	4	6	4
EW19	22	iii	18	4	24	9	5	66	43	90.6	4	3	4	4	6
EW20	16	iii	1	4	14	3	4	34	67	58.5	6	5	4	4	6
EW23	19	iii	18	5	4	3	1	46	23	9.5	5	5	5	9	4
EW41	6	iii	0	2	14	10	2	50	69	13.3	5	4	2	4	5
EW42	24	iii	15	3	28	10	4	34	40	25.6	3	5	5	7	3
EW43	11	iii	12	4	29	9	2	62	76	87.3	5	4	2	5	6
KM32	2	iii	24	3	27	2	5	54	54	74.6	2	4	4	2	2
KM33	2	iii	17	3	29	6	3	73	30	64.7	4	4	4	4	5
KM35	3	iii	18	3	23	10	3	64	63	79.0	4	2	3	4	4
KM39	3	iii	6	3	9	2	4	39	74	123.7	6	6	4	4	3
KM40	1	iii	45	4	25	12	4	57	49	103.8	5	6	5	4	2
KW34	4	iii	6	3	45	14	7	23	60	62.9	5	6	4	6	7
KW36	3	iii	6	3	27	13	5	66	61	14.5	4	4	4	5	5
KW37	3	iii	13	3	29	18	5	71	43	31.6	4	4	5	5	4
KW38	3	iii	18	3	41	18	3	55	55	30.8	3	5	4	6	8
NM 2	6	iii	40	3	8	4	2	1	62	39.6	4	7	4	5	7
NM 3	6	iii	25	3	42	11	6	50	44	76.5	4	4	5	4	3
NM 6	6	iii	68	5	26	2	6	8	23	60.5	4	6	6	6	6
NM 7	5	iii	23	3	14	5	2	27	69	37.7	4	4	3	5	5

Table B.4: *Continued*

Pers	INR	State	VAS	GR	MIAK	AU12	REP2	G%	S%	GAR	Mi	Ga	Sp	Ges	Man
NM 9	5	III	58	3	31	9	5	22	28	35.3	5	5	5	5	8
NM11	5	III	66	4	12	2	4	16	49	30.0	6	5	5	7	7
NM13	5	III	33	5	6	1	1	40	52	27.8	6	4	8	5	4
NM14	4	III	53	5	26	8	6	50	53	26.4	6	5	4	7	4
NM17	5	III	47	5	16	2	4	9	40	15.2	3	6	4	5	6
NW 4	3	III	40	7	10	2	3	39	65	59.6	4	6	4	4	6
NW 5	6	III	19	3	37	13	6	65	70	46.7	4	5	5	6	4
NW 8	5	III	18	3	18	8	4	64	62	32.3	4	4	4	4	6
NW10	2	III	66	6	18	4	3	25	22	48.1	5	5	5	6	8
NW18	6	III	38	5	14	2	3	27	44	16.9	4	4	5	5	6
NW19	6	III	17	3	25	3	6	42	36	60.7	3	4	5	6	6
NW20	6	III	43	3	17	8	2	46	52	17.9	4	3	2	3	5

Table B.5: *Frequencies of occurrence of single Action Units (other abbreviations see Table B.3). Values arranged according to subgroups.*

Pers	INR	State	VAS	1+2	4	12	9	10	14	15	17	18	20	23	24	28
EM 5	2	I	112	0	0	1	0	0	1	1	0	1	1	0	11	0
EM 5	18	II	25	6	1	5	0	2	1	2	1	0	0	0	3	0
EM 5	24	III	20	6	2	6	0	0	2	5	0	0	2	0	0	0
EM 6	6	I	55	1	3	2	0	0	3	5	0	0	5	0	1	0
EM 6	32	II	44	8	5	7	0	0	2	0	0	0	1	0	0	0
EM 6	37	III	25	1	1	10	0	0	7	0	1	1	5	0	0	0
EM 7	1	I	104	6	0	0	0	2	0	0	0	0	0	0	0	2
EM 7	14	II	25	3	0	5	0	0	0	0	0	0	1	0	0	4
EM 7	16	III	12	3	3	6	0	3	0	0	0	0	0	0	0	0
EM 8	13	I	72	1	0	2	0	0	2	0	0	0	0	0	0	1
EM 8	2	II	69	2	0	1	0	0	7	0	1	0	1	0	9	4
EM 8	19	III	39	1	3	3	0	0	15	0	0	0	0	0	0	4
EM13	2	I	71	1	15	8	0	0	0	10	0	0	7	0	0	0
EM13	11	III	49	2	14	1	0	0	0	0	1	0	12	0	12	0
EM14	2	I	90	1	3	1	0	2	2	2	1	0	0	0	0	2
EM14	14	II	16	1	0	2	0	0	2	0	0	0	0	0	0	1
EM14	16	III	0	0	0	0	0	1	2	0	0	0	0	0	0	0
EM16	2	I	111	0	1	2	0	0	6	0	3	3	3	1	1	5
EM16	5	III	12	1	0	5	0	0	17	0	0	2	0	0	0	1
EM17	2	I	63	2	0	6	0	0	4	1	1	0	0	0	3	1
EM17	8	II	32	8	1	9	0	2	1	1	0	1	1	3	2	0
EM17	12	III	15	2	4	7	0	2	0	0	1	0	2	0	1	2
EM22	1	I	94	0	0	0	0	0	0	1	0	0	0	15	1	1
EM22	19	II	12	3	3	10	0	0	0	1	3	2	2	4	1	8
EM22	17	III	1	0	0	0	0	1	0	0	0	0	3	5	1	11
EW 9	3	I	110	8	1	0	0	1	1	0	0	0	2	0	3	0
EW 9	27	II	19	14	0	4	0	0	0	0	0	0	0	0	0	1
EW 9	36	III	13	22	2	4	0	1	0	0	2	0	0	1	0	0
EW10	2	I	113	6	11	1	1	3	0	0	2	0	15	0	2	3
EW10	41	II	19	5	1	9	0	0	0	0	0	0	0	0	6	0
EW10	15	III	12	14	4	3	0	0	0	0	0	2	0	0	0	6
EW11	2	I	93	5	5	1	0	0	0	0	0	0	6	0	0	1

Table B.5: *Continued*

Pers	INR	State	VAS	1+2	4	12	9	10	14	15	17	18	20	23	24	28
EW11	15	II	48	1	6	0	0	0	4	0	0	1	5	0	0	8
EW11	34	III	25	0	3	14	0	0	0	1	1	0	1	0	8	2
EW15	3	I	92	1	1	3	0	1	0	1	0	0	0	0	3	4
EW15	13	II	22	3	2	5	0	0	0	2	0	0	0	0	1	0
EW15	15	III	12	2	0	4	0	1	0	3	1	0	1	0	3	9
EW18	2	I	50	7	0	2	0	0	0	6	0	6	1	0	4	0
EW18	13	II	33	4	1	2	1	0	4	8	0	8	0	0	0	3
EW18	15	III	24	12	0	4	0	0	11	1	0	0	0	0	0	1
EW19	2	I	89	0	0	1	0	0	15	0	0	0	0	0	2	0
EW19	22	III	18	1	5	9	0	0	4	0	0	0	2	0	2	1
EW20	2	I	77	3	3	0	0	4	1	1	0	0	0	0	1	2
EW20	12	II	2	5	2	5	1	1	0	0	1	0	0	0	0	0
EW20	16	III	1	4	2	3	0	2	1	1	0	1	0	0	0	0
EW23	2	I	64	0	0	0	0	0	0	0	2	0	10	0	0	0
EW23	19	III	18	0	1	3	0	0	0	0	0	0	0	0	0	0
EW41	8	I	113	0	0	0	0	0	0	0	0	0	2	0	0	1
EW41	21	II	8	1	0	8	0	0	0	0	0	0	0	0	0	0
EW41	6	III	0	0	0	10	0	0	0	0	0	3	0	0	0	1
EW42	2	I	108	2	1	0	0	0	10	0	3	0	0	0	0	4
EW42	24	III	15	5	0	10	0	0	8	0	4	0	0	0	0	1
EW43	2	I	110	15	0	0	0	0	0	0	1	0	0	5	2	1
EW43	11	III	12	17	0	9	0	0	1	1	0	0	0	0	0	1
KM32	3	I	27	10	3	11	0	0	3	1	0	0	0	0	0	2
KM32	2	III	24	10	0	2	0	0	5	1	1	1	0	0	5	2
KM33	3	I	24	9	0	12	0	0	0	0	0	2	0	0	0	2
KM33	2	III	17	19	0	6	0	1	0	0	0	0	0	0	2	1
KM35	2	I	20	3	0	12	2	1	4	1	0	0	0	0	0	2
KM35	3	III	18	5	1	10	0	5	0	0	0	0	0	0	1	1
KM39	2	I	9	5	0	4	0	0	0	0	0	0	2	0	2	0
KM39	3	III	6	2	0	2	0	0	0	0	3	0	0	0	2	0
KM40	2	I	49	3	0	12	0	5	0	0	0	0	0	0	15	0
KM40	1	III	45	0	0	12	0	4	0	1	0	1	0	0	5	2
KW34	2	I	7	3	0	19	0	0	0	0	1	6	1	0	12	0
KW34	4	III	6	3	1	14	0	1	0	3	4	5	0	1	8	5
KW36	2	I	7	0	0	18	0	0	0	5	2	1	0	0	10	0
KW36	3	III	6	0	0	13	0	0	0	4	2	0	0	0	6	2
KW37	2	I	13	4	2	23	0	5	9	8	4	1	6	0	0	6
KW37	3	III	13	2	2	18	0	0	0	0	0	1	0	0	4	2
KW38	2	I	20	17	3	12	0	0	0	0	0	4	1	0	14	0
KW38	3	III	18	10	1	18	0	0	0	0	0	1	0	0	11	0
NM 2	3	I	75	0	0	12	1	0	0	0	0	0	0	0	1	0
NM 2	5	II	55	1	0	7	0	0	1	0	0	0	0	0	1	0
NM 2	6	III	40	3	0	4	0	0	0	0	0	0	1	0	0	0
NM 3	3	I	78	11	0	3	1	0	0	1	1	0	9	0	0	0
NM 3	5	II	29	10	0	14	0	5	0	0	2	0	0	0	0	0
NM 3	6	III	25	12	3	11	1	5	0	0	3	0	6	0	0	1
NM 6	1	I	108	15	8	0	0	5	0	2	0	0	1	0	0	1
NM 6	6	II	75	17	4	1	0	3	0	0	2	0	0	0	0	9
NM 6	6	III	68	8	2	2	0	1	0	6	0	3	1	0	0	3
NM 7	3	I	111	0	0	0	0	0	0	0	0	0	4	0	8	0
NM 7	6	II	83	0	0	0	0	0	0	0	0	1	2	1	4	0
NM 7	5	III	23	1	0	5	0	1	0	1	1	1	1	3	0	0

Table B.5: *Continued*

Pers	INR	State	VAS	1+2	4	12	9	10	14	15	17	18	20	23	24	28
NM 9	2	I	107	2	4	0	0	0	0	0	1	2	20	0	0	0
NM 9	6	II	63	5	2	14	0	3	0	0	3	13	1	0	0	5
NM 9	5	III	58	0	0	9	0	0	0	2	5	7	1	0	6	1
NM11	3	I	85	6	0	11	0	0	0	1	0	0	2	0	1	8
NM11	6	II	68	5	0	4	0	0	4	4	0	0	4	0	1	1
NM11	5	III	66	3	2	2	0	0	0	0	1	0	0	1	0	3
NM13	1	I	81	4	2	0	0	0	0	0	0	0	0	0	1	0
NM13	7	II	73	4	0	1	0	2	0	0	2	0	0	0	3	0
NM13	5	III	33	1	0	1	0	0	0	0	0	0	0	0	0	4
NM14	1	I	99	0	4	2	0	0	0	0	3	1	5	0	3	4
NM14	6	II	68	9	5	4	0	3	0	0	1	0	0	0	0	1
NM14	4	III	53	4	3	8	0	0	0	0	0	1	3	0	2	5
NM17	2	I	113	3	111	6	0	5	0	1	0	1	4	1	1	1
NM17	6	II	78	0	0	3	0	2	13	0	0	0	0	1	0	0
NM17	5	III	47	1	2	2	0	3	1	0	0	0	5	0	1	1
NW 4	6	I	103	1	2	12	0	2	1	2	0	1	0	3	0	0
NW 4	4	II	102	4	1	6	0	0	1	1	1	0	0	0	7	1
NW 4	3	III	40	1	0	2	0	0	2	0	1	0	1	0	0	3
NW 5	1	I	60	3	1	15	0	0	2	0	0	1	2	0	0	1
NW 5	3	II	19	10	0	13	0	0	2	2	3	0	0	0	0	0
NW 5	6	III	19	6	2	13	0	1	8	1	2	1	0	1	2	0
NW 8	2	I	67	5	0	3	0	1	9	1	0	0	0	0	0	0
NW 8	7	II	36	0	0	7	1	1	6	2	1	0	0	0	0	0
NW 8	5	III	18	4	2	8	1	0	2	1	0	0	0	0	0	0
NW10	1	I	91	0	0	3	0	2	7	0	8	0	1	0	0	1
NW10	7	II	68	4	0	2	0	0	2	0	1	0	3	0	2	5
NW10	2	III	66	0	1	4	0	2	9	0	1	0	0	0	0	1
NW18	2	I	113	3	1	2	0	2	20	0	2	0	0	0	0	2
NW18	5	II	74	0	0	6	0	2	21	2	2	0	0	1	0	1
NW18	6	III	38	6	0	2	0	1	5	0	0	0	0	0	0	0
NW19	3	I	102	2	4	5	0	2	11	1	1	0	0	3	0	2
NW19	4	II	61	1	3	5	0	3	6	2	3	0	3	0	0	1
NW19	6	III	17	5	2	3	0	4	6	3	1	0	1	0	0	0
NW20	3	I	88	3	4	2	0	0	6	0	0	0	0	0	1	0
NW20	5	II	43	15	4	6	0	0	2	0	4	0	0	0	0	3
NW20	6	III	43	1	6	8	0	0	1	0	0	0	0	1	0	0

Table B.6: *Centroid values of Action Units within clusters of facial patterns*

	CLUSTER									
	I		II		III		IV		V	
AU	$\bar{x}$	s	$\bar{x}$	s	$\bar{x}$	s	$\bar{x}$	s	$\bar{x}$	s
1+2	.01	.03	.12	.09	.54	.11	.18	.13	.11	.13
4	.02	.06	.11	.11	.07	.10	.06	.09	.03	.06
12	.01	.03	.15	.11	.10	.10	.42	.17	.20	.12
20	.47	.30	.11	.10	.04	.10	.02	.04	.01	.04

Table B.6: *Continued*

	CLUSTER									
	I		II		III		IV		V	
AU	$\bar{x}$	s	$\bar{x}$	s	$\bar{x}$	s	$\bar{x}$	s	$\bar{x}$	s
14	.01	.03	.07	.09	.02	.05	.03	.05	.45	.17
18	.04	.05	.03	.06	.01	.02	.03	.07	.01	.02
15	.01	.03	.07	.09	.01	.02	.03	.04	.02	.03
17	.03	.07	.03	.04	.03	.04	.03	.06	.05	.08
23	.02	.05	.04	.15	.02	.06	.01	.04	.01	.02
24	.31	.34	.06	.09	.05	.07	.10	12	.02	.04
28/32	.06	.14	.16	.16	.07	.08	.02	.03	.05	.06
9	.00	.00	.00	.01	.00	.01	.01	.02	.00	.01
10	.00	.00	.04	.07	.04	.06	.04	.07	.05	.07

Table B.7: *Grouping of individuals into clusters on admission, discharge and follow up. Clusters I to V = arabic numbers*

Group	Sex	Pers.	Adm.	Grouping on Disch.	Follow up
E	M	5	1	4	2
		6	2	4	5
		7	3	2	4
		8	2	5	5
		13	2	2	–
		14	2	5	5
		16	2	5	–
		17	5	4	2
		22	2	2	2
E	W	9	3	3	3
		10	2	3	4
		11	2	2	4
		15	2	4	2
		18	2	2	5
		19	5	4	–
		20	2	4	4
		23	1	4	–
		41	1	4	N
		42	5	5	–
		43	3	3	–
N	M	12	4	4	4
		3	3	4	4
		6	3	3	2
		7	1	4	1

Table B.7: *Continued*

Group	Sex	Pers.	Adm.	Grouping on Disch.	Follow up
		9	1	4	4
		11	2	2	2
		13	3	2	4
		14	2	2	4
		17	2	2	5
N	W	4	2	4	4
		5	4	4	5
		8	5	4	5
		10	5	5	2
		18	5	5	5
		19	5	2	2
		20	5	3	4
K	M	32	3	4	
		33	3	4	
		35	4	4	
		39	4	4	
		40	4	4	
K	W	34	4	4	
		36	4	4	
		37	2	4	
		38	4	4	

Table B.8: *Gaze and speech of patients and interviewers*

Relative amounts of gaze and speech activity (in %) and rating (rat.) of patients' gaze and speech behaviour. I = interviewer, P = patient, st = standardized, fr = free part of the interview. −1 = missing data. (Other abbreviations see Table B.3).

					Gaze (%)					Speech (%)				
					Interv		Patient			Interv		Patient		
Pers	INR	Days	VAS	GR	st	fr	st	fr	Rt	st	fr	st	fr	Rt
EM 5	1	1	−1	8	−1	−1	4	12	−1	9	25	47	31	−1
EM 5	2	4	112	8	86	81	28	26	7	11	32	27	12	7
EM 5	3	6	108	8	87	95	11	19	7	9	36	23	18	7
EM 5	4	8	108	8	93	97	28	9	7	14	20	36	27	7
EM 5	5	11	102	8	94	97	27	13	7	11	17	33	33	7
EM 5	6	13	98	8	90	97	1	3	7	17	41	14	21	7
EM 5	7	15	100	8	88	93	9	13	7	13	28	16	7	7
EM 5	8	18	102	8	91	87	34	20	5	15	18	20	25	5
EM 5	9	20	100	8	90	96	33	20	5	14	23	40	51	3
EM 5	10	22	103	8	90	85	9	5	7	19	37	16	10	7
EM 5	11	25	96	8	88	89	28	29	5	13	28	51	58	7

Table B.8: *Continued*

| Pers | INR | Days | VAS | GR | Gaze (%) | | | | | Speech (%) | | | | |
| | | | | | Interv | | Patient | | | Interv | | Patient | | |
					st	fr	st	fr	Rt	st	fr	st	fr	Rt
EM 5	12	27	86	8	91	87	37	38	5	13	34	54	34	5
EM 5	14	32	90	8	90	82	18	17	5	11	35	31	39	5
EM 5	16	46	27	5	78	−1	71	−1	3	12	−1	74	−1	5
EM 5	17	53	38	3	89	91	51	68	3	18	33	48	48	5
EM 5	18	60	25	3	87	95	53	53	1	16	19	66	75	3
EM 5	19	1	29	3	84	96	55	69	3	16	32	54	72	3
EM 5	20	3	24	3	96	90	48	41	3	13	25	68	71	3
EM 5	21	5	25	3	94	86	42	60	3	16	43	65	50	5
EM 5	22	8	23	3	85	94	57	64	3	10	18	51	66	3
EM 5	23	10	30	3	93	84	36	53	5	12	24	54	47	3
EM 5	24	12	20	3	77	98	45	45	5	11	15	73	79	3
EM 6	1	1	61	5	89	−1	37	−1	−1	16	−1	61	−1	5
EM 6	2	6	59	5	76	63	27	40	5	9	8	55	63	5
EM 6	3	8	60	5	−1	84	−1	25	5	−1	16	−1	63	5
EM 6	4	11	44	3	96	91	32	33	3	8	13	69	75	2
EM 6	5	13	53	3	88	88	33	11	5	13	18	64	67	5
EM 6	6	15	55	3	90	87	10	4	5	11	16	45	53	5
EM 6	7	18	54	5	88	85	10	4	7	11	33	45	34	7
EM 6	8	20	55	5	78	76	4	18	5	10	50	39	25	7
EM 6	9	22	52	3	86	84	10	10	5	12	25	41	47	5
EM 6	10	25	51	3	91	86	5	15	5	12	22	22	43	5
EM 6	11	27	52	3	95	84	22	29	5	20	12	41	57	5
EM 6	12	29	49	5	81	75	3	9	5	15	23	24	28	5
EM 6	15	36	54	5	91	69	6	6	7	14	25	32	23	7
EM 6	18	43	55	5	67	90	12	16	5	16	28	33	38	3
EM 6	20	50	52	5	71	91	6	21	5	14	26	34	43	5
EM 6	23	57	55	3	85	77	29	47	5	8	28	52	38	5
EM 6	26	64	46	3	98	−1	24	22	5	12	16	42	40	3
EM 6	32	78	44	3	97	94	27	25	5	15	16	47	55	5
EM 6	33	85	45	3	98	85	12	15	5	10	30	44	34	5
EM 6	34	92	40	3	−1	94	−1	34	5	−1	3	−1	58	3
EM 6	35	1	27	2	−1	−1	20	50	−1	8	16	73	79	3
EM 6	37	6	25	3	−1	−1	15	19	5	15	7	57	79	5
EM 7	1	1	104	8	88	100	24	37	5	10	27	4	5	7
EM 7	2	12	50	5	79	89	46	60	5	6	27	52	51	3
EM 7	3	21	21	3	78	92	48	36	5	16	20	67	63	3
EM 7	5	26	23	3	93	96	49	51	5	14	35	52	37	5
EM 7	6	28	28	3	95	84	46	49	5	12	27	43	22	5
EM 7	7	30	29	2	91	90	45	56	5	11	31	55	40	5
EM 7	8	33	18	2	90	98	42	44	5	13	32	54	48	5
EM 7	9	35	26	3	96	88	48	53	5	11	30	66	48	5
EM 7	10	37	28	3	69	96	39	37	5	10	18	60	62	3
EM 7	11	40	24	5	93	88	37	45	5	11	34	67	59	5
EM 7	12	42	24	3	97	78	43	44	5	9	42	58	28	5
EM 7	13	44	25	3	88	72	38	58	3	10	61	60	21	5
EM 7	14	47	25	3	90	90	47	42	5	11	18	68	76	5
EM 7	15	1	10	3	86	−1	48	53	5	13	14	58	80	3
EM 7	16	4	12	3	89	93	52	62	5	15	15	67	76	5
EM 7	17	6	17	3	82	−1	44	−1	3	8	−1	62	−1	3

Table B.8: *Continued*

Pers	INR	Days	VAS	GR	Gaze (%)					Speech (%)				
						Interv		Patient			Interv		Patient	
					st	fr	st	fr	Rt	st	fr	st	fr	Rt
EM 7	18	8	17	3	85	92	43	49	5	8	26	60	53	5
EM 7	19	11	17	3	89	86	42	55	4	13	27	69	72	4
EM 7	20	13	20	3	89	88	40	60	4	15	32	62	66	5
EM 7	21	15	23	3	79	90	41	59	3	8	35	76	64	4
EM 8	1	1	70	5	68	88	20	22	7	10	18	49	52	5
EM 8	2	3	69	5	91	98	39	36	5	10	14	34	39	5
EM 8	3	5	64	5	84	86	28	25	3	9	23	44	35	5
EM 8	4	8	63	5	91	94	30	27	5	8	20	42	48	5
EM 8	5	10	68	5	92	93	37	35	7	12	29	35	32	7
EM 8	6	12	70	5	86	89	34	36	5	10	27	43	42	7
EM 8	7	15	70	5	77	96	39	38	3	15	26	28	33	5
EM 8	8	17	66	5	72	95	35	26	5	16	20	20	34	5
EM 8	9	19	68	5	90	97	29	26	5	11	17	39	32	7
EM 8	10	22	69	5	88	91	32	26	3	12	16	27	50	7
EM 8	11	31	70	5	91	73	29	33	5	11	26	39	38	5
EM 8	12	36	70	5	94	94	33	39	5	10	26	41	27	7
EM 8	13	43	72	5	92	95	33	38	7	11	26	41	22	5
EM 8	16	1	41	4	60	69	30	32	6	15	29	23	37	5
EM 8	17	3	49	4	78	97	24	26	5	8	23	18	31	5
EM 8	18	6	46	4	84	89	22	26	5	9	39	17	22	5
EM 8	19	10	39	4	81	82	23	35	5	11	28	26	24	5
EM 8	20	13	40	3	83	91	30	36	6	12	23	20	20	6
EM13	1	1	91	6	74	78	36	23	4	12	13	66	66	4
EM13	2	4	71	6	79	88	37	46	5	8	12	74	65	3
EM13	3	7	74	6	84	87	48	51	5	13	21	67	56	5
EM13	4	11	66	7	87	95	30	29	5	8	9	71	70	3
EM13	5	14	65	7	88	98	36	40	5	5	8	72	76	3
EM13	6	18	53	5	78	79	69	64	4	13	30	57	46	4
EM13	7	21	62	6	82	92	42	45	5	8	26	60	50	3
EM13	8	25	55	4	77	96	62	55	5	11	20	46	34	4
EM13	9	28	55	5	83	98	46	58	5	7	24	57	58	5
EM13	10	32	53	4	85	93	70	80	4	14	20	55	50	4
EM13	11	35	49	4	90	97	56	64	4	7	26	56	57	4
EM13	12	39	53	4	83	93	78	83	2	30	23	50	60	4
EM13	13	42	50	4	87	96	70	76	4	7	18	68	60	4
EM13	14	46	50	4	85	97	87	86	3	13	12	68	69	4
EM14	1	1	94	7	78	93	68	61	4	21	34	43	44	4
EM14	2	5	90	6	80	97	56	46	5	15	14	41	44	4
EM14	3	8	88	6	85	95	53	45	4	16	27	45	46	4
EM14	4	12	107	6	90	91	56	44	4	16	20	48	52	4
EM14	5	15	63	6	86	91	57	48	4	13	18	58	66	2
EM14	6	19	105	6	84	98	39	44	4	10	26	52	63	4
EM14	7	22	34	5	89	96	37	44	5	10	21	62	63	2
EM14	8	26	31	3	80	99	46	40	4	8	33	54	47	4
EM14	9	29	13	4	91	−1	32	−1	5	12	−1	57	−1	3
EM14	12	40	13	3	75	90	43	42	4	11	30	50	51	4
EM14	13	43	14	3	84	99	48	40	5	13	15	42	67	3
EM14	14	47	16	3	77	95	49	33	4	10	35	53	35	5
EM14	15	1	14	4	92	88	57	66	5	12	29	57	59	4

Table B.8: *Continued*

					Gaze (%)					Speech (%)				
						Interv	Patient				Interv	Patient		
Pers	INR	Days	VAS	GR	st	fr	st	fr	Rt	st	fr	st	fr	Rt
EM14	16	5	0	3	85	86	59	66	4	19	26	66	59	3
EM14	17	8	0	3	94	98	55	53	4	11	8	77	81	3
EM14	18	12	1	3	94	97	51	46	3	5	9	81	82	3
EM16	1	1	61	6	93	93	72	47	4	27	22	34	51	4
EM16	2	5	111	8	86	84	44	59	5	22	43	18	31	4
EM16	3	9	17	5	83	90	49	45	4	14	39	51	42	3
EM16	4	13	57	6	93	86	45	66	3	11	32	58	60	3
EM16	5	17	12	4	76	87	62	54	4	19	27	58	57	3
EM16	6	20	19	4	92	90	57	39	5	12	21	57	65	4
EM16	7	24	32	4	72	84	46	73	4	17	50	65	40	3
EM16	8	27	49	6	91	92	53	62	6	12	40	56	23	5
EM16	9	31	7	3	79	83	61	54	3	16	36	55	43	3
EM16	10	34	2	3	91	84	52	53	5	16	40	50	43	5
EM16	11	38	6	3	69	77	46	36	4	24	50	42	36	4
EM17	1	1	65	5	70	92	28	19	5	16	12	40	54	6
EM17	2	4	63	6	83	90	33	36	5	11	19	49	57	5
EM17	3	8	45	5	78	85	49	44	3	20	18	46	53	4
EM17	4	11	58	5	79	88	59	60	5	21	26	53	64	5
EM17	5	15	56	4	58	67	73	56	4	24	46	51	35	5
EM17	6	18	43	3	86	90	62	50	5	30	28	52	56	4
EM17	7	22	35	3	68	76	75	67	4	26	25	55	60	3
EM17	8	25	32	3	83	81	84	73	4	32	25	45	56	4
EM17	9	1	21	3	69	90	80	64	4	20	23	43	63	3
EM17	10	5	20	3	72	89	88	78	4	19	19	48	57	4
EM17	11	8	18	3	79	89	82	85	5	30	42	50	63	4
EM17	12	12	15	3	80	85	82	65	5	24	27	45	47	4
EM17	13	15	14	3	−1	88	−1	75	4	−1	47	−1	55	4
EM22	1	1	94	8	82	97	36	30	6	14	23	46	47	5
EM22	2	5	25	4	94	98	34	32	3	19	27	43	33	6
EM22	3	9	59	6	89	100	49	30	4	18	19	41	53	4
EM22	4	16	52	7	91	99	26	18	6	15	16	30	29	6
EM22	5	19	48	6	91	98	42	36	5	26	35	37	18	5
EM22	6	23	64	6	90	96	51	37	4	23	31	39	22	5
EM22	7	26	42	6	90	100	37	46	6	16	50	34	23	5
EM22	8	30	33	6	86	95	66	68	5	16	25	35	31	5
EM22	9	33	72	7	92	92	61	55	6	13	26	36	16	6
EM22	10	37	51	6	65	92	62	53	5	20	39	25	25	6
EM22	11	40	51	5	91	94	53	43	4	22	31	31	21	4
EM22	12	47	30	5	75	90	60	58	3	25	28	31	30	5
EM22	13	51	50	5	86	94	67	56	3	25	25	28	30	4
EM22	14	54	47	6	90	95	53	54	5	17	21	27	35	5
EM22	15	58	34	5	90	98	28	26	5	24	30	39	26	4
EM22	16	61	37	4	88	98	53	50	4	16	37	42	40	4
EM22	17	65	1	4	88	99	48	32	4	13	21	53	50	4
EM22	18	68	2	3	91	99	41	43	4	11	16	56	59	4
EM22	19	1	12	3	59	98	46	41	2	23	32	48	58	4
EM22	20	5	6	3	76	95	47	45	4	25	35	41	36	5
EW 9	1	1	81	5	89	98	48	71	2	8	20	53	41	3
EW 9	2	4	100	7	−1	94	−1	82	4	−1	52	−1	31	5

Table B.8: *Continued*

Pers	INR	Days	VAS	GR	Gaze (%)					Speech (%)				
					Interv		Patient			Interv		Patient		
					st	fr	st	fr	Rt	st	fr	st	fr	Rt
EW 9	3	7	110	7	91	98	51	55	3	15	19	40	56	4
EW 9	4	9	110	8	90	94	21	32	5	10	27	50	40	4
EW 9	5	11	112	7	90	92	27	50	5	15	48	46	24	3
EW 9	6	14	105	5	90	87	32	54	5	14	41	67	36	2
EW 9	7	16	102	5	90	96	51	43	5	15	19	63	60	3
EW 9	8	18	95	6	90	96	68	60	2	9	21	67	51	1
EW 9	9	21	98	7	90	96	22	38	6	12	29	65	51	5
EW 9	10	23	98	7	92	89	6	35	7	11	32	65	46	6
EW 9	11	25	80	6	90	95	29	58	5	16	36	53	47	4
EW 9	12	28	89	6	90	-1	35	-1	5	12	-1	53	-1	5
EW 9	13	30	77	6	90	99	45	45	6	9	31	52	50	5
EW 9	14	32	81	6	91	95	39	41	6	12	24	55	54	4
EW 9	15	35	75	6	93	98	54	55	4	9	31	59	38	3
EW 9	16	37	67	5	93	98	46	61	5	10	34	60	50	4
EW 9	17	39	65	5	85	91	50	66	3	8	32	59	50	3
EW 9	18	44	63	6	85	86	55	57	4	8	9	70	71	3
EW 9	19	46	55	6	83	88	53	65	5	12	27	59	52	4
EW 9	20	51	44	6	89	94	67	64	3	24	24	54	58	3
EW 9	21	53	38	6	87	83	57	70	4	14	35	53	42	3
EW 9	22	56	29	5	87	95	47	53	5	10	37	54	36	4
EW 9	23	58	-1	5	87	90	44	52	5	16	29	44	43	4
EW 9	24	63	40	5	91	94	47	47	4	11	26	63	46	5
EW 9	25	65	34	6	90	92	35	36	6	16	35	40	41	4
EW 9	26	70	22	5	83	89	48	55	5	12	28	50	37	3
EW 9	27	74	19	5	90	96	42	55	6	10	19	52	57	4
EW 9	28	77	20	5	91	92	34	63	4	12	23	57	69	3
EW 9	29	81	21	5	81	96	40	50	6	15	9	50	70	3
EW 9	30	84	22	5	92	94	60	55	5	10	24	66	64	4
EW 9	31	88	21	6	85	84	52	63	5	15	26	48	50	5
EW 9	32	95	26	5	81	91	62	70	4	12	37	66	53	3
EW 9	33	98	24	4	91	93	51	60	5	11	29	63	61	3
EW 9	34	1	12	3	89	91	66	68	4	15	31	63	58	4
EW 9	35	4	14	5	86	96	62	60	3	9	16	53	67	4
EW 9	36	7	13	3	91	92	54	53	5	16	22	47	53	4
EW 9	37	11	11	4	80	91	56	60	3	13	20	51	60	4
EW 9	38	14	11	3	90	81	52	67	4	21	60	61	36	4
EW10	1	1	103	8	88	99	4	14	8	5	19	77	67	2
EW10	2	2	113	8	86	76	18	54	6	7	40	43	48	2
EW10	3	5	103	7	84	98	44	64	5	6	30	84	62	3
EW10	4	9	97	8	87	-1	54	-1	5	15	-1	58	-1	1
EW10	5	12	108	8	81	92	0	10	7	11	19	19	42	6
EW10	6	15	60	6	85	86	51	47	5	11	26	44	43	5
EW10	7	16	78	8	91	79	1	24	6	9	13	40	57	3
EW10	8	19	50	7	88	92	29	32	5	8	15	47	50	2
EW10	9	23	91	8	69	94	13	20	6	8	29	49	41	4
EW10	10	26	71	8	93	97	42	34	6	10	21	73	63	2
EW10	11	30	65	7	92	89	49	62	4	7	25	60	59	2
EW10	12	33	21	6	81	86	52	37	4	8	21	57	55	3
EW10	13	37	21	5	94	89	48	61	5	13	35	65	59	2

Table B.8: *Continued*

Pers	INR	Days	VAS	GR	Gaze (%)					Speech (%)				
					Interv		Patient			Interv		Patient		
					st	fr	st	fr	Rt	st	fr	st	fr	Rt
EW10	14	40	47	6	90	99	51	36	5	12	13	80	84	2
EW10	15	44	12	5	92	97	55	49	5	7	32	66	64	2
EW10	16	47	15	5	91	91	43	56	5	9	20	76	75	2
EW10	17	51	3	3	82	89	43	55	3	9	32	73	76	2
EW10	18	54	19	5	99	96	51	59	4	17	9	82	90	2
EW10	19	58	22	5	84	98	47	41	3	11	29	68	66	2
EW10	20	61	28	5	93	−1	37	−1	5	11	−1	74	−1	2
EW10	21	65	−1	6	93	99	35	17	5	11	14	73	69	2
EW10	22	68	50	6	84	98	32	23	6	15	19	73	63	3
EW10	23	72	34	5	88	91	51	51	4	10	30	58	47	2
EW10	24	75	54	8	92	88	0	0	8	25	16	54	61	5
EW10	25	79	21	−1	84	84	51	42	−1	−1	−1	−1	−1	−1
EW10	26	82	36	5	88	91	42	56	4	8	18	74	81	4
EW10	27	86	34	5	91	95	42	49	3	7	16	67	68	2
EW10	28	89	42	5	86	99	38	54	6	13	21	58	79	4
EW10	30	96	39	4	93	99	51	53	5	9	26	75	65	5
EW10	31	107	35	4	87	90	41	45	4	9	28	68	47	2
EW10	32	110	41	7	94	88	0	3	7	8	25	45	41	5
EW10	33	117	40	5	−1	91	−1	60	5	−1	19	−1	58	4
EW10	34	121	40	5	84	−1	51	−1	−1	12	−1	60	−1	4
EW10	35	124	40	5	81	80	51	64	5	9	27	57	55	5
EW10	36	128	39	6	87	92	55	54	4	8	27	59	44	3
EW10	37	131	32	4	87	93	38	60	4	9	40	70	58	4
EW10	38	138	43	4	87	96	34	69	3	13	34	67	49	3
EW10	39	145	34	4	89	96	61	67	5	13	28	62	66	4
EW10	40	152	30	4	−1	93	−1	52	4	−1	18	−1	59	4
EW10	41	1	19	3	90	96	77	71	4	16	22	68	78	2
EW10	42	4	39	5	80	96	68	64	4	15	26	59	67	3
EW10	43	7	42	5	87	87	62	73	4	14	24	63	68	3
EW10	44	11	50	6	80	95	73	87	2	10	51	54	24	4
EW10	45	14	59	6	87	84	41	39	5	12	21	51	46	4
EW10	46	18	56	7	85	94	41	22	6	19	22	52	48	4
EW10	47	21	42	5	91	87	43	61	5	14	43	62	47	4
EW10	48	39	37	3	82	88	66	73	4	23	18	57	76	4
EW10	49	42	33	3	84	92	59	57	4	24	18	68	76	3
EW11	1	1	111	8	76	80	2	0	8	10	22	55	54	5
EW11	2	5	93	6	91	90	5	7	8	8	16	58	43	4
EW11	3	8	88	6	78	98	7	6	7	9	37	38	27	5
EW11	4	12	97	7	−1	100	−1	0	8	−1	20	−1	37	3
EW11	6	19	81	7	83	98	2	1	8	11	21	59	43	4
EW11	9	29	83	6	83	94	5	9	7	9	46	42	27	4
EW11	10	33	85	6	76	83	4	0	8	12	16	58	56	4
EW11	11	36	79	6	80	−1	2	−1	7	10	−1	49	−1	4
EW11	12	47	58	4	83	97	4	6	6	11	26	56	63	4
EW11	14	57	58	5	63	90	2	12	6	13	24	44	61	4
EW11	15	61	48	6	76	93	3	3	8	11	14	55	59	4
EW11	16	64	75	6	85	94	3	10	5	9	20	65	57	4
EW11	17	68	59	2	60	78	1	1	8	9	22	48	49	4
EW11	19	75	82	7	82	84	1	1	8	8	32	53	41	3

Table B.8: *Continued*

					Gaze (%)					Speech (%)				
					Interv		Patient			Interv		Patient		
Pers	INR	Days	VAS	GR	st	fr	st	fr	Rt	st	fr	st	fr	Rt
EW11	20	78	57	6	−1	90	−1	6	7	−1	42	−1	50	4
EW11	22	85	75	6	86	89	1	1	7	11	15	57	59	4
EW11	25	96	63	5	75	98	7	2	7	12	46	54	33	3
EW11	27	103	62	3	68	97	1	13	7	7	19	72	71	4
EW11	28	110	75	5	76	88	21	15	6	11	34	60	46	4
EW11	29	113	76	5	−1	73	−1	2	6	−1	14	−1	70	4
EW11	30	117	72	5	73	87	2	15	7	14	24	70	64	3
EW11	31	120	63	4	44	32	1	7	7	14	28	65	64	3
EW11	32	1	56	5	30	60	5	2	8	13	12	67	75	2
EW11	33	5	36	3	62	74	18	6	6	17	17	59	70	2
EW11	34	8	25	3	44	91	5	6	7	14	22	59	68	4
EW15	1	1	110	6	76	95	39	34	4	19	18	41	59	3
EW15	2	5	79	5	85	92	35	37	5	22	35	34	39	5
EW15	3	8	92	6	86	89	11	40	5	21	25	31	32	5
EW15	4	12	70	5	78	94	51	54	4	26	15	49	56	3
EW15	5	19	89	5	77	90	40	68	4	21	18	35	36	3
EW15	6	22	92	6	84	79	37	44	5	20	30	23	42	5
EW15	7	23	64	3	67	90	54	67	4	17	28	27	53	4
EW15	8	26	92	5	66	83	57	63	4	20	26	39	39	4
EW15	9	30	75	5	84	93	64	73	3	16	24	40	46	4
EW15	10	47	70	4	73	85	53	82	4	29	41	36	31	4
EW15	11	57	27	3	83	92	61	76	2	22	30	48	46	4
EW15	12	64	59	4	86	90	66	79	4	23	28	35	43	5
EW15	13	66	22	3	85	94	65	85	2	23	22	39	53	2
EW15	14	1	20	3	69	83	63	61	5	23	28	36	60	4
EW15	15	3	12	3	76	86	76	53	4	30	20	35	65	4
EW15	16	6	10	3	82	93	47	50	3	20	17	44	58	3
EW15	17	10	20	4	76	82	61	52	4	31	27	38	49	3
EW15	18	13	10	3	85	95	57	63	4	26	18	41	55	4
EW18	1	1	22	5	86	89	80	70	3	8	20	50	53	5
EW18	2	4	50	6	84	95	88	93	3	12	29	33	36	6
EW18	3	7	35	6	92	98	81	85	3	10	33	48	33	6
EW18	4	11	25	5	82	68	74	89	2	11	59	53	19	5
EW18	5	14	41	5	90	91	84	88	3	21	47	51	27	4
EW18	6	18	52	5	84	81	69	81	3	11	49	50	35	4
EW18	7	21	45	6	87	88	76	84	4	24	36	60	50	4
EW18	8	25	43	5	81	65	77	94	2	11	53	54	18	4
EW18	9	33	36	3	86	69	85	89	3	11	39	54	33	4
EW18	10	36	46	6	89	86	72	82	4	19	43	58	54	4
EW18	11	39	42	4	80	61	78	87	2	15	40	47	30	4
EW18	12	42	36	4	77	85	77	83	4	20	39	49	36	4
EW18	13	46	33	4	80	84	70	90	4	18	45	58	35	4
EW18	14	1	29	3	71	83	79	82	4	23	45	41	42	4
EW18	15	6	24	3	83	97	78	78	3	20	14	46	62	4
EW18	16	10	21	3	78	90	78	79	3	21	20	50	47	4
EW18	17	13	18	3	89	96	75	51	3	20	16	60	59	3
EW19	1	1	110	8	76	93	42	49	5	14	21	36	51	5
EW19	2	4	89	7	87	87	49	60	5	28	42	33	28	5
EW19	3	8	47	6	88	87	64	66	4	19	29	37	41	4

Table B.8: *Continued*

Pers	INR	Days	VAS	GR	Gaze (%)					Speech (%)				
					Interv Patient					Interv Patient				
					st	fr	st	fr	Rt	st	fr	st	fr	Rt
EW19	4	11	41	4	83	83	44	52	4	24	47	42	35	4
EW19	5	15	35	6	82	90	57	46	5	14	28	42	39	4
EW19	6	18	37	4	93	91	57	62	3	18	21	45	34	4
EW19	7	22	30	6	82	71	49	62	4	16	58	44	21	4
EW19	8	25	45	6	84	94	58	55	4	16	11	43	47	5
EW19	9	29	67	6	78	86	54	62	4	19	29	36	35	4
EW19	10	32	46	5	90	98	65	77	3	17	20	41	47	4
EW19	11	36	26	5	85	90	65	60	4	20	27	43	37	4
EW19	12	39	33	4	87	98	67	56	2	13	10	50	56	4
EW19	13	43	37	7	85	91	46	30	5	26	26	43	33	5
EW19	14	46	41	7	85	94	53	28	5	13	12	37	31	6
EW19	16	53	27	4	88	95	48	40	3	9	12	52	41	5
EW19	17	57	22	4	80	86	63	69	5	15	52	43	23	4
EW19	18	60	19	2	86	92	61	65	4	17	28	39	38	4
EW19	19	64	20	4	87	98	68	57	2	18	12	43	50	4
EW19	20	67	25	5	91	92	61	63	4	17	19	45	43	5
EW19	21	71	17	3	84	86	72	66	3	18	16	50	49	3
EW19	22	74	18	4	91	97	66	51	3	14	13	43	53	4
EW19	23	78	15	3	76	90	82	65	4	33	30	40	42	4
EW20	1	1	99	7	89	90	72	58	5	16	30	56	59	2
EW20	2	5	77	5	93	95	86	56	4	14	15	57	62	4
EW20	3	9	51	5	89	88	72	63	4	11	21	59	72	2
EW20	4	12	41	6	94	100	66	34	5	14	12	69	72	3
EW20	5	16	30	5	93	89	68	60	4	10	14	59	69	3
EW20	6	19	35	5	96	99	63	53	4	10	11	68	70	3
EW20	7	23	22	5	91	95	78	62	4	13	28	65	64	3
EW20	8	26	20	5	91	100	67	43	4	15	11	64	75	3
EW20	9	30	15	5	90	100	62	46	3	12	4	65	85	3
EW20	10	33	12	5	94	98	38	25	5	12	11	71	87	3
EW20	11	37	6	3	92	96	66	47	3	11	12	62	73	2
EW20	12	40	2	3	90	97	63	65	3	11	8	64	79	2
EW20	13	44	0	3	86	93	73	43	4	17	13	66	70	3
EW20	14	1	3	3	85	93	75	56	4	20	30	64	64	4
EW20	15	6	0	3	94	93	56	39	4	18	13	72	77	2
EW20	16	10	1	4	86	74	34	33	5	27	36	67	53	4
EW20	17	13	1	4	93	100	55	38	4	15	8	75	88	3
EW23	1	1	55	8	85	99	6	1	9	19	20	25	22	7
EW23	2	4	64	7	89	100	58	53	7	11	9	25	31	5
EW23	3	8	59	8	86	99	34	22	7	13	27	19	19	6
EW23	19	99	18	5	65	99	46	37	5	20	31	23	21	5
EW23	20	106	14	5	70	99	11	50	6	18	24	25	37	5
EW41	1	1	26	5	89	97	59	66	4	7	19	65	58	4
EW41	2	4	22	3	90	100	61	55	5	12	11	70	83	2
EW41	3	8	21	5	80	93	61	73	2	8	21	65	70	4
EW41	4	11	16	3	86	97	41	59	4	5	14	77	74	2
EW41	5	22	13	3	88	-1	46	-1	4	6	-1	68	-1	2
EW41	6	25	0	2	91	97	50	59	4	9	22	69	60	2
EW41	7	29	83	7	85	98	27	41	5	10	30	38	29	6
EW41	8	32	113	7	85	-1	6	-1	7	12	-1	19	-1	7

Table B.8: *Continued*

Pers	INR	Days	VAS	GR	Gaze (%)					Speech (%)				
					Interv		Patient			Interv		Patient		
					st	fr	st	fr	Rt	st	fr	st	fr	Rt
EW41	9	43	83	6	87	−1	59	−1	6	29	−1	30	−1	6
EW41	10	57	52	6	80	99	68	76	4	18	36	39	32	5
EW41	11	60	53	7	86	−1	54	−1	5	21	−1	42	−1	5
EW41	12	64	30	3	92	96	56	67	4	11	20	68	68	3
EW41	15	85	0	2	88	98	59	51	4	15	15	61	76	4
EW41	16	92	0	3	77	93	50	48	3	20	37	55	40	4
EW41	17	99	14	5	81	96	61	82	4	20	52	33	24	6
EW41	18	109	11	4	88	91	49	57	5	19	46	39	38	5
EW41	19	113	4	5	90	94	58	70	4	24	36	49	33	4
EW41	20	1	12	2	90	97	45	47	5	20	24	72	77	2
EW41	21	5	8	5	83	82	53	59	4	26	29	41	51	4
EW42	1	1	107	8	74	64	45	32	3	9	9	49	61	5
EW42	2	3	108	8	89	94	31	23	7	14	14	45	60	5
EW42	3	5	113	8	71	84	22	28	7	14	21	41	29	5
EW42	4	8	112	8	89	96	29	32	5	15	31	37	56	5
EW42	5	10	88	5	65	75	18	24	5	8	19	47	24	5
EW42	6	12	106	8	70	98	11	15	7	7	20	37	55	5
EW42	7	15	87	8	85	97	15	29	7	12	21	49	29	7
EW42	8	17	87	8	−1	97	6	6	7	43	23	29	17	5
EW42	9	19	87	8	99	97	25	21	5	10	35	55	23	7
EW42	10	22	77	8	98	96	17	42	7	8	31	54	35	5
EW42	11	24	58	8	91	89	12	17	5	8	26	43	37	5
EW42	12	26	52	8	87	93	12	27	7	7	29	45	37	7
EW42	14	31	58	5	88	92	10	15	5	8	18	55	48	7
EW42	15	33	58	5	82	88	15	19	5	12	38	33	12	7
EW42	16	43	53	8	86	93	30	17	5	14	26	42	35	7
EW42	18	57	57	8	76	96	27	27	7	10	18	40	42	5
EW42	19	64	50	5	89	48	19	20	7	13	32	45	35	5
EW42	20	71	49	5	82	52	11	9	5	7	20	48	31	7
EW42	21	78	54	5	90	90	10	18	5	9	33	37	31	5
EW42	22	85	54	3	92	92	18	27	5	10	36	40	29	5
EW42	23	92	53	3	91	93	26	52	5	15	38	32	23	5
EW42	24	108	15	3	92	82	34	35	5	12	22	40	43	5
EW43	1	1	85	6	80	95	40	36	4	18	17	67	57	3
EW43	2	3	110	7	83	96	17	35	5	12	16	66	76	2
EW43	3	6	96	7	91	93	12	30	5	8	20	81	75	5
EW43	4	10	77	7	93	87	16	11	6	12	19	67	46	5
EW43	5	17	75	5	72	87	30	24	6	10	18	47	44	3
EW43	6	22	58	3	76	95	55	42	5	8	6	76	81	2
EW43	7	24	45	3	78	100	46	47	4	8	8	68	77	2
EW43	8	27	37	3	82	99	55	45	4	8	8	72	81	2
EW43	9	31	30	3	83	98	61	46	4	7	5	81	84	3
EW43	11	38	12	4	85	85	62	68	4	11	36	76	63	2
KM32	2	5	24	3	71	95	54	45	4	17	16	54	67	4
KM32	3	8	27	3	90	87	59	67	2	15	20	52	56	3
KM33	1	1	10	3	72	92	85	77	4	21	14	29	48	5
KM33	2	3	17	3	79	95	73	73	4	17	16	30	51	4
KM33	3	6	24	3	84	−1	79	−1	2	20	−1	32	−1	4
KM35	1	1	39	3	71	90	51	49	4	11	10	50	74	5

Table B.8: *Continued*

Pers	INR	Days	VAS	GR	Gaze (%) Interv st	fr	Patient st	fr	Rt	Speech (%) Interv st	fr	Patient st	fr	Rt
KM35	2	4	20	3	79	99	52	51	5	10	5	55	74	5
KM35	3	7	18	3	88	97	64	57	2	14	8	63	81	3
KM35	4	11	23	3	80	99	60	61	4	11	14	62	74	4
KM39	1	1	10	3	86	95	51	59	6	8	20	76	64	4
KM39	2	4	9	3	86	96	48	53	4	13	16	71	79	5
KM39	3	7	6	3	87	96	39	56	6	7	11	74	76	4
KM39	4	11	7	3	88	99	48	53	4	7	14	77	80	3
KM40	1	1	45	4	84	99	57	37	6	11	10	49	78	5
KM40	2	3	49	4	82	99	63	50	4	9	10	60	81	4
KW34	1	1	12	3	84	89	31	20	6	9	21	72	61	4
KW34	2	4	7	3	90	96	31	40	7	8	21	69	62	4
KW34	4	11	6	3	84	99	23	40	6	14	23	60	70	4
KW36	1	1	6	3	74	97	60	44	3	15	16	56	66	4
KW36	2	5	7	3	86	99	78	62	3	16	18	57	68	2
KW36	3	8	6	3	71	97	66	45	4	20	18	61	62	4
KW36	4	11	3	3	80	95	72	59	4	25	19	49	62	5
KW37	1	1	46	3	65	98	64	74	3	25	23	52	52	4
KW37	2	5	13	3	84	99	63	67	2	20	25	36	49	5
KW37	3	8	13	3	84	98	71	70	4	15	24	43	57	4
KW37	4	12	4	3	63	99	58	64	2	17	21	40	55	4
KW38	2	1	20	3	84	98	44	52	4	14	20	53	62	4
KW38	3	4	18	3	60	92	55	46	5	18	20	55	65	4
NM 2	1	1	59	6	88	99	16	12	6	8	5	53	75	4
NM 2	2	5	68	6	−1	99	−1	7	6	−1	14	−1	54	5
NM 2	3	29	75	5	90	99	24	16	6	13	13	37	52	5
NM 2	4	63	55	4	93	−1	9	−1	6	7	−1	54	−1	4
NM 2	5	119	55	4	88	99	10	13	6	11	21	40	42	5
NM 2	6	−1	40	3	93	99	1	1	7	11	4	62	53	4
NM 3	1	1	28	6	88	99	55	43	4	8	61	63	26	3
NM 3	2	10	38	5	86	99	52	46	4	15	32	34	44	4
NM 3	3	27	78	6	82	99	55	42	6	20	21	43	57	6
NM 3	4	54	24	3	82	99	58	34	4	17	14	39	52	4
NM 3	5	103	29	3	89	99	55	42	4	12	25	38	52	3
NM 3	6	−1	25	3	91	99	50	51	4	10	13	44	68	5
NM 6	1	1	75	7	91	99	7	3	7	15	26	18	9	7
NM 6	2	8	88	7	86	−1	5	−1	6	25	−1	19	−1	6
NM 6	4	66	108	6	90	98	1	2	6	9	23	31	49	4
NM 6	6	−1	68	5	86	94	8	2	6	14	25	23	38	6
NM 6	7	−1	68	6	88	99	7	4	6	18	18	22	59	5
NM 7	1	1	96	7	93	96	0	5	8	10	22	58	66	5
NM 7	2	7	71	7	90	97	8	13	6	8	30	70	57	2
NM 7	3	28	111	8	88	94	0	9	9	8	4	23	40	6
NM 7	4	61	55	4	92	99	25	22	6	9	24	65	56	4
NM 7	5	85	23	3	95	97	27	35	4	7	18	69	61	3
NM 7	6	−1	83	6	92	98	29	21	5	15	14	36	50	5
NM 7	7	−1	108	7	95	99	1	0	8	15	13	30	37	4
NM 9	1	1	112	7	87	99	8	6	7	16	18	17	17	7
NM 9	2	7	107	7	89	99	2	1	7	12	17	17	10	6
NM 9	4	74	68	6	91	99	10	2	6	11	24	22	15	6

Table B.8: *Continued*

Pers	INR	Days	VAS	GR	st	fr	st	fr	Rt	st	fr	st	fr	Rt
						Gaze (%)					Speech (%)			
					Interv		Patient			Interv		Patient		
NM 9	5	117	58	3	91	99	22	14	5	14	22	28	34	5
NM 9	6	−1	63	4	91	99	27	25	5	12	11	30	49	5
NM11	1	1	75	6	94	99	21	11	5	4	5	68	67	2
NM11	2	4	76	5	97	99	42	16	4	10	23	53	53	4
NM11	3	29	85	4	97	99	23	36	4	7	38	44	47	4
NM11	4	48	−1	5	96	99	21	28	5	8	7	36	34	4
NM11	5	95	66	4	95	98	16	7	5	12	10	49	40	5
NM11	6	−1	68	6	95	99	11	11	4	8	13	45	69	5
NM11	7	−1	89	6	96	97	24	13	5	11	15	37	38	5
NM13	1	1	81	8	91	98	29	30	5	11	22	48	47	5
NM13	2	13	25	5	79	90	44	37	4	16	13	60	72	4
NM13	3	30	40	5	89	99	31	29	4	16	18	54	41	4
NM13	4	44	21	3	88	99	41	62	4	17	38	52	47	4
NM13	5	57	33	5	87	99	40	55	4	15	20	52	72	8
NM13	7	−1	73	3	91	97	39	53	3	17	17	44	65	5
NM14	1	1	99	8	96	93	40	76	5	7	37	50	29	4
NM14	2	8	90	7	96	97	42	33	−1	8	11	45	36	5
NM14	3	41	70	6	94	99	42	42	4	8	12	53	41	5
NM14	4	64	53	5	95	−1	50	−1	5	9	−1	53	−1	4
NM14	5	107	79	5	81	94	29	34	5	9	19	49	44	5
NM14	6	−1	68	6	89	99	27	40	4	9	8	44	53	4
NM17	1	1	87	6	97	94	8	1	7	5	19	47	21	4
NM17	2	7	113	7	93	96	1	0	7	7	21	42	25	5
NM17	3	31	115	7	88	−1	1	−1	8	13	−1	13	−1	6
NM17	4	57	49	6	85	86	1	0	8	12	19	31	22	5
NM17	5	94	47	5	83	96	9	16	6	7	10	40	66	4
NM17	6	−1	78	3	89	99	4	0	8	15	8	42	49	4
NW 4	1	1	73	7	96	96	35	36	4	5	6	77	77	2
NW 4	2	14	54	6	96	99	47	50	4	6	4	64	73	3
NW 4	3	40	40	7	95	70	39	14	6	6	3	65	52	4
NW 4	4	62	102	7	93	99	16	24	6	5	10	52	71	4
NW 4	5	112	68	6	91	99	40	51	5	11	18	64	77	4
NW 4	6	−1	103	6	93	99	39	55	4	11	15	60	70	4
NW 5	1	1	60	3	92	99	77	57	4	9	14	64	75	3
NW 5	2	7	16	3	93	93	60	72	4	8	21	74	65	4
NW 5	3	18	19	3	90	99	52	40	4	11	11	75	82	4
NW 5	4	36	25	3	95	99	61	57	4	9	8	62	71	4
NW 5	5	79	29	3	93	99	44	39	4	14	10	50	74	4
NW 5	6	−1	19	3	90	99	65	51	5	14	7	70	92	5
NW 5	7	−1	52	5	92	99	45	36	4	13	15	70	79	4
NW 8	1	1	59	5	98	99	42	52	4	6	26	49	46	4
NW 8	2	7	67	5	96	99	41	27	5	5	12	62	50	4
NW 8	3	35	13	3	92	99	57	49	4	6	11	47	66	4
NW 8	4	46	29	3	88	99	52	82	4	12	23	64	63	4
NW 8	5	64	18	3	92	99	64	49	4	13	3	62	96	4
NW 8	7	−1	36	3	94	99	48	58	3	15	10	56	82	4
NW10	1	1	91	7	90	98	40	4	6	15	7	30	26	6
NW10	2	7	66	6	87	95	25	14	5	12	11	22	27	5
NW10	3	23	71	7	90	95	7	7	6	13	23	21	16	6

Table B.8: *Continued*

Pers	INR	Days	VAS	GR	Gaze (%)					Speech (%)				
					Interv		Patient			Interv		Patient		
					st	fr	st	fr	Rt	st	fr	st	fr	Rt
NW10	5	129	49	4	92	96	42	55	4	11	21	22	34	5
NW10	6	−1	78	4	93	98	37	57	5	14	20	15	34	5
NW10	7	−1	68	7	88	98	10	3	7	18	30	17	18	7
NW18	1	1	53	6	95	99	50	45	5	8	8	75	67	4
NW18	2	7	113	7	91	96	3	2	7	8	10	62	61	4
NW18	3	21	48	5	92	99	32	53	5	8	14	56	60	5
NW18	4	46	34	4	93	99	35	27	5	11	20	66	53	5
NW18	5	74	74	4	86	96	25	43	5	19	27	36	55	5
NW18	6	−1	38	5	94	99	27	35	4	12	10	44	65	5
NW19	1	1	108	6	91	99	36	21	5	13	16	44	51	5
NW19	2	8	90	6	93	98	19	18	5	10	11	57	60	4
NW19	3	20	102	6	92	96	23	29	4	8	24	54	39	5
NW19	4	42	61	4	91	97	41	42	4	11	19	56	66	4
NW19	5	69	88	6	89	96	13	36	4	16	34	46	40	4
NW19	6	−1	17	3	93	99	42	36	4	13	8	36	61	5
NW20	1	1	88	7	94	96	11	15	6	10	14	73	68	4
NW20	2	6	43	5	96	98	42	43	5	4	22	90	62	4
NW20	3	22	88	6	97	97	22	10	6	5	16	85	77	2
NW20	5	85	43	3	92	99	42	57	4	7	25	78	68	3
NW20	6	−1	43	3	93	99	46	46	3	10	5	52	84	2

Table B.9 *Individual correlations of gaze, speech, and subjective wellbeing*

Pers (see table B3)
Correlations between relative amounts of gaze (G%) and speech activity (S%) with subjective wellbeing, indicated on Visual Analogue Scale (VAS) and Global Clinical Rating (GR) for each patient (n1), for behavioural measurements (n2) and for subjective data (n3).

Pers	G% vs. VAS	GR	S% vs. VAS	KE	S% vs. B%	ZB vs. KE	n1	n2 (B/S)	n3 (Z/K)
EM 5	.80	.75	.84	.75	.78	.94	25	21	24
EM 6	−.01	.31	.36	.41	.76	.56	39	20	39
EM 7	.71	.69	.81	.70	.60	.86	21	20	21
EM 8	.50	.42	.69	.69	.07	.93	18	18	18
EM13	.71	.87	−.48	−.65	−.47	.71	14	14	14
EM14	−.23	−.28	.68	.50	−.08	.92	18	16	18
EM16	.18	.15	.64	.57	.01	.95	11	11	11
EM17	.84	.88	−.09	.09	.20	.84	13	12	13
EM22	−.07	.00	.45	.49	−.37	.89	20	20	20
EW 9	.50	.50	−.07	.16	.14	.72	38	37	37
EW10	.52	.64	.41	.43	.38	.78	49	45	47

Table B.9: *Continued*

Pers	G% vs. VAS	GR	S% vs. VAS	KE	S% vs. B%	ZB vs. KE	n1	n2 (B/S)	n3 (Z/K)
EW11	.21	.20	.21	.22	.00	.76	34	22	34
EW15	.62	.70	.33	.25	.31	.89	18	18	18
EW18	−.02	−.01	.14	.00	−.58	.63	17	17	17
EW19	.60	.62	.62	.51	.22	.73	23	22	23
EW20	−.49	−.14	.67	.33	−.62	.80	17	17	17
EW23	−.24	.09	.22	.33	−.21	.77	5	5	16
EW41	.55	.25	.65	.79	.29	.78	21	19	21
EW42	−.16	−.06	−.08	−.20	.10	.56	24	22	24
EW43	.89	.91	.33	.22	.32	.85	11	10	11
NM 2	−.98	−.79	.81	.37	−.75	.62	7	5	7
NM 3	−.06	−.03	.10	−.49	.09	.63	6	6	6
NM 6	.98	.17	−.67	.50	−.75	.24	5	5	5
NM 7	.76	.82	.78	.61	.38	.92	7	7	7
NM 9	.81	.91	.91	.95	.97	.86	6	5	6
NM11	−.38	.11	.39	.16	.15	.10	7	7	6
NM13	.63	.65	.78	−.07	.38	.51	7	6	7
NM14	.19	−.09	.34	.27	.63	.88	7	6	7
NM17	.45	.40	.28	.42	.57	.49	6	6	6
NW 4	.61	.62	.49	−.13	.51	−.07	6	6	6
NW 5	−.20	.48	.21	−.18	.19	.52	7	7	7
NW 8	.92	.80	−.08	.12	.11	.92	6	6	6
NW10	−.06	.65	−.34	−.40	.35	.39	7	6	7
NW18	.76	.36	.04	−.48	.37	.64	6	6	6
NW19	.58	.77	−.51	−.44	−.36	.96	6	6	6
NW20	.96	.91	−.21	−.44	−.22	.77	7	5	7

Table B.10: *Gestural behaviour*

Frequencies of object (ob), speech (sp) and ambiguously (am) related gestures. Gestures with large (la) and small (sm) spatial extensions and their frequencies adjusted for amount of speech (r). Tot = total number of gestures.
Rating of the amount of gestural activity (Ge) and manipulations (Ma).
Values arranged according to groups.

Pers	INR	State	VAS	Relation				Rel. to am. of speech				Rating	
				ob	sp	am	la	sm	larr	smar	Tot	Ge	Ma
EM 5	2	I	112	1	3	1	2	9	16.7	25.0	41.7	5	9
EM 5	18	II	25	11	19	0	11	3	14.7	25.3	40.0	5	3
EM 5	24	III	20	15	32	1	18	1	22.8	38.0	60.8	5	5
EM 6	6	I	55	2	7	1	2	5	3.8	15.1	18.9	9	7
EM 6	32	II	44	7	19	1	5	3	9.1	40.0	49.1	7	5
EM 6	37	III	25	3	9	1	1	1	1.3	15.2	16.5	5	5
EM 7	1	I	104	0	0	0	0	1	.0	.0	.0	9	7
EM 7	14	II	25	1	10	1	2	1	2.6	10.5	13.2	7	5
EM 7	16	III	12	5	13	1	5	1	6.6	18.4	25.0	6	6
EM 8	13	I	72	0	11	0	0	5	.0	50.0	50.0	7	3
EM 8	2	II	69	0	9	0	0	3	.0	23.1	23.1	9	3
EM 8	19	III	39	2	21	1	2	2	8.3	91.7	100.0	5	6
EM13	2	I	71	10	40	4	9	8	13.8	69.2	83.1	5	4
EM13	11	III	49	9	49	6	16	3	28.1	84.2	112.3	4	5
EM14	2	I	90	5	14	2	5	9	11.4	36.4	47.7	5	6
EM14	14	II	16	8	11	7	8	1	22.9	37.1	60.0	6	7
EM14	16	III	0	28	16	2	30	1	50.8	35.6	86.4	3	5
EM16	2	I	111	15	15	4	23	9	74.2	35.5	109.7	4	4
EM16	5	III	12	25	31	11	37	3	64.9	52.6	117.5	3	6
EM17	2	I	63	7	47	7	2	3	3.5	103.5	107.0	5	8
EM17	8	II	32	21	9	1	24	1	42.9	12.5	55.4	5	8
EM17	12	III	15	18	4	0	8	1	17.0	29.8	46.8	5	6
EM22	1	I	94	6	3	0	6	5	12.8	6.4	19.1	8	3
EM22	19	II	12	24	12	3	21	1	36.2	31.0	67.2	4	1
EM22	17	III	1	3	9	0	4	1	8.0	16.0	24.0	4	5
EW 9	3	I	110	7	5	2	6	7	10.7	14.3	25.0	7	1
EW 9	27	II	19	15	10	0	18	2	31.6	12.3	43.9	5	7
EW 9	36	III	13	23	24	2	22	1	41.5	50.9	92.5	5	6
EW10	2	I	113	17	10	3	27	7	56.3	6.3	62.5	7	7
EW10	41	II	19	29	19	1	18	1	23.1	41.0	64.1	3	5
EW10	15	III	12	16	15	0	7	3	10.9	37.5	48.4	6	6
EW11	2	I	93	0	1	0	0	3	.0	2.3	2.3	9	7
EW11	15	II	48	7	7	1	10	4	16.9	8.5	25.4	8	4
EW11	34	III	25	3	4	0	3	1	4.4	5.9	10.3	6	6
EW15	3	I	92	1	5	2	0	8	.0	25.0	25.0	8	2
EW15	13	II	22	3	9	1	2	3	3.8	20.8	24.5	6	6
EW15	15	III	12	0	5	0	0	1	.0	7.7	7.7	4	5
EW18	2	I	50	11	16	0	5	2	13.9	61.1	75.0	5	5
EW18	13	II	33	3	23	0	7	2	20.0	54.3	74.3	6	6
EW18	15	III	24	3	29	0	3	1	4.8	46.8	51.6	6	4
EW19	2	I	89	12	4	3	10	1	35.7	32.1	67.9	7	6
EW19	22	III	18	3	39	6	3	2	5.7	84.9	90.6	4	6
EW20	2	I	77	19	27	6	8	7	12.9	71.0	83.9	4	5
EW20	12	II	2	46	19	6	36	4	45.6	44.3	89.9	2	6
EW20	16	III	1	23	7	1	19	2	35.8	22.6	58.5	4	6

Table B.10: *Continued*

Pers	INR	State	VAS	Relation				Rel. to am. of speech				Rating	
				ob	sp	am	la	sm	larr	smar	Tot	Ge	Ma
EW23	2	I	64	0	0	0	0	6	.0	.0	.0	9	1
EW23	19	III	18	1	1	0	1	1	4.8	4.8	9.5	9	4
EW41	8	I	113	0	0	0	0	7	.0	.0	.0	8	7
EW41	21	II	8	3	5	2	4	1	7.8	11.8	19.6	6	3
EW41	6	III	0	4	2	2	4	1	6.7	6.7	13.3	4	5
EW42	2	I	108	21	5	5	22	5	36.7	15.0	51.7	5	7
EW42	24	III	15	0	11	0	1	3	2.3	23.3	25.6	7	3
EW43	2	I	110	33	20	8	48	7	63.2	17.1	80.3	2	8
EW43	11	III	12	31	20	5	35	3	55.6	31.7	87.3	5	6
KM32	3	I	27	22	10	1	26	1	46.4	12.5	58.9	3	6
KM32	2	III	24	26	17	7	35	1	52.2	22.4	74.6	2	2
KM33	3	I	24	2	3	1	3	1	9.4	9.4	18.8	4	5
KM33	2	III	17	24	9	0	19	1	37.3	27.5	64.7	4	5
KM35	2	I	20	28	33	11	15	1	20.3	77.0	97.3	5	2
KM35	3	III	18	33	23	8	39	1	48.1	30.9	79.0	4	4
KM39	2	I	9	7	65	2	0	1	.0	93.7	93.7	4	2
KM39	3	III	6	36	48	10	48	1	63.2	60.5	123.7	4	3
KM40	2	I	49	14	22	5	32	1	39.5	11.1	50.6	4	4
KM40	1	III	45	42	29	10	46	3	59.0	44.9	103.8	4	2
KW34	2	I	7	16	10	5	22	1	35.5	14.5	50.0	6	7
KW34	4	III	6	32	10	2	32	1	45.7	17.1	62.9	6	7
KW36	2	I	7	4	14	1	4	1	5.9	22.1	27.9	3	4
KW36	3	III	6	1	8	0	0	1	.0	14.5	14.5	5	5
KW37	2	I	13	2	10	0	1	1	2.0	22.4	24.5	6	6
KW37	3	III	13	4	11	3	0	2	.0	31.6	31.6	5	4
KW38	2	I	20	12	5	3	11	1	17.7	14.5	32.3	4	5
KW38	3	III	18	6	10	4	9	1	13.8	16.9	30.8	6	8
NM 2	3	I	75	4	12	6	11	5	21.2	21.2	42.3	7	8
NM 2	5	II	55	12	4	3	10	2	23.8	21.4	45.2	6	8
NM 2	6	III	40	11	4	6	9	1	17.0	22.6	39.6	5	7
NM 3	3	I	78	28	6	9	22	6	38.6	36.8	75.4	4	7
NM 3	5	II	29	16	18	6	7	1	13.5	63.5	76.9	4	6
NM 3	6	III	25	36	13	3	20	1	29.4	47.1	76.5	4	3
NM 6	4	I	108	20	12	3	14	6	28.6	42.9	71.4	5	5
NM 6	1	II	75	3	8	0	1	5	11.1	111.1	122.2	8	6
NM 6	6	III	68	2	21	0	2	5	5.3	55.3	60.5	6	6
NM 7	3	I	111	8	19	0	14	5	35.0	32.5	67.5	4	4
NM 7	6	II	83	1	4	0	5	5	10.0	.0	10.0	5	7
NM 7	5	III	23	11	12	0	21	3	34.4	3.3	37.7	5	5
NM 9	2	I	107	6	2	0	1	6	10.0	70.0	80.0	7	9
NM 9	6	II	63	10	19	5	7	3	14.3	55.1	69.4	6	5
NM 9	5	III	58	6	2	4	6	2	17.6	17.6	35.3	5	8
NM11	3	I	85	8	6	0	8	5	17.0	12.8	29.8	6	5
NM11	6	II	68	4	3	4	6	3	8.7	7.2	15.9	6	5
NM11	5	III	66	3	4	5	2	5	5.0	25.0	30.0	7	7
NM13	1	I	81	22	10	9	16	3	34.0	53.2	87.2	5	4
NM13	7	II	73	33	4	1	9	1	13.8	44.6	58.5	3	3
NM13	5	III	33	16	2	2	13	7	18.1	9.7	27.8	5	4
NM14	1	I	99	7	3	3	2	7	6.9	37.9	44.8	5	7
NM14	6	II	68	6	11	0	0	5	.0	32.1	32.1	8	7
NM14	4	III	53	7	5	2	2	7	3.8	22.6	26.4	7	4

Table B.10: *Continued*

Pers	INR	State	VAS	Relation					Rel. to am. of speech				Rating	
				ob	sp	am	la	sm	larr	smar	Tot		Ge	Ma
NM17	2	I	113	2	0	0	2	8	8.0	.0	8.0	7	8
NM17	6	II	78	2	1	0	2	1	4.1	2.0	6.1	7	6
NM17	5	III	47	1	9	0	1	2	1.5	13.6	15.2	5	6
NW 4	6	I	103	25	18	1	39	7	55.7	7.1	62.9	3	3
NW 4	4	II	102	2	23	0	5	7	7.0	35.2	42.3	6	5
NW 4	3	III	40	8	23	0	6	8	111.5	448.1	59.6	4	6
NW 5	1	I	60	9	37	0	22	1	229.3	332.0	61.3	3	5
NW 5	3	II	19	9	25	0	14	3	17.1	24.4	41.5	4	5
NW 5	6	III	19	14	29	0	27	3	29.3	17.4	46.7	6	4
NW 8	2	I	67	5	7	0	9	6	18.0	6.0	24.0	6	6
NW 8	7	II	36	42	3	2	40	1	48.8	8.5	57.3	4	4
NW 8	5	III	18	15	16	0	21	2	21.9	10.4	32.3	4	6
NW10	1	I	91	1	9	0	2	3	7.7	30.8	38.5	7	8
NW10	7	II	68	1	2	0	0	1	.0	16.7	16.7	8	8
NW10	2	III	66	4	9	0	11	3	40.7	7.4	48.1	6	8
NW18	2	I	113	1	9	0	4	2	6.6	9.8	16.4	7	5
NW18	5	II	74	7	4	0	7	5	12.7	7.3	20.0	7	6
NW18	6	III	38	3	8	0	4	1	6.2	10.8	16.9	5	6
NW19	3	I	102	10	6	0	13	5	33.3	7.7	41.0	5	7
NW19	4	II	61	9	14	0	8	1	12.1	22.7	34.8	5	7
NW19	6	III	17	17	20	0	14	1	23.0	37.7	60.7	6	6
NW20	3	I	88	9	18	1	12	5	15.6	20.8	36.4	6	7
NW20	5	II	43	11	14	0	19	1	27.9	8.8	36.8	5	5
NW20	6	III	43	9	6	0	5	1	6.0	11.9	17.9	3	5

Table B.11: *Pearson correlations*

N = 90 interviews from states I and III
(correlations r > 0.30 marked by *)

VARIABLE	1	2	3	4	5	6	7	8	9	10	11
1 Visual Anal. Scale	—										
2 Global Clinical Rating	0.82	—									
3 Wellbeing	0.80	0.78	—								
4 Concentr. Efficiency	0.77	0.79	0.81	—							
5 Activity Soc. contact	0.65	0.75	0.64	0.67	—						
6 Emotion Future expect.	0.63	0.70	0.64	0.64	0.71	—					
7 Somat. compl. Sleep	0.55	0.63	0.70	0.63	0.52	0.49	—				
8 Gen. fac. act. MIAX	−0.11	−0.20	−0.17	−0.16	−0.16	−0.15	−0.18	—			
9 AU 12 (Smile)	−0.47	−0.57	−0.45	−0.45	−0.42	−0.43	−0.37	−0.57	—		
10 Fac. Repertoire 2	−0.05	−0.15	−0.07	−0.07	−0.10	−0.10	−0.13	0.68	0.30	—	
11 Gaze (G%) of Patient	−0.55	−0.44	−0.46	−0.37	−0.27	−0.38	−0.27	0.12	0.33	0.09	—
12 Speech Activity (S%)	−0.42	−0.42	−0.39	−0.35	−0.35	−0.42	−0.28	0.06	0.25	0.04	0.24
13 Rel. Gest. Act. (GAR)	−0.10	−0.03	−0.16	−0.09	0.11	0.03	−0.21	0.16	−0.04	0.13	0.22
14 Rat. Facial Variability	0.45	0.57	0.43	0.50	0.39	0.49	0.44	−0.33	−0.41	−0.23	−0.21
15 Rating of Gaze	0.47	0.50	0.38	0.39	0.44	0.45	0.35	−0.15	−0.32	−0.20	−0.67
16 Rating of Speech Act.	0.33	0.36	0.30	0.31	0.33	0.38	0.27	−0.16	−0.24	−0.07	−0.33
17 Rat. Interruptions	0.36	0.27	0.34	0.26	0.22	0.22	0.23	−0.21	−0.18	−0.03	−0.38
18 Rat. of Gestural Act.	0.36	0.38	0.34	0.34	0.17	0.32	0.36	−0.08	−0.25	−0.04	−0.45
19 Rat. of Manipulations	0.21	0.18	0.19	0.12	0.18	0.06	0.18	0.04	−0.07	−0.01	−0.29
20 Rat. Foot/Leg Movem.	0.01	0.02	0.07	0.08	0.10	0.01	0.09	0.02	−0.08	0.01	0.03
21 Rat. Position Change	0.13	0.13	0.16	0.16	0.13	0.16	0.13	−0.08	−0.16	0.00	−0.04

VARIABLE	12	13	14	15	16	17	18	19	20	21
12 Speech Activity (S%)	—									
13 Rel. Gest. Act. (GAR)	0.12	—								
14 Rat. Facial Variability	−0.32	−0.07	—							
15 Rating of Gaze	−0.21	−0.11	0.30	—						
16 Rating of Speech Act.	−0.62	−0.11	0.41	0.37	—					
17 Rat. Interruptions	−0.33	−0.27	0.35	0.30	0.51	—				
18 Rat. of Gestural Act.	−0.40	−0.48	0.46	0.46	0.43	0.43	—			
19 Rat. of Manipulations	−0.14	−0.09	−0.02	0.28	0.09	0.09	0.14	—		
20 Rat. Foot/Leg Movem.	−0.01	0.00	−0.07	−0.04	−0.15	−0.17	−0.14	0.06	—	
21 Rat. Position Change	−0.06	0.05	−0.12	0.02	−0.06	−0.14	−0.14	0.26	0.42	—

Table B.11: *Continued*

N = 90 interviews from states I and III
(correlations r > 0.30 marked by *)

VARIABLE	1	2	3	4	5	6	7	8	9	10	11
1 Visual Anal. Scale	–										
2 Global Clinical Rating	0.86	–									
3 Wellbeing	0.82	0.81	–								
4 Concentr. Efficiency	0.81	0.80	0.82	–							
5 Activity Soc. contact	0.69	0.76	0.68	0.68	–						
6 Emotion Future expect.	0.67	0.66	0.66	0.64	0.75	–					
7 Somat. compl. Sleep	0.60	0.65	0.70	0.64	0.57	0.51	–				
8 Gen. fac. act. MIAK	–0.17	–0.26	–0.23	–0.21	–0.18	–0.17	–0.22	–			
9 AU 12 (Smile)	–0.49	–0.60	–0.47	–0.48	–0.45	–0.42	–0.39	0.60	–		
10 Fac. Repertoire 2	–0.08	–0.17	–0.11	–0.08	–0.09	–0.09	–0.13	0.66	0.33	–	
11 Gaze (G%) of Patient	–0.52	–0.40	–0.41	–0.38	–0.26	–0.31	–0.26	0.16	0.33	0.12	–
12 Speech Activity (S%)	–0.41	–0.41	–0.45	–0.38	–0.36	–0.41	–0.34	0.09	0.26	0.06	0.18
13 Rel. Gest. Act. (GAR)	–0.08	–0.02	–0.12	–0.08	0.09	0.06	–0.24	0.11	–0.09	0.12	0.21
14 Rat. Facial Variability	0.48	0.57	0.46	0.52	0.44	0.52	0.44	–0.39	–0.45	–0.25	–0.20
15 Rating of Gaze	0.47	0.48	0.35	0.40	0.47	0.39	0.36	–0.23	–0.34	–0.19	–0.67
16 Rating of Speech Act.	0.28	0.31	0.28	0.34	0.35	0.33	0.31	–0.22	–0.22	–0.13	–0.24
17 Rat. Interruptions	0.28	0.25	0.28	0.29	0.21	0.19	0.24	–0.31	–0.14	–0.09	–0.24
18 Rat. of Gestural Act.	0.35	0.36	0.34	0.36	0.21	0.28	0.39	–0.13	–0.21	–0.07	–0.41
19 Rat. of Manipulations	0.22	0.18	0.22	0.10	0.17	0.06	0.15	0.09	–0.06	0.05	–0.35
20 Rat. Foot/Leg Movem.	0.01	0.05	0.10	0.08	0.13	0.04	0.09	0.02	–0.09	–0.03	0.01
21 Rat. Position Change	0.19	0.22	0.27	0.24	0.19	0.25	0.20	–0.05	–0.19	0.00	–0.07

VARIABLE	12	13	14	15	16	17	18	19	20	21
12 Speech Activity (S%)	–									
13 Rel. Gest. Act. (GAR)	0.16	–								
14 Rat. Facial Variability	–0.35	–0.08	–							
15 Rating of Gaze	–0.15	–0.10	0.30	–						
16 Rating of Speech Act.	–0.61	–0.13	0.42	0.31	–					
17 Rat. Interruptions	–0.33	–0.32	0.38	0.21	0.48	–				
18 Rat. of Gestural Act.	–0.37	–0.51	0.49	0.43	0.39	0.45	–			
19 Rat. of Manipulations	–0.12	–0.10	–0.06	0.26	0.06	0.08	0.13	–		
20 Rat. Foot/Leg Movem.	–0.06	0.02	–0.09	0.01	–0.14	–0.23	–0.21	0.10	–	
21 Rat. Position Change	–0.08	0.06	–0.10	0.08	–0.08	–0.15	–0.21	0.32	0.40	

Table B.12: *Change ratios for nonverbal parameters and subjective wellbeing on Visual Analogue Scale*

(Abbreviations see Appendix A 2)

Change ratios (III-I):I

Pers	VAS	MIAX	AU12 6	REP2	G%	S%	GAR
EM 5	−.82	.44	5.00	5.00	.61	1.70	.46
EM 6	−.55	.30	4.00	−.40	.50	.27	−.13
EM 7	−.88	.50	6.00	.33	1.17	15.75	25.00
EM 8	−.46	3.33	.50	1.00	−.30	−.37	1.00
EM13	−.31	.02	−.88	.00	.51	−.24	.35
EM14	−1.00	−.79	−1.00	−.80	.05	.61	.81
EM16	−.89	.04	1.50	−.50	.41	2.22	.07
EM17	−.76	.17	.17	.50	1.48	−.08	−.56
EM22	−.99	.17	.00	2.00	.33	.15	.25
EW 9	−.88	1.00	4.00	.33	.06	.18	2.70
EW10	−.89	−.34	2.00	−.29	2.06	.53	−.23
EW11	−.73	.67	13.00	.33	.00	.02	3.43
EW15	−.87	.71	.33	.67	5.91	.13	−.69
EW18	−.52	.12	1.00	−.40	−.11	.39	−.31
EW19	−.80	.33	8.00	1.50	.35	.30	.33
EW20	−.99	−.07	3.00	.00	−.60	.18	−.30
EW23	−.72	−.67	3.00	−.50	−.21	−.08	9.52
EW41	−1.00	3.67	10.00	1.00	7.33	2.63	13.33
EW42	−.86	.40	10.00	.00	.10	−.11	−.50
EW43	−.89	.21	9.00	−.33	2.65	.15	.09
KM32	−.11	−.10	−.82	.00	−.08	.04	.27
KM33	−.29	.16	−.50	−.25	−.08	−.06	2.45
KM35	−.10	−.08	−.17	−.40	.23	.15	−.19
KM39	−.33	−.31	−.50	.00	−.19	.04	.32
KM40	−.08	−.29	.00	.00	−.10	−.18	1.05
KW34	−.14	.07	−.26	.75	−.26	−.13	.26
KW36	−.14	−.25	−.28	.25	−.15	.07	−.48
KW37	.00	−.57	−.22	−.44	.13	.19	.29
KW38	−.10	−.20	.50	−.40	.25	.04	−.05
NM 2	−.47	−.43	−.67	1.00	−.96	.68	−.06
NM 3	−.68	.62	2.67	1.00	−.09	.02	.01
NM 6	−.37	−.19	2.00	.50	7.00	−.26	−.15
NM 7	−.79	.17	5.00	.00	27.00	2.00	−.44
NM 9	−.46	.07	9.00	.25	10.00	.65	−.56
NM11	−.22	−.59	−.82	.00	−.30	.11	.01
NM13	−.59	−.14	1.00	−.50	.38	.08	−.68
NM14	−.46	.18	3.00	.00	.25	.06	−.41
NM17	−.58	−.53	−.67	−.20	8.00	−.05	.89
NW 4	−.61	−.58	−.83	−.40	.00	.08	−.05
NW 5	−.68	.48	−.13	.50	−.16	.09	−.24
NW 8	−.73	−.05	1.67	.33	.56	.00	.35
NW10	−.27	−.18	.33	−.25	−.38	−.27	.25
NW18	−.66	−.56	.00	−.50	8.00	−.29	.03
NW19	−.83	−.19	−.40	−.14	.83	−.33	.48
NW20	−.51	.06	3.00	−.50	1.09	−.39	−.51

Change Ratios (II-I):I

Pers	VAS	MIAX	AU12 6	REP2	G%	S%	GAR
EM 5	−.78	.31	4.00	4.00	.89	1.44	−.04
EM 6	−.20	.15	2.50	−.20	1.70	.04	1.60

Table B.12: *Continued*

(Abbreviations see Appendix A 5)

Change ratios (II-I):I

Pers	VAS	MIAX	AU12 6	REP2	G%	S%	GAR
EM 7	−.76	.30	5.00	.00	.96	16.00	13.16
EM 8	−.04	3.17	−.50	1.00	.18	−.17	−.54
EM14	−.82	−.57	1.00	−.60	−.13	.29	.26
EM17	−.49	.61	.50	.25	1.55	−.08	−.48
EM22	−.87	1.06	10.00	7.00	.28	.04	2.51
EW 9	−.83	.19	4.00	−.33	−.18	.30	.75
EW10	−.83	−.52	8.00	−.57	3.28	.58	.03
EW11	−.48	.39	−1.00	.33	−.40	−.05	9.93
EW15	−.76	−.07	.67	.33	4.91	.26	−.02
EW18	−.34	.19	.00	.20	−.20	.76	−.01
EW20	−.97	.00	5.00	−.25	−.27	.12	.07
EW41	−.93	2.00	8.00	.00	7.83	1.16	19.61
NM 2	−.27	−.29	−.42	.00	−.58	.08	.07
NM 3	−.63	.19	3.67	.33	.00	−.12	.02
NM 6	−.31	.13	1.00	.25	6.00	−.42	.71
NM 7	−.25	−.33	.00	.00	29.00	.57	−.85
NM 9	−.41	.59	14.00	.75	12.50	.76	−.13
NM11	−.20	−.21	−.64	.25	−.52	.02	−.46
NM13	−.10	.71	1.00	1.00	.34	−.08	−.33
NM14	−.31	.05	1.00	−.33	−.32	−.12	−.28
NM17	−.31	−.44	−.50	−.40	3.00	.00	−.23
NW 4	−.01	−.08	−.50	−.40	−.59	−.13	−.33
NW 5	−.68	.20	−.13	.25	−.32	.17	−.32
NW 8	−.46	−.05	1.33	.00	.17	−.10	1.39
NW10	−.25	−.14	−.33	.50	−.75	−.43	−.57
NW18	−.35	.09	2.00	−.17	7.33	−.42	.22
NW19	−.40	−.13	.00	.00	.78	.04	−.15
NW20	−.51	1.13	2.00	.50	.91	−.08	.01

Table B.13: *Median values*

Median differences from comparing medians for female and male subjects. E, N = patients, C = controls (abbreviations see Appendix A5)

MEDIAN VALUES

	Group	Total			Male			Female			Med-Diff Fem-Male		
		I	II	III	I	II	III	I	II	III	I	II	III
MIAK E	18	18	21	25	17.5	23	23	17.5	19	28	0	−4.0	+5.0
N	25	25	23	18	26	22	16	24	27	17.8	−2.0	+5.0	+1.8
E+N	19.5	19.5	22.5	23.5	19	22.7	22	19.5	21.5	24	+0.5	−1.2	+2.0
C	35	35	–	28	28	–	25	46.5	–	35	+18.5	–	+10
AU 12 E	0.9	0.9	5.0	4.5	1.7	5.8	5	0.4	4.8	4.3	−1.3	−1.0	−0.7
N	2.9	2.9	5.5	4.0	2	3.8	4	3.3	6	4	+1.3	+2.2	0
E+N	1.6	1.6	5.1	4.3	1.8	4.5	4.5	1.5	5.5	4.3	−0.3	+1	−0.2
C	12.0	12.0	–	12.0	11.7	–	6	18.5	–	16	+6.8	–	+10
REP 2 E	3.3	3.3	3.8	3.8	3.8	4.3	3.7	3.1	3.3	3.9	−0.7	−1.0	+0.2
N	4.0	4.0	4.5	3.8	3.7	4	4.5	4.3	5.5	3.3	+0.6	+1.5	−1.2
E+N	3.7	3.7	4.1	3.8	3.7	4.1	3.9	3.7	4.0	3.7	0	−0.1	−0.2
C	4.4	4.4	–	4.3	4.3	–	3.8	4.5	–	5	+0.2	–	+1.2
G% E	33	33	51	53	34.3	47	52	31	63	54	−3.3	+16	+2
N	24	24	27	33	23	23	22	39	41	42	+16	+18	+20
E+N	30	30	41	46	28.5	34	42.5	35	45	48	+6.5	+11	+5.5
C	59	59	–	57	59	–	57	53.5	–	60.5	−5.5	–	+3.5
S% E	41	41	53	57	44.5	48	57	40	55	47	−4.5	+7	−10
N	46	46	43	51	42	40	49	61.5	55	52	+19.5	+15	+3
E+N	43	43	45	52	41.5	44	53	49.5	55.5	49.5	+8.0	+11.5	−3.5
C	55	55	–	55	55	–	54	55	–	57.5	0	–	+3.5
GAR E	49	49	47	50	47.7	49	61	51.7	44	48.4	+4	−5	−12.6
N	44	44	39	37	67.5	45.2	35.3	38.5	36.8	46.7	−29	−8.4	+11.4
E+N	45	45	41	40	48.9	47.2	39	39.7	39.1	47.5	−9.2	−8.1	+8.5
C	50	50	–	65	58.9	–	79	30.1	–	31.2	−28.8	–	−48.9

Table B.14: *Reduction and substantial change in nonverbal parameters*

Number (n) and proportions (p) of individuals showing reduced values or substantial change in respective behavioural parameters at different states (I to III). Medians for Change Ratios. (abbreviations see Appendix A5)

		Reduction						Substantial change									
		n			p			Increase (+)				Decrease (−)				Median change ratio C R	
								n		p		n		p			
	Group	I	II	III	I	II	III	I-II	I-III	I-II	I-III	I-II	I-III	I-II	I-III	I-II	I-III
MIAK	E	15	8	7	.75	.57	.35	5	9	.36	.45	2	3	.14	.15	+.25	+.17
	N	7	7	10	.44	.44	.63	3	2	.19	.13	2	5	.13	.31	−.01	−.14
	E+N	22	15	17	.61	.50	.47	8	11	.27	.31	4	8	.13	.22	–	–
	C	1	–	1	.11	–	.11	–	0	–	0	–	1	–	.11	–	−.20
AU12	E	18	4	7	.90	.29	.35	10	14	.71	.70	1	2	.07	.10	+4.0	+.33
	N	10	5	7	.63	.31	.44	8	8	.50	.50	1	4	.06	.26	+.50	0
	E+N	28	9	14	.78	.30	.39	18	22	.60	.61	2	6	.07	.17	–	0
	C	0	–	2	0	–	.22	–	0	–	0	–	1	–	.11	–	0
REP2	E	6	3	4	.30	.21	.20	3	6	.21	.30	2	1	.14	.05	0	+.33
	N	3	2	4	.19	.13	.25	4	2	.26	.13	0	0	0	0	0	0
	E+N	9	5	8	.25	.17	.22	7	8	.23	.22	2	1	.07	.03	–	0
	C	0	–	0	0	–	0	–	1	–	.11	–	–	–	0	–	–
G%	E	11	2	5	.55	.14	.25	7	12	.50	.60	0	2	.0	.10	+.89	+.38
	N	10	10	8	.63	.63	.50	8	9	.50	.56	6	3	.38	.19	+.25	+.47
	E+N	21	12	13	.58	.40	.36	15	21	.50	.58	6	5	.20	.14	–	−.09
	C	1	–	1	.11	–	.11	–	0	–	0	–	0	–	0	–	–
S%	E	8	1	2	.40	.07	.10	8	9	.57	.45	0	2	0	.10	+.27	+.18
	N	4	3	3	.25	.19	.19	2	3	.13	.19	3	5	.19	.31	−.08	+.04
	E+N	12	4	5	.33	.13	.14	10	12	.33	.33	3	7	.10	.19	–	+.04
	C	1	–	1	.11	–	.11	–	0	–	0	–	0	–	0	–	–
GAR	E	6	2	5	.30	.14	.25	5	5	.36	.25	0	0	0	0	−.16	+.29
	N	2	4	3	.13	.25	.19	1	0	.06	0	0	0	0	0	−.19	+.27
	E+N	8	7	8	.22	.23	.22	6	5	.20	.14	0	0	0	0	–	+.27
	C	1	–	1	.11	–	.11	–	1	–	.11	–	0	–	0	–	–

References

Abraham, K. (1968). "Notes on the psycho-analytical investigation and treatment of manic-depressive insanity and allied conditions (1911)". In W. Gaylin (ed.), *The meaning of despair: Psychoanalytic contributions to the understanding of depression* New York: Science House.

Addington, D. W. (1968). "The relationship of selected vocal characteristics to personality perception". Speech Monographs, 35, 492-503.

Ahrens, R. (1954). "Beitrag zur Entwicklung des Physiognomie-und Mimikerkennens". Teil I und II. *Zeitschrift für experimentelle und angewandte Psychologie*, 2, 412-54.

Akiskal, H.S. (1979). "A biobehavioral approach to depression". In R.A. Depue (ed.), *The psychobiology of depressive disorders* (pp. 409-37). New York: Academic Press.

Akiskal, H.S., & McKinney, W.T. (1975). "Overview of recent research in depression: Integration of the conceptual models into a comprehensive clinical frame". *Archives of General Psychiatry*, 32, 285-305.

Allport, G.W. (1937). *Personality: A psychological interpretation.* New York: Holt.

Altmann, S.A. (1967). "The structure of primate social communication". In S.A. Altmann (ed.), *Social communication among primates* (pp. 325-62). University of Chicago Press.

Ambrose, J.A. (1961). "The development of the smiling response in early infancy". In B.M. Foss (ed.), *Determinants of infant behaviour.* vol. I. (pp. 179-201). London: Methuen.

American Psychiatric Association (1980). *Diagnostic and statistical manual of mental disorders* (3rd. edn.) Washington, DC: Author.

Anderson, N.H. (1979). "Algebraic rules in psychological measurement". *American Scientist*, 67, 555-63.

Angst, J. (1980). "Verlauf unipolarer depressiver, bipolarer manisch-depressiver und schizo-affektiver Erkrankungen und Psychosen – Ergebnisse einer prospektiven Studie". *Fortschritte der Neurologie und Psychiatrie*, 48, 3-30.

Angst, J., Battegay, R., Bente, D., Berner, P., Broeren, W., Cornu, F., Dick, P., Engelmeier, M.P., Heimann, H., Heinrich, K., Helmchen, H., Hippius, H., Pöldinger, W., Schmidlein, P., Schmitt, W., Weiss, P. (1986). "Das Dokumentations-System der Arbeitsgemeinschaft Methodik und Dokumentation in der Psychiatrie (AMP)". *Arzneimittel-Forschung*, 18, 3-8.

Argyle, M. (1969). *Social interaction.* London: Methuen.

Argyle, M. (1970). "Eye-contact and distance: A reply to Stephenson and Rutter". *British Journal of Psychology*, 61, 395-6.

Argyle, M. (1975). *Bodily communication.* London: Methuen.

Argyle, M. (1979). "New developments in the analysis of social skills". In A. Wolfgang (ed.), *Nonverbal behavior.* (pp. 139-58). New York: Academic Press.

Argyle, M. & Cook, M. (1976). *Gaze and mutual gaze.* Cambridge University Press.

Argyle, M, & Dean, J. (1965) "Eye-contact, distance, and affiliation". *Sociometry*, 28, 289-304.

Argyle M. & Ingham, R. (1972) "Gaze, mutual gaze, and proximity". *Semiotica*, 6, 32-49.

Arieti, S. (1974). "Affective disorders: Manic-depressive psychosis and psychotic depression". In S. Arieti & E.B. Brody (eds.), *American handbook of psychiatry*, vol. 3: *Adult clinical psychiatry.* (pp. 449-90). New York: Basic Books.

Aronson, H., & Weintraub, W. (1967). "Verbal productivity as a measure of change in affective status". *Psychological Reports*, 20, 483-7.

Aronson, H., & Weintrab, W. (1972). "Personal adaptation as reflected in verbal behavior". In A.W. Siegman & B. Pope (eds.), *Studies in dyadic communication* (pp. 265-79). New York: Pergamon Press.

Asendorpf, J., & Wallbott, H.G. (1979). "MaBe der Beobachterübereinstimmung: Ein systematischer Vergleich". *Zeitschrift für Sozialpsychologie*, 10, 243-52.

Avarello, M. (1983). "Nonverbales Verhalten in klinisch-diagnostischen Gesprächssituationen – Eine Eindrucksstudie". Dissertation, Leopold-Franzens-Universität, Innsbruck.

Beattie, G.W. (1978a). "Sequential temporal patterns of speech and gaze in dialogue". *Semiotica*, 23, 30-52.

Beattie, G.W. (1978b). "Floor apportionment and gaze in conversational dyads". *The British Journal of Social and Clinical Psychology*, 17, 7-16.

Beattie, G.W. (1979). "Planning units in spontaneous speech: some evidence from hesitation in speech and speaker gaze direction in conversation". *Linguistics*, 17, 61-78.

Beattie, G.W. (1981). "Sequential temporal patterns of speech and gaze in dialogue". In A. Kendon (ed.), *Nonverbal communication, interaction, and gesture* (pp. 297-320). The Hague: Mouton.

Beattie, G.W., & Bradbury, R.J. (1979). "An experimental investigation of the modificability of the temporal structure of spontaneous speech". *Journal of Psycholinguistic Research*, 8, 225-48.

Beck, A.T. (1974). "The development of depression: A cognitive model". In J. Friedmann & M.M. Katz (eds.), *The psychology of depression: Contempory theory and research* (pp. 3-20). New York: Wiley.

Beck, A.T., Ward, C.H., Mendelson, M., Mock, J., & Erbaugh, J. (1961). "An inventory for measuring depression". *Archives of General Psychiatry*, 4, 561-71.

Bem, D.J. (1983). "Further *déjà vu* in the search for cross-situational consistency: A response to Mischel and Peake". *Psychological Review*, 90, 390-3.

Bem D.J., & Allen, A. (1974). "On predicting some of the people some of the time: The search for cross-situational consistencies in behaviour". *Psychological Review*, 81, 506-20.

Bem, D.J., & Funder, D.C. (1978). "Predicting more of the people more of the time: Assessing the personality of situations". *Psychological Review*, 85, 485-501.

Berger, C.R. (1979). "Beyond initial interaction: Uncertainty, understanding, and the development of interpersonal relationships". In H. Giles & R.N. StClair (eds.), *Language and social psychology* (pp. 122-44). Oxford: Basil Blackwell.

Best, D. (1978). *Philosophy and human movement*. London: George Allen & Unwin.

Bleuler, E. (1969). *Lehrbuch der Psychiatrie*. (11th edn). Berlin: Springer.

Blöschl, L. (1976). "Zur intra-und extrafamiliären Kontaktstruktur depressiver Patientinnen". *Psychologische Beiträge*, 18, 465-80.

Blöschl, L. (1978). *Psychosoziale Aspekte der Depression*. Bern: Huber.

Bond, M.H., & Komai, H. (1976). "Targets of gazing and eye contact during interviews: Effects on Japanese nonverbal behavior". *Journal of Personality and Social Psychology*, 34, 1276-85.

Boomer, D.S. (1963). "Speech disturbance and body movement in interviews". *Journal of Nervous and Mental Disease*, 136, 263-6.

Boomer, D.S. & Dittmann, A.T. (1964). "Speech rate, filled pause, and body movement in interviews". *Journal of Nervous and Mental Disease*, 139, 324-7.

Bouhuys, A.L. & Mulder-Hajonides van der Meulen, W.R.E. (1984). "Speech timing measures of severity, psychomotor retardation, and agitation in endogenously depressed patients". *Journal of Communication Disorders*, 17 , 277-88.

Boyd, J.H. & Weissmann, M.M. (1982). "Epidemiology". In E.S. Paykel (ed.) *Handbook of affective disorders* (pp. 109-25). Edinburgh: Churchill Livingstone.

Brähler, E., & Zenz, H. (1977). "Die automatische Analyse des Sprech-Pausen-Verhaltens im psychotherapeutischen Gespräch". In D. Wegner (ed.), *Gesprächsanalysen* (pp. 229-323). Hamburg: Buske.

Broadbent, D.E. (1958). *Perception and communication*. London: Pergamon Press.

Brown, G.W., Birley, J.L.T. & Wing, J.K. (1972). "Influence of family life on the course of schizophrenic disorders: A replication". *British Journal of Psychiatry*, 121, 241-58.

Brunner, L.J. (1979). "Smiles can be back-channels". *Journal of Personality and Social Psychology*, 37, 728-34.

Brunswik, E. (1956). *Perception and the representative design of psychological experiments*. Los Angeles: University of California Press.

Buck, R. (1979). "Individual differences in nonverbal sending accuracy and electrodermal responding: The externalizing-internalizing dimension". In R. Rosenthal (ed.) *Skill in nonverbal communication*. (pp. 140-70). Cambridge, Mass.: Oelgeschlager, Gunn, & Hain.

Bühler, K. (1965). *Sprachtheorie*. Stuttgart: Fischer (1st. edn. 1934).

Bühler, K. (1968). *Ausdruckstheorie*. Stuttgart: Fischer (1st. edn. 1933).

Bunney, W.E., & Hamburg, D.A. (1963). "Methods for reliable longitudinal observation of behavior". *Archives of General Psychiatry*, 9, 280-94.

Burrows, A., & Schumacher, J. (1979). *Doktor Diamonds Bildnisse von Geisteskranken*. Frankfurt: Syndikat.

Butterworth, B., & Beattie, J. (1978). "Gesture and silence as indicators of planning in speech". In R.N. Campbell & P.T. Smith (eds.), *Recent advances in the psychology of language – formal and experimental approaches* (pp. 347-60). New York: Plenum.

Byrne, D.G. (1976). "Vigilance and arousal in depressive states". *The British Journal of Social and Clinical Psychology*, 15, 267-74.

Cappella, J. (1981). "Mutual influence in expressive behavior: Adult-adult and infant-adult dyadic interaction". *Psychological Bulletin*, 89, 101-23.

Carney, R.M., Hong, B.A., O'Connell, M.F., & Amado, H. (1981). "Facial electromyography as a predictor of treatment outcome in depression". *British Journal of Psychiatry*, 138, 454-9.

Cary, M.S. (1978). "The role of gaze in the unitization of conversation". *Social Psychology*, 41, 269.

Castellan, N.J. (1973). "Comments on the 'lens model' equation and the analysis of multiple-cue judgment task". *Psychometrica*, 38, 87-100.

Chance, M.R.A. (1962). "An interpretation of some agonistic postures: The role of 'cut-off' acts and postures". In *Evolutionary aspects of animal communication. Symposium of the Zoological Society of London*. No. 8 (pp. 71-89).

Chance, M.R.A. (1967). "Attention structure as the basis of primate rank orders". *Man*, 2, 503-18.

Chapple, E.D. (1940). "Measuring human relations". *Genetic Psychological Monographs*, 22, 3-147.

Chapple, E.D. (1949). "The interaction chronograph: Its evolution and present application". *Personnel*, 25, 295-307.

Chapple, E.D., Chapple, M.F., Wood, L.A., Miklowitz, A., Kline, N.S., & Saunders, J.C. (1960). "Interaction chronograph method for analysis of differences between schizophrenics and controls". *AMA Archives of General Psychiatry*, 3, 160-7.

Chapple, E.D., & Lindemann, E. (1942). "Clinical implications of measurements of interaction rates in psychiatric interviews". *Applied Anthropology*, 1, 1-11.

Cherry, C. (1961). *On human communication – A review, a survey, and a criticism*. New York: Wiley (First published 1957).

Chevalier-Skolnikoff, S. (1973). "Facial expression of emotion in nonhuman primates". In P. Ekman (ed.), *Darwin and facial expression* (pp. 11-89). New York: Academic Press.

CIPS – Collegium Internationale Psychiatriae Scalarum (ed.) (1981). *Internationale Skalen für Psychiatrie*. Weinheim: Beltz.

Clarke, A.H., & Ellgring, H. (1983). "Computer-aided video". In P. Dowrick & S.J. Biggs (eds.), *Using video* (pp. 47-60) New York: Wiley.

Clarke, A.H., Wagner, H., & Ellgring, J.H. (1984) "A syntactic approach to the analysis of nonverbal behaviour". In T. Borbe (ed.), *Semiotics unfolding* (Part 2: Semiotics and social interaction) (pp. 453-60). Berlin: Mouton.

Cohen, A.A., & Harrison, R.P. (1973). "Intentionality in the use of hand illustrators in face-to-face communication situations". *Journal of Personality and Social Psychology*, 28, 276-9.

Costello, C.G. (1977). "The adaptive function of depression". *Canada's Mental Health*, 25, 20-1.

Coutts, L.M., Irvine, M., & Schneider, F.W. (1977). "Nonverbal adjustments to changes in gaze and orientation". *Psychology*, 14, 28-32.

Coutts, L.M., & Schneider, F.W. (1975). "Visual behavior in an unfocussed interaction as a function of sex and distance". *Journal of Experimental Social Psychology*, 11, 64-77.

Coutts, L.M., & Schneider, F.W. (1976). "Affiliative conflict theory: An investigation of the intimacy equilibrium and compensation hypothesis". *Journal of Personality and Social Psychology*, **34**, 1135-42.

Coyne, J.A. (1976). "Depression and the response of others". *Journal of Abnormal Psychology*, **85**, 186-93.

Coyne, J.C. (1976) "Toward an interactional description of depression". *Psychiatry*, **39**, 28-40.

Cranach, M. von & Ellgring, H. (1973). "Problems in the recognition of gaze direction". In M. von Cranach, & I. Vine (eds.), *Social communication and movement* (pp. 419-44). London: Academic Press.

Cranach, M. von & Vine, I (1973). "Introduction". In M. von Cranach & I. Vine (eds.), *Social communication and movement* (pp. 1-25). London: Academic Press.

Dabbs, J.M., Jr. (1980). "Temporal patterning of speech and gaze in social and intellectual conversation". In H. Giles & W.P. Robinson (eds.), *Language – social psychological perspectives* (pp. 307-10). Oxford: Pergamon.

Dabbs, J.M. Jr., Evans, M.S., Hopper, C.H., & Purvis, J.A. (1980). "Self-monitors in conversation: What do they monitor?", *Journal of Personality and Social Psychology*, **39**, 278-84.

Darwin, C (1965). *The expression of the emotions in Man and animals.* (1872). The University of Chicago Press.

Davison, G.C., & Neale, J.M. (1986). *Abnormal psychology.* New York: Wiley.

Dawes, R.M. (1979). "The robust beauty of improper linear models in decision making". *American Psychologist* **34**, 571-82.

Day, M.E. (1964). "An eye movement phenomenon relating to attention, thought, and anxiety". *Perceptual and Motor Skills*, **19**, 443-6.

De Jong, R., & Ferstl, R. (1980). "Die Entwicklung eines Therapieprogrammes für depressive Patienten: Erste Ergebnisse", In R. De Jong, N. Hoffman & M. Linden (eds.), *Verhaltensmodifikation bei Depressionen.* (pp. 171-96). Munich: Urban & Schwarzenberg.

De Jong, R., Henrich,G., & Ferstl, R. (1981). "Behavioural treatment programme for neurotic depression". *Behavioural Analysis and Modification*, **4**, 275-87.

Deutsch, F. (1951). "Thus speaks the body: III. Analytic posturology". *Psychoanalytic Quarterly*, **20**, 338-9.

Dilling, H., & Weyerer, S. (1978). *Epidemiologie psychischer Störungen and psychiatrische Versorgung.* Munich: Urban & Schwarzenberg.

Dittmann, A.T. (1962). "The relationship between body movements and moods in interviews". *Journal of Consulting Psychology*, **26**, 480.

Dittmann, A.T. (1963) "Kinesic research and therapeutic processes: Further discussion". In P.H. Knapp (ed.), *Expression of the emotions in man* (pp. 140-7). New York: International Universities Press.

Dittman, A.T., & Llewellyn, L.G. (1969). "Body movement and speech rhythm in social conversation". *Journal of Personality and Social Psychology*, **11**, 98-106.

Dörr, P., von Zerssen, D., Fischler, M., & Schulz, H. (1979). "Relationship between mood changes and adrenal cortical activity in a patient with 48 hour unipolar-depressive cycles". *Journal of Affective Disorders*, **1**, 93-104.

Duke, J.D. (1968). "Lateral eye movement behaviour". *The Journal of General Psychology*, **78**, 189-95.

Duncan, S. (1969). "Nonverbal communication". *Psychological Bulletin*, 72, 118-37.

Duncan, S. (1972). "Some signals and rules for taking speaking turns in conversations". *Journal of Personality and Social Psychology*, 23, 283-92.

Duncan, S., & Fiske, D.W. (1977). *Face-to-face interaction: Research, methods, and theory*. New York: Wiley.

Dutka, W., Hartmann-Zeilberger, J., Linden, M., & Hoffman, N. (1978). "Die Sozialpartner von Depressiven". *Zeitschrift für Klinische Psychologie und Psychotherapie*, 26, 247-55.

Dzida, W., & Kiener, F. (1978). "Strategien der Verwertung nonverbaler Informationen zur Persönlichkeitsbeurteilung". *Zeitschrift für experimentalle und angewandte Psychologie*, 25, 552-63.

Efron, D. (1972). *Gesture, race and culture*. (1st ed: *Gesture and environment*. New York: Kings Crown Press, 1941). The Hague: Mouton.

Ehrlichman, H., & Weinberger, A. (1978). "Lateral eye movements and hemispheric asymmetry: A critical review". *Psychological Bulletin*, 85, 1080-101.

Eibl-Eibesfeldt, I. (1972). "Similarities and differences between cultures in expressive movements". In R.A. Hinde (ed.), *Nonverbal communication* (pp. 297-314). Cambridge University Press.

Eibl-Eibesfeldt, I. (1978). *Grundriss der vergleichenden Verhaltensforschung – Ethologie*. Munich: Piper.

Eibl-Eibesfeldt, I. (1984). *Die Biologie des menschlichen Verhaltens – GrundriB der Humanethologie*. Munich: Piper.

Einhorn, H.J. & Hogarth, R.M. (1978). "Confidence in judgment: Persistence of the illusion of validity". *Psychological Review*, 85, 395-416.

Einhorn, H.J., & Hogarth, R.M. (1981). "Behavioral decision theory: Processes of judgement and choice". *Annual Review of Psychology*, 32, 53-88.

Ekman, P. (1972). "Universals and cultural differences in facial expression of emotion". In J.B. Cole (ed.), *Nebraska Symposium on Motivation* (pp. 207-83). Lincoln: University of Nebraska Press.

Ekman, P. (ed.) (1973). *Darwin and facial expression: A century of research in review*. New York: Academic Press.

Ekman, P. (1979). "About brows: Emotional and conversational signals". In M. von Cranach, K. Foppa, W. Lepenies & D. Ploog (eds.), *Human ethology* (pp. 169-202). Cambridge University Press.

Ekman, P., & Friesen, W.V. (1969a). "The repertoire of nonverbal behavior – Categories, origins, usage, and coding". *Semiotica*, 1, 49-98.

Ekman, P., & Friesen, W.V. (1969b). "Nonverbal leakage and clues to deception". *Psychiatry* 32 88-106.

Ekman, P., & Friesen, W.V. (1972). "Hand movements". *The Journal of Communication*, 22 353-74.

Ekman, P., & Friesen, W.V. (1974). "Nonverbal behavior and psychopathology". In R.J. Friedman & M.M. Katz (eds.) *The psychology of depression: Contemporary theory and research*. (pp. 203-32) Washington DC: Winston and Sons.

Ekman, P., & Friesen, W.V. (1975). *Unmasking the face*. Englewood Cliffs, NJ: Prentice Hall.

Ekman, P., & Friesen, W.V. (1978). *Manual for the facial action code*. Palo Alto: Consulting Psychologist Press.

Ekman, P., Friesen, W.V., & Ancoli, S. (1980). "Facial signs of emotional experience". *Journal of Personality and Social Psychology*, 39, 1125-34.

Ekman, P., Friesen, W.V., O'Sullivan, M., & Scherer, K.R. (1980). "Relative importance of face, body, and speech in judgments of personality and affect". *Journal of Personality and Social Psychology*, 38, 270-7.

Ekman, P., Hager, J.C. & Friesen, W.V (1981). "The symmetry of emotional and deliberate facial actions". *Psychophysiology*, 18, 101-6.

Ekman, P., & Oster, H. (1979). "Facial expression of emotion". *Annual Review of Psychology*, 30 527-54.

Ekman, P., Roper, G., & Hager, J.C. (1980). "Deliberate facial movement". *Child development*, 51, 886-91.

Ellgring, H. (1975). "Blickverhalten und Sprechaktivität – Untersuchungen zum sprachlichen und nichtsprachlichen Verhalten in Zwei-Personen-Situationen". (Dissertation). Philipps-Universität, Marburg/L.

Ellgring, H. (1977). "Kommunikatives Verhalten im Verlauf depressiver Erkrankungen". In W.H. Tack (ed.), *Bericht über den 30. Kongress der Deutschen Gesellschaft für Psychologie in Regensburg 1976, vol. 2.* (pp. 190-2) Göttingen: Hogrefe.

Ellgring, H. (1981). "Psychische Beanspruchung durch Sprache und Blickzuwendung in Gesprächs-und Leistungssituationen". In L. Tent (ed.), *Erkennen – Wollen Handeln. Beiträge zur Allgemeinen und Angewandten Psychologie* (pp. 276-90). Göttingen: Hogrefe.

Ellgring, H. (1982). "Video-unterstützte Therapie und Supervision. Ein Überblick". In B. Kügelgen (ed.), *Video und Medizin.* (pp. 213-20). Erlangen: Perimed.

Ellgring, H. (1983). "Kommunikation". In D. Frey & S. Greif (eds.), *Sozialpsychologie – Ein Handbuch in Schlüsselbegriffen* (pp. 196-203). Munich: Urban & Schwarzenberg.

Ellgring, H. (1984). "Nonverbale Indikatoren des psychischen Befindens". In A. Hopf & H. Beckmann (eds.), *Forschungen zur biologischen Psychiatrie* (pp. 79-84). Berlin: Springer.

Ellgring, H. (1986). "Nonverbal expression of psychological states in psychiatric patients". *European Archives of Psychiatric and Neurological Sciences*, 236, 31-4.

Ellgring, H., & Clarke, A.H. (1978). "Verlaufsbeobachtungen anhand standardisierter Videoaufzeichnungen bei depressiven Patienten". In H. Helmchen & E. Renfordt (eds.), *Fernsehen in der Psychiatrie* (pp. 68-77). Stuttgart: Thieme.

Ellgring, H. & Ploog, D. (1985). "Sozialkommunikatives Verhalten in klinischer Perspektive". In D. Bente, H. Coper & S. Kanowski (eds.) *Hirnorganische Psychosyndrome – Methoden zur Objektivierung der therapeutischen Wirksamkeit.* (pp. 217-36). Berlin: Springer.

Ellgring, H., Derbolowsky, J., & von Dewitz, A. (1977). "Standardized interview for investigating the course of depression (SID)". *Scandinavian Journal of Behaviour Therapy*, 6, 56.

Ellgring, H. Derbolowsky, J., von Dewitz, A., & Hieke, S. (1978). "Standardisiertes Interview zur Depression (Mimeo)". Munich: Max-Planck-Institut für Psychiatrie.

Ellgring, H., Wagner, H., & Clarke, A.H. (1980). "Psychopathological states and their effects on speech and gaze behaviour". In H. Giles, W.P. Robinson, & P.M. Smith (eds.) *Language – Social psychological perspectives*. (pp. 267-73). Oxford: Pergamon Press.

Ellgring, J.H., & von Cranach, M. (1972). "Processes of learning in the recognition of eye-signals". *European Journal of Social Psychology*, 2 33-43.

Ellsworth, P.C., & Carlsmith, J.M. (1968). "Effects of eye-contact and verbal content on affective response to a dyadic interaction". *Journal of Personality and Social Psychology*, 10, 15-20.

Ellsworth, P.C. & Langer, E.J. (1976). "Staring and approach: An interpretation of the stare as a nonspecific activator". *Journal of Personality and Social Psychology*, 33, 117-22.

Ellsworth, P.C., & Ross, L. (1975). "Intimacy in response to direct gaze". *Journal of Experimental Social Psychology*, 11, 592-613.

Ellsworth, P.C., Carlsmith, J.M. & Henson, A. (1972). "The stare as a stimulus to flight in human subjects: A series of field experiments". *Journal of Personality and Social Psychology*, 21, 302-11.

Emerson, J.D., & Strenio, J. (1983). "Boxplots and batch comparison". In D.C. Hoaglin, F. Mosteller & J.W. Tukey (eds.), *Understanding robust and exploratory data analysis* (pp. 58-96). New York: Wiley.

Engel, B.T. (1960). "Stimulus-response and individual-response specificity". *Archives of General Psychiatry*, 2, 305-13.

Engel, B.T., & Bickford, A.F. (1961). "Response specificity – Stimulus-response and individual-response specificity in essential hypertensives". *Archives of General Psychiatry*, 5, 82-93.

Enke, W. (1930). "Die Psychomotorik der Konstitutionstypen". *Zeitschrift für angewandte Psychologie*, 36, 238-87.

Exline, R. (1972). "Visual interaction: The glance of power and preference". In J.R. Cole (ed.) *Nebraska Symposium on Motivation*, 1971 (pp. 163-206). Lincoln, Nebraska: University of Nebraska Press.

Exline, R.V. (1963). "Explorations in the process of person perception: Visual interaction in relation to competition, sex, and need for affiliation". *Journal of Personality*, 31, 1-20.

Exline, R.V., & Fehr, B.J. (1982). "The assessment of gaze and mutual gaze". In K.R. Scherer & P. Ekman (eds.), *Handbook of methods in nonverbal behavior research* (pp. 91-135). Cambridge University Press.

Exline, R.V., Gray, F., & Schuette, D. (1965). "Visual behaviour in a dyad as affected by interview content and sex of respondent". *Journal of Personality and Social Psychology*, 1, 201-9.

Exline, R.V., Thibaut, J., Hickey, C.B., & Gumpert, P. (1970). "Visual interaction in relation to machiavellianism and an unethical act". In R. Christie & F.L. Geis (eds.) *Studies in machiavellianism*. (pp. 53-76). New York: Academic Press.

Exline, R.V., & Winters, L.C. (1965). "Affective relations and mutual glances in dyads". In S.S. Tomkins & C.E. Izard (eds.), *Affect, cognition, and personality* (pp. 319-50). New York: Springer.

Fahrenberg, J., Walschburger, P., Förster, F., Myrtek, M., & Müller, W. (1979). *Psychophysiologische Aktivierungsforschung*. Munich: Minerva.

Feldstein, S. (1964). "Vocal patterning of emotional expression". In J.H. Masserman (ed.), *Science and psychoanalysis*. vol. 7. (pp. 193-210). New York: Grune & Stratton.

Feldstein, S., & Welkowitz, J. (1978). "A chronography of conversation: In defense of an objective approach". In A.W. Siegman & S. Feldstein (eds.), *Nonverbal behavior and communication* (pp. 329-78). New York: Wiley.

Ferguson, N. (1977). "Simultaneous speech, interruptions and dominance". *The British Journal of Social and Clinical Psychology*, **116**, 295-302.

Ferster, C.B. (1973). "A functional analysis of depression". *American Psychologist*, **28** 857-70.

Feyereisen, P. (1982). "Temporal distribution of co-verbal hand movements". *Ethology and Sociobiology*, **3**, 1-9.

Fisch, H.U.,Frey, S. & Hirsbrunner, H.P. (1983). "Analyzing nonverbal behavior in depression". *Journal of Abnormal Psychology*, **92**, 307-18.

Fischer-Cornelssen, K.A., & Abt, K. (1980). "Videotape recording in psychiatry and psychopharmacology". *Acta Psychiatrica Scandinavia*, **61**, 228-38.

Folstein, M.F., & Luria, R. (1973). "Reliability, validity, and clinical applications of the visual analogue mood scale". *Psychological Medicine*, **3**, 479-86.

Forrest, M., & Hokanson, J.E. (1975). "Depression and autonomic arousal reduction accompanying self-punitive behavior". *Journal of Abnormal Psychology*, **84**,346-57.

Freedman, N. (1972). The analysis of movement behavior during the clinical interview. In A.W. Siegman, & B. Pope (eds.), *Studies in dyadic communication*. (pp. 153-75). New York: Pergamon Press.

Freedman, N. (1977). "Hands, words, and mind: On the structuralization of body movements during discourse and the capacity for verbal representation". In N. Freedman & S. Grand (eds.) *Communicative structures and psychic structures* (pp. 109-32). New York: Plenum Press.

Freedman, N. Blass, T., Rifkin, A., & Quitkin, F. (1973). "Body movement and the verbal encoding of aggressive affect". *Journal of Personality and Social Psychology*, **26**, 72-83.

Freedman, N., & Hoffman, S.P. (1967). "Kinetic behavior in altered clinical interviews." *Perceptual and Motor Skills*, **24**, 527-39.

Frey, S. (1975). "Tonic aspects of behavior in interaction". In A. Kendon, R.M. Harris, & M.R. Key (eds.), *Organization of behavior in face-to-face interaction* (pp. 127-50). The Hague: Mouton.

Fridlund, A.J. & Izard, C.E. (1983). "Electromyographic studies of facial expression of emotions and patterns of emotions". In J.T. Cacioppo & R.E. Petty (eds.) *Social Psychophysiology* (pp. 243-86). New York: Guilford Press.

Friesen, W. & Ekman, P. (1984). "EMFACS-7" (Unpublished manuscript). San Francisco: Human Interaction Laboratory.

Friesen, W.V., Ekman, P., & Wallbott, H.G. (1979). "Measuring hand movements". *Journal of Nonverbal Behavior*, **4**. 97-112.

Frijda, N.H. (1968). "Recognition of emotion". In L. Berkowitz (ed.), *Advances in experimental social psychology, 4*. New York: Academic Press.

Gauron, E.F. & Dickinson, J.K. (1969). "The influence of seeing the patient first on diagnostic decision making in psychiatry". *American Journal of Psychiatry*, **126**, 199-205.

Gaylin, W. (ed.) (1968). *The meaning of despair: Pychoanalytic contributions to the understanding of depression*. New York: Science House.

Gershon, E., Cromer, M., & Klerman, G. (1968). "Hostility and depression. Psychiatry," **31**, 224-35.

Gerstenbrand, F. (1967). *Das traumatische apallische Syndrom*. Vienna: Springer.

Giles, H., Robinson, W.P., & Smith, P.M. (eds.) (1980). *Language: Social psychological perspectives*. Oxford: Pergamon.

Glaister, J., Feldstein, S., & Pollack, H. (1980). "Chronographic speech patterns of acutely psychotic patients: A preliminary note". *Journal of Nervous and Mental Disease*, **168**, 219-23.

Godfrey, H.P., & Knight, R.G. (1984) "The validity of actometer and speech activity measures in the assessment of depressed patients". *British Journal of Psychiatry*, **145** 159-63.

Goffman, E. (1959). *The presentation of the self in everyday life*. Golden City, NY: Doubleday Anchor.

Goffman, E. (1969). *Strategic interaction*. University of Philadelphia Press.

Goldberg, L.R. (1970). "Man versus model of man: A rationale, plus some evidence for a method of improving on clinical inferences". *Psychological Bulletin*, **73**, 422-32.

Goldfried, M.R. (1976). "Behavioral assessment". In J.B. Weiner (ed.), *Clinical methods in psychology* (pp. 281-330).

Goldman-Eisler, F. (1952). "Individual differences between interviewers and their effect on interviewers' conversation behavior". *Journal of Mental Sciences*, **98**, 660-71.

Goldman-Eisler, F. (1968). *Psycholinguistics: Experiments in spontaneous speech*. New York: Academic Press.

Goldstein, I.B. (1965). "The relationship of muscle tension and autonomic activity to psychiatric disorders". *Psychosomatic Medicine*, **27**, 39-52.

Gottschalk, L.A., Wingert, L., & Gleser, C. (1970). *Manual of instructions for using the Gottschalk-Gleser Content Analysis Scales: Anxiety, hostility, social alienation, personal disorganisation*. Berkeley: University of California Press.

Graham, J.A., & Argyle, M. (1975). "A cross-cultural study of the communication of extraverbal meaning of gestures". *International Journal of Psychology*, **10**, 57-67.

Graham, J.A., & Heywood, S. (1975). "The effects of elimination of hand gestures and of verbal codability on speech performance". *European Journal of Social Psychology*, **5**, 189-95.

Greden, J.E., Albala, A.A., Smohler, I.A., Gardner, R., & Carroll, B.J. (1981). "Speech pause time: A marker of psychomotor retardation among endogenous depressives". *Biological Psychiatry*, **16**, 851-9.

Greden, J.F., Genero, N., & Price, H.L. (1985). "Agitation-increased electomyogram activity in the corrugator muscle region: A possible explanation of the 'Omega sign'?", *American Journal of Psychiatry*, **142**, 348-51.

Greden, J.F., Price, L., Genero, H., Feinberg, M., & Levine, S. (1984). "Facial EMG activity levels predict treatment outcome in depression". *Psychiatry Research*, **13**, 345-52.

Grinker, R.R., Miller, J., Gabshin, M., Nunn, R., & Nunnally, J.C. (1961). *The phenomena of depressions*. New York: Harper & Row.

Günthner, B. (1981). "Motorisches Verhalten depressiver Personen im Interview". Unpublished dissertation. Psychologisches Institut der Ludwig-Maximilians-Universität, Munich.

Hänni, R. (1974). "Auswirkungen der Störung von Sprechpausen". In L.H. Eckensberger & U.S. Eckensberger (eds.), *Bericht über den 28. Kongress der Deutschen Gesellschaft für Psychologie in Saarbrücken, 1972. Vol. 1: Wissenschaftstheorie und Psycholinguistik* (pp. 109-19). Göttingen: Hogrefe.

Hall, E.T. (1969). *The hidden dimension*. Garden City, NJ: Doubleday.

Hall, J.A. (1979). "Gender, gender roles, and nonverbal communication skills". In R. Rosenthal (ed.), *Skills in nonverbal communication: Individual differences*. Cambridge, Mass: Oelgeschlager, Gunn & Hain.

Hall, J.A. (1984). *Nonverbal sex differences: Communication accuracy and expressive style*. Baltimore, MD: John Hopkins University Press.

Hall, J.A., Rosenthal, R., Archer, D., DiMatteo, M.R., & Rogers, P.L. (1978). "Profile of nonverbal sensitivity". In P. McReynolds (ed.), *Advances in psychological assessment* (pp. 179-221). San Francisco: Jossey-Bass, 4.

Hamilton, M. (1960). A rating scale for depression. Journal of Neurology, Neurosurgery and Psychiatry, 23, 56-62.

Hammen, C.L. & Peters, S.D. (1978). "Interpersonal consequences of depression: Responses to men and women enacting a depressed role". *Journal of Abnormal Psychology*, **87**, 322-32.

Hammond, K.R., Hursch, C.J., & Todd, F.J. (1964). "Analyzing the components of clinical inference". *Psychological Review*, **71**, 438-56.

Hardy, P., Jouvent, R., & Wildlöcher, D. (1984). "Speech pause time and the retardation rating scale for depression (ERD). Towards a reciprocal validation". *Journal of Affective Disorders*, **16**, 123-7.

Hayduk, L.A. (1983). "Personal space: Where we now stand". *Psychological Bulletin*, **94**, 293-335.

Helfrich, H., & Dahme, B. (1974). "Sind Verzögerungsphänomene beim spontanen Sprechen Indikatoren persönlichkeitsspezifischer Angstverarbeitung". *Zeitschrift für Sozialpsychologie*, **5**, 55-65.

Henderson, A.I. (1975). "A note on the interference between verbal output and a cognitive task". *Acta Psychologica*, **39**, 495-7.

Henderson, A.I., Goldman-Eisler, F., & Skarbek, A. (1965). "Temporal patterns of cognitive activity and breath control in speech". *Language and Speech*, **8**, 236-42.

Henley, N.M., & LaFrance, M. (1984). "Gender as culture: Difference and dominance in nonverbal behavior". In A. Wolfgang (ed.), *Nonverbal behavior*, (pp.351-71). Lewiston, New York: Hogrefe.

Hess, E.H. (1965). "Attitude and pupil size". *Scientific American*, **212**, 46-55.

Hiebinger, S. (1982). "Kommunikatives Verhalten im Verlauf der endogenen Depression". Dissertation. Universität Salzburg.

Hill, D. (1974). Non-verbal behavior in mental illness. *British Journal of Psychiatry*, **124**, 221-30.

Hinchliffe, M.K., Hooper, D., & Roberts. F.J. (1978). *The melancholy marriage. – Depression in marriage and psychosocial approaches to therapy.* Chichester: Wiley.

Hinchliffe, M.K., Hooper, D., Roberts, F.J., & Vaughan, P.W. (1975). "A study of the interaction between depressed patients and their spouses". *British Journal of Psychiatry*, **126**, 164-72.

Hinchliffe, M.K., Lancashire, M., & Roberts, F.J. (1970). "Eye-contact and depression – A preliminary report". *British Journal of Psychiatry*, **117**, 571-2.

Hinchliffe, M.K., Lancashire, M., & Roberts, F.J. (1971a). "A study of eye-contact changes in depressed and recovered psychiatric patients". *British Journal of Psychiatry*, **119**, 213-15.

Hinchliffe, M.K., Lancashire, M., & Roberts, F.J. (1971b). Depression: Defence mechanisms in speech. British Journal of Psychiatry, 118, 471-472.

Hinchliffe, M.K., Vaughan, P.W., Hooper, D.R., & Roberts, J.F. (1977). "The melancholy marriage: An inquiry into the interaction of depression: II. Expressiveness". *British Journal of Medical Psychology*, **50**, 125-42.

Hinde, R.A. (ed.) (1972). *Non-verbal communication.* Cambridge University Press.

Hoffmann, G.M., Gonze, J.C., & Mendlewicz, J. (1985). "Speech pause time as a method for the evaluation of psychomotor retardation in depressive illness". *British Journal of Psychiatry*, **146**, 535-8.

Hoffmann, N., Schädrich, W., & Schiller, U. (1976). "Diagnostik bei Depressiven". In N. Hoffmann (ed.) *Depressives Verhalten* (pp. 192-217). Salzburg: O. Müller.

Hofstätter, P.R. (1957). *Psychologie.* Frankfurt: Fischer.

Holzkamp, K. (1969). "Reinforcement durch Blickkontakt: Eine experimentelle Studie". *Zeitschrift für experimentelle und angewandte Psychologie*, **16**, 538-60.

Hortsjö, C.-H. (1970). *Man's face and mimic language.* Malmö: Nordens Boktrycheri.

Howes, M.J., & Hokanson, J.E. (1979). "Conversational and social responses to depressive interpersonal behavior". *Journal of Abnormal Psychology*, **88**, 625-34.

Hursch, C.J., Hammond, K. & Hursch, J. (1964). "Some methodolical considerations in multiple-cue probability studies". *Psychological Review*, **71**, 42-60.

Hutt, C., & Ounsted, C. (1966). "The biological significance of gaze-aversion, with particular reference to the syndrome of infantile autism". *Behavioural Science*, **11**, 346-56.

Izard, C. (1971). *The face of emotion.* New York: Appleton-Century-Crofts.

Izard, C. (1972). *Patterns of emotions: A new analysis of anxiety and depression.* New York: Academic Press.

Izard, C.E. (1977). *Human emotions.* New York: Plenum Press.

Jaffe, J., & Feldstein, S. (1970). *Rhythms of dialogue.* New York: Academic Press.

Jones, J.H., & Pansa, M. (1979). "Some nonverbal aspects of depression and schizophrenia occurring during the interview". *Journal of Nervous and Mental Disease*, **167**, 402-9.

Kanfer, F.H. & Saslow, G. (1969). "Behavioral diagnostic". In C.M. Franks (ed.), *Behavior therapy: Appraisal and status* (pp. 417-44). New York: McGraw-Hill.

Kelly, G.A. (1955). *The psychology of personal constructs.* New York: Norton.

Kendell, R.E. (1970). "Relationship between aggression and depression: Epidemiological implications of a hypothesis". *Archives of General Psychiatry*, **22**, 308-18.

Kendell, R.E. (1976). "The classification of depressions: A review of contemporary confusion". *The British Journal of Psychiatry*, **129**, 15-28.

Kendon, A. (1967). "Some functions of gaze direction in social interaction". *Acta Psychologica*, **26**, 22-63.

Kendon, A. (1970). "Movement coordination in social interaction: Some examples described". *Acta Psychologica*, **32**, 101-25.

Kendon, A. (1973). "The role of visible behavior in the organization of social interaction". In M. von Cranach & I. Vine (eds.), *Social communication and movement*. (pp. 29-74). London: Academic Press.

Kendon, A. (1978). "Looking in conversation and the regulation of turns at talk: A comment on the papers of G. Beattie and D.R. Rutter et al". *The British Journal of Social and Clinical Psychology*, **17**, 23-4.

Kendon, A. (1980). "Gesticulation and speech: Two aspects of the process of utterance". In M. Ritchie Key (ed.) *The relationship of verbal and nonverbal communication* (pp. 207-27). The Hague: Mouton.

Kiener, F. (1962). *Hand, Gebärde und Charakter*. Munich: Ernst Reinhardt.

Kiritz, S.A. (1973). "Hand movement and clinical ratings at admission and discharge for hospitalized psychiatric patients". Dissertation, Medical Center, San Francisco.

Klaus, G. (1969). *Wörterbuch der Kybernetik*. Berlin: Dietz.

Kleinke, C.L., Meeker, F.B., & LaFong, L. (1974). "Effects of gaze, touch, and use of name on evaluation of 'engaged' couples". *Journal of Research in Personality*, **7**, 368-73.

Kleinke, C.L. & Pohlen, P.D. (1971). "Affective and emotional responses as a function of other person's gaze and cooperativeness in a two-person game". *Journal of Personality and Social Psychology*. **17**, 308-13.

Klerman, G.L. (1974). "Depression and adaptation". In R.J. Friedman & M.M. Katz (eds.),, *The psychology of depression: Contemporary theory and research*. (pp. 127-45). New York: Wiley.

Klerman, G.L. (1986). "Evidence for increase in rate of depression in North America and Western Europe in recent decades". In H. Hippius, G.L. Klerman & N. Matussek (eds.), *New results in depression research* (pp. 7-15). Berlin: Springer.

Klerman, G.L., Endicott, J., Spitzer, R., & Hirschfeld, R. (1979). "Neurotic depressions: A systematic analysis of multiple criteria and meanings". *The American Journal of Psychiatry*, **136**, 57-61.

Klos, T., Ellgring, H., & Scherer, K.R. "Vocal indicators of mood change in depression" (in preparation).

König, O. (1975). *Urmotiv Auge. Neuentdeckte Grundzüge menschlichen Verhaltens*. Munich: Piper.

Kohnen, R., & Lienert, G.A. (1976). "Freie und gebundene Wirkungsbeschreibung eines Schlafmittels (Flurazepam) durch gesunde Versuchspersonen". *Arzneimittel-Forschung (Drug Research)*, **26**, 1134-7.

Kraepelin, E. (1883). *Compendium der Psychiatrie*. Leipzig: Abel.

Kraepelin, E. (1896). *Psychiatrie – Ein Lehrbuch für Studierende und Ärzte*. Leipzig: Barth.

Krause, R. (1978). "Nonverbales interaktives Verhalten von Stotterern und ihren

Gesprächspartnern". *Schweizerische Zeitschrift für Psychologie und ihre Anwendungen*, 37, 177-201.

Krause, R. (1981). *Sprache und Affekt – Das Stottern und seine Behandlung*. Stuttgart: Kohlhammer.

Krause, R. (1983). "Zur Onto-und Phylogenese des Affektsystems und ihrer Beziehungen zu psychischen Störungen". *Psyche*, 37, 1016-43.

Krause, R. (1984). "Psychoanalyse als interaktives Geschehen". In U. Baumann (ed.) *Psychotherapie – Makro/Mikroperspektive* (pp. 146-58). Göttingen: Hogrefe.

Kraut, R.E. & Johnston, R.E. (1979). "Social and emotional messages of smiling: An ethological approach". *Journal of Personality and Social Psychology*, 37, 1539-53.

Kretschmer, E. (1967). *Körperbau und Charakter*. (25th edn.). Heidelberg: Springer.

Krout, M.H. (1935). "Autistic gestures: An experimental study in symbolic movement". *Psychological Monographs*, 46, 208.

Krout, M.H. (1937). "Further studies on the relation of personality and gesture: Nosological analysis of autistic gestures". *Journal of Experimental Psychology*, 20, 279-87.

Lacey, J.I. (1967). "Somatic response patterning and stress: Some revisions of activation theory". In M.H. Appley & R. Trumbull (eds.), *Psychological stress*. (pp. 14-42). New York: Appleton-Century-Crofts.

Lacey, J.I., & Lacey, B.C. (1958). "Verification and extension of the principle of autonomic response stereotypy". *American Journal of Psychology*, 71, 50-73.

Lamiell, J.T. (1981). "Toward an idiothetic psychology of personality". *American Psychologist*, 36, 276-89.

Landis, C. (1924). "Studies of emotional reactions. II. General behavior and facial expression". *Journal of Comparative Psychology*, 4, 447-509.

Lawick-Goodall, J., van (1968). "The behavior of free-living chimpanzees in the Gombe Stream Reserve". *Animal Behavior Monographs*, 1, 161-311.

Lay, C.H., & Burron, B.F. (1968). "Perception of the personality of the hesitant speaker". *Perception and Motor Skills*, 26, 951-6.

Lazarus, R.S. (1984). "On the primacy of cognition". *American Psychologist*, 39, 124-9.

Lazzerini, A.J., Stephenson, G.M., & Neave, H. (1978). "Eye-contact in dyads: A test of the independence hypothesis". *British Journal of Social and Clinical Psychology*, 17, 227-9.

Leff, J., & Vaughan, Ch. (1985). *Expressed emotion in families – its significance for mental illness*. New York: Guilford.

Lewinsohn, P.M. (1974). "A behavioral approach to depression". In R.J. Friedman & M.M. Katz (eds.), *The psychology of depression: Contemporary theory and research* (pp. 157-78). New York: Wiley.

Lewinsohn, P.M., & Libet, J. (1972). "Pleasant events, activity schedules, and depression". *Journal of Abnormal Psychology*, 79, 291-6.

Lewinsohn, P.M., Youngren, M.A., & Grosscup, S.J. (1979). "Reinforcement and depression". In R.A. Depue (ed.), *The psychobiology of depressive disorders: Implications for the effects of stress* (pp. 291-316). New York: Academic Press.

Leyhausen, P. (1967). "Biologie von Ausdruck und Eindruck". *Psychologische Forschung*, **31**, 113-76.

Libby, W., & Yaklevich, D. (1973). "Personality determinants of eye contact and duration of eye contact and duration of gaze aversion". *Journal of Personality and Social Psychology*, **27**, 197-206.

Libet, J.M., & Lewinsohn, P.M. (1973). "Concept of social skill with special reference to the behavior of depressed persons". *Journal of Consulting and Clinical Psychology*, **40**, 304-12.

Linden, M. (1976). "Depression als aktives Verhalten". In N. Hoffmann (ed.), *Depressives Verhalten – Psychologische Modelle zur Ätiologie und Therapie* (pp. 108-49). Salzburg: Otto Müller.

Little, J.C., & McPhail, N.J. (1973). "Measures of depressive mood at monthly intervals". *British Journal of Psychiatry*, **122**, 447-52.

Loeb, F. (1968). "The fist: The microscopic film analysis of the function of a recurrent behavioral pattern in the psychotherapeutic session". *Journal of Nervous and Mental Disease*, **147**, 605-18.

Lorenz, K. (1963). *Das sogenannte Böse*. Vienna: Borotha-Schoeler.

Lorenz, K. (1965). *Über tierisches und menschliches Verhalten*. vol. I. Munich Piper.

Lorr, M., McNair, D.M., Klett, C.J., & Lasky, J.J. (1962). *Impatient Multidimensional Psychiatric Scale (IMPS)*. Palo Alto: Consulting Psychologist Press.

Lubin, B. (1965). "Adjective checklist for measurement of depression". *Archives of General Psychiatry*, **12**, 57-62.

Luria, A. (1932). *The nature of human conflicts*. New York: Liveright.

MacKay, D.M. (1972). "Formal analysis of communicative processes". In R.A. Hinde (ed.), *Non-verbal communication*. (pp. 3-25). Cambridge University Press.

MacKey, W.C. (1976). "Parameters of the smile as a social signal". *The Journal of Genetic Psychology*, **129**, 125-30.

Magnus, H. (1885). *Die Sprache der Augen*. Wiesbaden: Bergmann.

Mahl, G.F. (1956). "Disturbances and silences in the patient's speech in psychotherapy". *Journal of Abnormal and Social Psychology*, **53**, 1-15.

Mahl, G.F. (1968). "Gestures and body movements in interviews". In J.M. Schlien (ed.), *Research in psychotherapy*. (pp. 295-346). Washington, DC: American Psychological Association.

Mahl, G.F. (1977). "Body movement, ideation, and verbalization during psychoanalysis". In N. Freedman & S. Grand (eds.) *Communicative structures and psychic structures*. (pp. 291-310). New York: Plenum Press.

Mahl, G.F., & Schulze, G. (1964). "Psychological research in the extralinguistic area". In T.A. Sebeok, A.S. Hayes, & M.S. Bateson (eds.), *Approaches to semiotics* (pp. 51-124). The Hague: Mouton.

Matarazzo, J.D. & Saslow, G. (1961). "Difference in interview interaction behavior among normal and deviant groups". In I.A. Berg & B.M. Bass (eds.), *Conformity and deviation* (pp. 286-327). New York: Harper & Row.

Matarazzo, J.D., & Wiens, A.N. (1972). *The interview: Research on its anatomy and structure*. Chicago: Aldine-Atherton.

Matarazzo, J.D., & Wiens, A.N. (1977). "Speech behavior as an objective correlate of empathy and outcome in interview and psychotherapy research". *Behavior Modification*, **1**, 453-80.

Matsumoto, D., Ekman, P., & Friesen, W.V. (1983). *Depression and facial expression*. University of California, Berkeley (Mimeo).

Mayer-Gross, W., Slater, E., & Roth, M. (1969). *Clinical psychiatry*. London: Bailliere, Tindall & Cassel.

Meehl, P.E. (1954). *Clinical versus statistical prediction*. Minneapolis: University of Minnesota Press.

Mehrabian, A. (1969). "Significance of posture and position in the communication of attitude and status relationships". *Psychological Bulletin*, 71, 359-72.

Mehrabian, A. (1972). *Nonverbal communication*. Chicago: Aldine-Atterton.

Mehrabian, A., & Wiener, M. (1967). "Decoding of inconsistent communication". *Journal of Personality and Social Psychology*, 6, 109-14.

Meltzer, L., Morris, W.N., & Hayes, D.P. (1971). "Interruption outcomes and vocal amplitude: Explorations in social psychophysics". *Journal of Personality and Social Psychology*, 18, 392-402.

Miller, R.E., Ranelli, C.J., & Levine, J.M. (1977). "Nonverbal communication as an index of depression". In I. Hanin & E. Usdin (eds.), *Animal models in psychiatry and neurology* (pp. 171-80). New York: Pergamon.

Miller, W.R. (1975). "Psychological deficit in depression". *Psychological Bulletin*, 82, 238-60.

Mischel, W. (1968). *Personality and assessment*. New York: Wiley.

Mischel, W. (1973). "Toward a cognitive social learning reconceptualization of personality". *Psychological Review*, 80, 252-83.

Mischel, W. (1983). "Alternatives in the pursuit of the predictability and consistency of persons: Stable data that yield unstable interpretations". *Journal of Personality*, 51, 578-604.

Mombour, W. (1974). "Symptomhäufigkeiten bei psychiatrischen Erkrankungen". *Archiv für Psychiatrie und Nervenkrankheiten*, 219, 133-52.

Murray, D.C. (1971). "Talk, silence, and anxiety". *Psychological Bulletin*, 75, 244-60.

Neuburger, E. (1970). *Kommunikation der Gruppe: Ein Beitrag zur Informationstheorie*. Munich: Oldenbourg.

Newman, S.S., & Mather, V.G. (1938). "Analysis of spoken language of patients with affective disorders". *American Journal of Psychiatry*, 94, 913-42.

Nichols, K., & Champness, B. (1971). "Eye gaze and the G.S.R.", *Journal of Experimental Social Psychology*, 7, 623-6.

Nielsen, G. (1962). *Studies in self-confrontation: Viewing of a sound motion picture of self and another person in a stressful dyadic situation*. Copenhagen: Munksgaard.

Norwine, A.C., & Murphy, O.J. (1938). "Characteristic time intervals in telephonic conversation". *Bell System Technical Journal*, 17, 281-91.

O'Connor, N., & Hermelin, B. (1967). "The selective visual attention of psychotic children". *Journal of Child Psychology and Psychiatry*, 8, 167-79.

Oliveau, D., & Willmuth, R. (1979). "Facial muscle electromyography in depressed and nondepressed hospitalized subjects: A partial replication". *American Journal of Psychiatry*, 136, 548-50.

Osgood, C.E. (1966). "Dimensionality of the semantic space for communication via facial expression". *Scandinavian Journal of Psychology*, 7, 1-30.

Oster, H. (1978). "Facial expression and affect development". In M. Lewis & R. Rosenblum (eds.), *The development of affect* (pp. 43-76). New York: Plenum Press.

Pansa-Henderson, M., & Jones, J.H. (1982). "Gaze and gaze avoidance as perceived by psychiatrists during clinical interviews with schizophrenic, depressed, and anxious patients". *Journal of Nonverbal Behavior*, 7, 69-78.

Pansa-Henderson, M., de L'Horne, D., & Jones, I.H. (1982). "Nonverbal behavior as a supplement to psychiatric diagnosis in schizophrenia, depression, and anxiety neurosis". *Journal of Psychiatric Treatment & Evaluation*, 4, 489-96.

Papousek, H. & Papousek, M., (1977). Mothering and cognitive head-start: Psychobiological considerations. In H.R. Schaffer (ed.), *Studies in mother-infant interaction* (pp. 63-85). New York: Academic Press.

Pattay, S. (1982). "Stimmungsbeeinflussung und Stimmausdruck – Lässt sich die Befindlichkeit des Patienten aus der Stimme des Therapeuten erkennen?, Unpublished dissertation, Ludwig-Maximilians-Universität, Munich.

Patterson, M.L. (1976). "An arousal model of interpersonal intimacy". *Psychological Review*, 83, 235-45.

Petrinovich, L. (1979). "Probabilistic functionalism: A conception of research method". *American Psychologist*, 34, 373-90.

Phelps, R.H. & Shanteau, J. (1978). "Livestock judges: How much information can an expert use?", *Organizational Behavior and Human Performance*, 21, 209-19.

Ploog, D. (1958). "Über das Hervortreten angeborener Verhaltensweisen in akuten schizophrenen Psychosen". *Psychiatria et Neurologia*, 136, 157-64.

Ploog, D. (1964). "Verhaltensforschung und Psychiatrie". In H.W. Gruhle, R. Jung, W. Mayer-Gross & M. Müller (eds.), *Psychiatrie der Gegenwart*, vol. I/1B. (pp. 291-443). Heidelberg: Springer.

Ploog, D. (1969). "Verhaltensbiologische Hypothesen zur Entstehung endogener Psychosen". In G. Huber & H. Kranz (eds.), *Schizophrenie und Zyklothymie* (pp. 19-28). Stuttgart: Thieme.

Ploog, D. (1972). "Breakdown of the social communication system: A key process in the development of schizophrenia? Prospects for research on schizophrenia". *Neurosciences Research Progress Bulletin*, 10, 394-5.

Ploog, D. (1977). "Phonation, emotion, cognition, with reference to the brain mechanisms involved". In Ciba Foundation (ed.), *Brain and mind* (pp. 79-98). Amsterdam: Elsevier.

Ploog, D. (1980). "Der Ausdruck der Gemütsbewegungen bei Mensch und Tieren". In Max-Planck-Gesellschaft (ed.), *Jahrbuch 1980* (pp. 66-97). Göttingen: Vanderhöck & Ruprecht.

Plutchik, R. (1980). "A general psychoevolutionary theory of emotion". In R. Plutchik, & H. Kellerman (eds.), *Emotion theory research and experience* (pp. 3-33). New York: Academic Press.

Pope, B., Blass, T., Siegman, A.W., & Raher, J. (1970). "Anxiety and depression in speech". *Journal of Consulting and Clinical Psychology*, 35, 128-33.

Prkachin, K.M., Craig, K.D., Papageorgis, D., & Reith, G. (1977). "Nonverbal communication deficits and response to performance feedback in depression". *Journal of Abnormal Psychology*, 86, 224-34.

Prusoff, B., Klerman, G. & Paykel, E. (1972). "Concordance between clinical assessments and patients self-report in depression". *Archives of General Psychiatry*, **26**, 546-52.

Rado, S. (1928). "The problem of melancholia". *International Journal of Psycho-Analysis*, **9**, 420-38.

Redican, W.K. (1982). "An evolutionary perspective on human facial displays". In P. Ekman (ed.), *Emotion in the human face* (2nd edn., pp. 212-80). Cambridge University Press.

Redlich, F.C., & Freedman, D.X. (1970). *Theorie and Praxis der Psychiatrie*. Frankfurt: Suhrkamp.

Regler, G. (1982). "Das Back-Channel-Verhalten von Therapeuten in Abhängigkeit von der Befindlichkeit ihrer depressiven Gesprächspartner". Unpublished dissertation Ludwig-Maximilians-Universität, Munich.

Renfordt, E., & Busch, H. (1976). "Neue Strategien psychiatrischer Urteilsbildung durch Anwendung audiovisueller Techniken". *Pharmakopsychiatrie und Neuro-Psychopharmakologie*, **9**, 67-75.

Renfordt, E., Busch, H., Fähndrich, E., & Müller-Örlingshausen, B. (1976). "Untersuchung einer neuen antidepressiven Substanz (Vilogazin) mit Hilfe der Zeit-Reihen-Analyse TV-gespeicherter Interviews". *Arzneimittel-Forschung*, **26**, 1114-16.

Renfordt, E., & Ulrich, G. (1986). "Relations among psychopathology, nonverbal behavior (speech activity), and neurophysiology (topography of alpha power) under antidepressive drug treatment". *Pharmacopsychiatry*, **19**, 202-3.

Rennschmid, M. (1979). "Blickverhalten und Sprechaktivität in gestörten und nicht gestörten Partnerbeziehungen". Unpublished dissertation, Max-Planck-Institut für Psychiatrie, Munich.

Riemer, M.D. (1955). "Abnormalities of the gaze: A classification". *Psychiatry Quarterly*, **29**, 659-72.

Rinn, W.E. (1984). "The neuropsychology of facial expression: A review of the neurological and psychological mechanisms for producing facial expressions". *Psychological Bulletin*, **95**, 52-77.

Rochester, S.R. (1973). "The significance of pauses in spontaneous speech". *Journal of Psycholinguistic Research*, **2**, 51-81.

Roessler, R., & Lester, J.W. (1976). "Voice predicts affect during psychotherapy". *The Journal of Nervous and Mental Disease* **163**, 166-76.

Rohracher, H. (1963). *Einführung in die Psychologie* (8 Auflage). Vienna: Urban & Schwarzenberg.

Rosenfeld, H.M. (1966). "Approval-seeking and approval-inducing functions of verbal and non-verbal responses in the dyad". *Journal of Personality and Social Psychology*, **4**, 597-605.

Rosenthal, R., Hall, J.A., DiMatteo, M.R., Rogers, P.L., & Archer, D. (1979). *Sensitivity to nonverbal communication: The PONS test*. Baltimore: Johns Hopkins University Press.

Rubinstein, S.L. (1959). *Grundlagen der allgemeinen Psychologie*. Berlin: Volk und Wissen.

Ruesch, J. (1980). "Communication and psychiatry". In H.J. Kaplan, A.M. Freedman, B.J.Sadock (eds.), *Comprehensive textbook of psychiatry*, vol. 1 (pp. 443-58). Baltimore: Williams & Wilkins.

Russo, N.F. (1975). "Eye contact, interpersonal distance and the equilibrium theory". *Journal of Personality and Social Psychology*, 31, 497-502.

Rutter, D.R. (1973). "Visual interaction in psychiatric patients: A review". *The British Journal of Psychiatry*, 123, 193-202.

Rutter, D.R. (1976). "Visual interaction in recently admitted and chronic long-stay schizophrenic patients". *British Journal of Social & Clinical Psychology*, 15, 295-303.

Rutter, D.R. (1977a). Visual interaction and speech patterning in remitted and acute schizophrenic patients. *The British Journal of Social and Clinical Psychology*, 16, 357-62.

Rutter, D.R. (1977b). "Speech patterning in recently admitted and chronic long-stay schizophrenic patients". *British Journal of Social and Clinical Psychology*, 16, 47-56.

Rutter, D.R. (1984). *Looking and seeing: The role of visual communication in social interaction*. New York: Wiley.

Rutter, D.R., & Stephenson, G.M. (1972a). "Visual interaction in a group of schizophrenic and depressive patients: A follow-up study". *British Journal of Social and Clinical Psychology*, 11, 410-11.

Rutter,D.R., & Stephenson, G.M. (1972b). "Visual interaction in a group of schizophrenic and depressive patients". *British Journal of Social and Clinical psychology*, 11, 57-65.

Rutter, D.R., Stephenson, G.M., & Dewey, M.E. (1981). "Visual communication and the content and style of conversation". *British Journal of Social Psychology*, 20, 41-52.

Rutter, D.R., Stephenson, G.M., Ayling, K., & White, P.A. (1978). "The timing of looks in dyadic conversation". *British Journal of Social and Clinical Psychology*, 17, 17-22.

Rutter, D.R., Stephenson, G.M., Lazzerini, A.J., Ayling, K., & White, P.A. (1977). "Eye-contact: A chance product of individual looking?", *The British Journal of Social and Clinical Psychology*, 16, 191-2.

SPSS-X (1986). *User's guide* (2nd edn.). New York: McGraw Hill.

Sader, M. (1961). *Möglichkeiten und Grenzen psychologischer Testverfahren*. Bern: Huber.

Sainsbury, P. (1954). "A method of measuring spontaneous movements by time-sampling motion pictures". *Journal of Mental Science*, 100, 742-8.

Sainsbury, P. (1955). "Gestural movement during psychiatric interview". *Psychosomatic Medicine*, 17, 458-69.

Sandifer, M.G., Hordorn, A., & Green, L.M. (1970). "The psychitric interview: The impact of the first three minutes". *American Journal of Psychiatry*, 126, 968-73.

Sawyer, J. (1966). "Measurement and prediction, clinical and statistical". *Psychological Bulletin*, 66, 178-200.

Scheflen, A.E. (1966). "Natural history method in psychotherapy". In L.A. Gottschalk, & A.H. Auerbach (eds.), *Methods of research in psychotherapy* (pp. 263-89). New York: Appleton Century Crofts.

Scheflen, A.E. (1973). *Communicational structure. Analysis of a psychotherapy transaction.* Bloomington: Indiana University Press.

Scherer, K.R. (1978). "Personality inference from voice quality: The loud voice of extraversion". *European Journal of Social Psychology*, 8, 467-87.

Scherer, K.R. (1979). "Non-linguistic vocal indicators of emotion and psychopathology". In C.E. Izard (ed.), *Emotions in personality and psychopathology* (pp. 493-529). New York: Plenum Press.

Scherer, K.R. (1979). "Personality markers in speech". In K.R. Scherer & H. Giles (eds.), *Social markers in speech* (pp. 147-201). Cambridge University Press.

Scherer, K.R. (1980). "The functions of nonverbal signs in conversation". In R. St. Clair & H. Giles (eds.), *The social and the psychological contexts of language* (pp. 225-44). Hillsdale, NJ: Erlbaum.

Scherer, K.R. (1981). "Vocal indicators of stress". In J.K. Darby (ed.) *The evaluation of speech in psychiatry.* (pp. 171-87). New York: Grune & Stratton.

Scherer, K.R. (1982). "Methods of research on vocal communication: Paradigms and parameters". In K.R. Scherer & P. Ekman (eds.), *Handbook of methods in nonverbal behaviour research* (pp. 136-98). Cambridge University Press.

Scherer, K.R. (1984). "On the nature and function of emotion: A component process approach". In K.R. Scherer & P. Ekman (eds.) *Approaches to emotion.* (pp. 293-317). Hillsdale, NJ: Lawrence Erlbaum.

Scherer, K.R. (1985). "Vocal affect signalling: a comparative approach". In J.S. Rosenblatt, C.Beer, M.C. Busnel & P.J.B. Slater (eds.), *Advances in the study of behaviour*, 15, (pp. 189-244). New York: Academic Press.

Scherer, K.R., & Scherer, U. (1979). "Nonverbales Verhalten von Beamten in der Interaktion mit dem Bürger: Erste Ergebnisse". In K.R. Scherer & H.G. Wallbott (eds.), *Nonverbale Kommunikation: Ausgewählte Beiträge zum Interaktionsverhalten* (pp. 307-14). Weinheim: Beltz.

Schlosberg, H. (1952). "The description of facial expression in terms of two dimensions". *Journal of Experimental Psychology*, 44, 229-37.

Schneider, F.W., & Hansvick, C.L. (1977). "Gaze and distance as a function of changes in interperonal gaze". *Social Behavior and Personality*, 5, 49-54.

Schuham, A.I. (1972). "Activity, talking time, and spontaneous agreement in disturbed and normal family interaction". *Journal of Abnormal Psychology*, 79, 68-75.

Schwartz, G.E., Fair, P.L., Mandel, M.R., Salt, P., Mieske, M., & Klerman, G.L. (1978). "Facial electromyography in the assessment of improvement in depression". *Psychosomatic Medicine*, 40, 355-60.

Schwartz, G.E., Fair, P.L., Salt, P. Mandel, M.R., & Klerman, G. (1976a). "Facial muscle patterning to affective imagery in depressed and nondepressed subject". *Science*, 192, 489-91.

Schwartz, G.E., Fair, P.L., Salt, P., Mandel, M.R., & Klerman, G.L. (1976b). "Facial expression and imagery in depression: An electromyographic study". *Psychosomatic Medicine*, 38, 337-47.

Schwartz, G.E., & Weinberger, D.A. (1980). "Patterns of emotional responses to affective situations: Relations among happiness, sadness, anger, fear, depression, and anxiety". *Motivation and Emotion*, 4, 175-91.

Schwarz, D., & Strian, F. (1972). "Psychometrische Untersuchungen zur Befindlichkeit psychiatrischer und intern-medizinischer Patienten". *Archiv für Psychiatrie und Nervenkrankheiten,* **216,** 70-81.

Shapiro, M., & Post, F. (1974). "Comparison of self-ratings of psychiatric patients with ratings made by a psychiatrist". *British Journal of Psychiatry,* **125,** 36-41.

Siegman, A.W. (1978a). "The telltale voice: Nonverbal messages of verbal communication". In A.W. Siegman & S. Feldstein (eds.), *Nonverbal behavior and communication.* (pp. 183-243). New York: Wiley.

Siegman, A.W. (1978b). "The meaning of silent pauses in the initial interview". *The Journal of Nervous and Mental Disease,* **166,** 642-54.

Siegman, A.W. & Feldstein, S. (1987). *Nonverbal behavior and communication* (2nd edn). Hillsdale, New Jersey: Lawrence Erlbaum.

Siegman, A. W. & Pope, B. (1965). "Effects of question specificity and anxiety – producing messages on verbal fluency in the initial interview". *Journal of Personality and Social Psychology,* **2,** 522-30.

Simmel, G. (1921). "Sociology of the senses: Visual interaction". In R.E. Park & E.W. Burgess, (eds.), *Introduction to the science of sociology* (pp. 356-60). University of Chicago Press.

Simmel, G. (1923). *Soziologie: Untersuchungen über die Formen der Vergesellschaftung.* Munich.

Slovic, P. & Lichtenstein, S. (1971). "Comparison os Bayesian and regression approaches to the study of information processing in judgement". *Organizational Behaviour and Human Performance,* **6,** 649-794.

Sommer, R. (1967). Small group ecology. *Psychological Bulletin* **67,** 145-52.

Spence, D.P., & Feinburg, C. (1967)."Forms of defensive looking: A naturalistic experiment". *Journal of Nervous and Mental Disease,* **145,** 261-71.

Spiegel, R. (1959). "Specific problems of communication in psychiatric conditions". In S. Arieti (ed.), *American handbook of psychiatry* (pp.909-49). New York: Basic Books.

Starkweather, J.A. (1967). "Vocal behaviour as an information channel of speaker status". In K. Salzinger & S. Salzinger (eds.), *Research in verbal behaviour and some neurophysiological implications* (pp. 253-65). New York: Academic Press.

Steiner, J.E. (1974). "Innate discriminative human facial expressions to taste and smell stimulation". *Annals of the New York Academy of Science,* **237,** 229-33.

Steinhausen, D., & Langer, K. (1977). *Clusteranalyse – Einführung in Methoden und Verfahren der automatischen Klassifikation.* Berlin: DeGruyter.

Stephenson, G.M., Ayling, K. & Rutter, D. (1976). "The role of visual communication in social exchange". *British Journal of Social and Clinical Psychology,* **15,** 113-20.

Strehle, H. (1960). *Mienen, Gesten und Gebärden – Analyse des Gebarens* (3rd edn.). Munich/Basle: Reinhardt.

Strongman, K.T., & Champness, B.G. (1968). "Dominance hierarchies and conflict in eye contact". *Acta Psychologica,* **28,** 376-86.

Szabadi, E., Bradshaw, C.M., & Besson, J.A. (1976). "Elongation of pause-time in speech: A simple, objective measure of motor retardation in depression". *British Journal of Psychiatry,* **129,** 592-7.

Szucko, J.J., & Kleinmutz, B. (1981). "Statistical versus clinical lie detection". *American Psychologist*, **36**, 488-96.

Teasdale, J.D., & Bancroft, J. (1977). "Manipulation of thought content as a determinant of mood and corrugator electromyographic activity in depressed patients". *Journal of Abnormal Psychology*, **86**, 235-41.

Teasdale, J.D., Fogarty, S.J., & Williams, J.M.G. (1980). "Speech rate as a measure of short-term variation in depression". *British Journal of Social and Clinical Psychology*, **19**, 271-8.

Teasdale, J.D., & Rezin, V. (1977). "Effect of thought-stopping on thoughts, mood and corrugator EMG in depressed patients". *Journal of Abnormal Psychology*, **86**, 235-41.

Thayer, S., & Schiff, W. (1974). "Observer judgement of social interaction: Eye contact and relationship inferences". *Journal of Personality and Social Psychology*, **30**, 110-14.

Thayer, S., & Schiff, W. (1977). "Gazing patterns and attribution of sexual involvement". *Journal of Social Psychology*, **101**, 235-46.

Thomsen, C.E. (1974). "Eye contact by non-human primates toward a human observer". *Animal Behaviour*, **22**, 144-9.

Tinbergen, N. (1951). *The study of instinct* (Deutsch: Instinktlehre, Berlin: Parey, 1966) Oxford University Press.

Tomkins, S.S. (1962). *Affect, imagery, and consciousness*. vol. I: *The positive affects*. New York: Springer.

Tomkins, S.S. (1963). *Affect, imagery, and consciousness*. vol. II: *The negative affects*. New York: Springer.

Tomkins, S.S. (1982). "Affect theory". In P. Ekman (ed.), *Emotion in the human face* (2nd edn., pp. 318-52). Cambridge University Press.

Treisman, A.M. (1964). "Verbal cues, language and meaning in selective attention". *American Journal of Psychology*, **77**, 206-19.

Trower, P., Bryant, B., & Argyle M. (1978). *Social skills and mental health*. London: Methuen.

Truax, C.B. (1971). "Normalization of verbal productivity and improvement in depressive status in schizophrenics". *Journal of Clinical Psychology*, **27**, 537-9.

Ulrich, G. (1979). "Über den Zusammenhang videoanalytisch gewonnener Maße des non-verbalen Verhaltens mit selbst eingeschätzter Befindlichkeit". *Schweizer Archiv für Neurologie, Neurochirurgie und Psychiatrie*, **125**, 349-59.

Ulrich, G. (1980). "Verhaltensphysiologische und vigilanztheoretische Aspekte des Handbewegungsverhaltens Depressiver in einer Interviewsituation". *Nervenarzt*, **51**, 294-301.

Ulrich, G. (1981). *Videoanalyse depressiver Verhaltensaspekte. Studien zum non-verbalen Verhalten in einer Interviewsituation*. Stuttgart: Enke.

Ulrich, G., & Harms, K. (1978). "Handbewegungsformen und ihr Lateralisationsverhalten im Behandlungsverlauf depressiver Syndrome". In H. Helmchem & E. Renfordt (eds.), *Fernsehen in der Psychiatrie*. (pp. 45-53). Stuttgart: Thieme.

Ulrich, G., Harms, K., & Fleischhauer, J. (1976). "Untersuchungen mit einer verhaltensorientierten Schätzskala für depressive Hemmung und Agitation". *Arzneimittel-Forschung (Drug Research)*, **26**, 1117-19.

Van Hoff, J.A.R.A.M. (1967). "The facial displays of the catarrhine monkeys and apes". In D. Morris (ed.), *Primate ethology* (pp.7-68). London: Weidenfeld & Nicholson.

Vanger, P. (1984). "Variations in the interactive behaviour of depressives". Unpublished doctoral dissertation. University of London.

Vanger, P., & Ellgring, H. "Minor nonverbal cues in the recognition of affect". (in preparation).

Vaughan, C.E., & Leff, J.P. (1976). "The influence of family and social factors on the course of psychiatric illness. A comparison of schizophrenic and depressed neurotic patients". *British Journal of Psychiatry*, **129**, 125.

Vrugt, A. (1987). "The meaning of nonverbal sex differences". *Semiotica* (in press).

Vrugt, A., & Kerkstra, A. (1982). *Differences between men and women in nonverbal behavior* (Mimeo). Universiteit van Amsterdam.

Wagner, H. (1981). "Die Ermittlung sozialer Signale: Methoden und Ergebnisse". Unpublished dissertation. Ludwig-Maximilians-Universität, Munich.

Wagner, H., Clarke, A.H., & Ellgring, H. (1980). "Qualitative and quantitative aspects of speech-gaze coordination". *Paper presented to the XXII. International Congress of Psychology, Leipzig*.

Wagner, H., Clarke, A.H., & Ellgring, H. (1983). "Eye-contact and individual looking – The role of chance". *British Journal of Social Psychology*, **22**, 61-2.

Wagner, H., Ellgring, H., & Clarke, A.H. (1980). "Binäre Kodierung von Sprechen und Blicken: Validität, Reliabilität und ihre Abhängigkeit von der zeitlichen Auflösung". *Zeitschrift für experimentelle und angewandte Psychologie*, **27**, 670-87.

Wagner, H., Ellgring, H., & Clarke, A.H. (1981). "Analyse des Blickverhaltens in sozialen Situationen". In P. Winkler (ed.), *Methoden der Analyse von Face-to-Face Situationen*. (pp. 330-43). Stuttgart: Metzler.

Wallbott, H.G. (1981). "Subjektive und objektive Aspekte gestischen Verhaltens". In P. Winkler (ed.). *Methoden der Analyse von face-to-face Situationen*. (pp. 285-301). Stuttgart: J.B. Metzler.

Wallbott, H.G. (1982). *Bewegungsstil und Bewegungsqualität: Untersuchungen zum Ausdruck und Eindruck gestischen Verhaltens* (in preparation). Weinheim: Beltz.

Watzlawick, P., Beavin, J.H., & Jackson, D.D. (1968). *Pragmatics of human communication*. London: Faber.

Waxer, P. (1974). "Nonverbal cues for depression". *Journal of Abnormal Psychology*, **83**, 319-22.

Waxer, P. (1976). "Nonverbal cues for depth of depression: Set versus no set". *Journal of Consulting and Clinical Psychology*, **44**, 493.

Waxer, P. (1979). "Therapist training in nonverbal behavior: Towards a curriculum". In A. Wolfgang (ed.). *Nonverbal behavior – Applications and cultural implications* (pp. 127-38). New York: Academic Press Inc.

Webb, J.T. (1970). "Interview synchrony: An investigation of two speech rate measures in an automated standardized interview": In A.W. Siegman & B. Pope (eds.), *Studies in dyadic communication: Proceedings of a Research Conference on the Interview* (pp. 115-31). New York: Pergamon Press.

Weissman, M.M., Myers, J.K., Leaf, P.J., Tischler, G.L., & Holzer, C.E. (1986). "The affective disorders: Results from the epidemiologic catchment area study (ECA)". In H. Hippius, G.L. Klerman & N. Matussek (eds.), *New results in depression research* (pp. 16-25). Berlin: Springer.

Weissman, M.M., & Paykel, E.S. (1974). *The depressed woman: A study of social relationships*. University of Chicago Press.

Weitbrecht, H.J. (1968). *Psychiatrie im Grundriss* (2nd edn.). Berlin: Springer.

Wessman, A.A. (1979). "Moods: Their personal dynamics and significance". In C.E. Izard (ed.), *Emotions in personality and psychopathology* (pp. 73-102). New York: Plenum Press.

Weygandt, W. (1902). *Atlas und Grundriss der Psychiatrie*. Munich: Lehmann.

Wickler, W. (1980). "Vocal dueting and the pair bond. I. Coyness and partner commitment. A hypothesis". *Zeitschrift für Tierpsychologie*, 52, 201-9.

Wickler, W., & Seibt, U. (1980). "Vocal dueting and the pair bond. II. Unisono dueting in the African Forest Weaver, Symplectes bicolor". *Zeitschrift für Tierpsychologie*, 52, 217-26.

Wiener, M., Devoe, S., Rubinow, S., & Geller, J. (1972). "Nonverbal behavior and nonverbal communication". *Psychological Review*, 70, 185-214.

Wiggins, J.C. (1973). *Personality and prediction: Principles of personality assessment*. Reading, Mass.: Addison Wesley.

Williams, J.G. Barlow, D.H., Agras, W.S., & Jackson, M. (1972). "Behavioral measurement of severe depression". *Archives of General Psychiatry*, 27, 330-3.

Wing, J.H., Cooper, J.E., & Sartorius, N. (1974). *Measurement and classifcation of psychiatric symptons – An instruction manual for the PSE and Catego Program*. Cambridge University Press.

Wolff, P., & Gutstein, J. (1972). "Effects of induced motor gestures on vocal output". *Journal of Communication*, 22, 277-88.

World Health Organization (1978). *Mental disorders: Glossary and guide to their classification in accordance with the Ninth Revision of the International Classification of Diseases*. Geneva: World Health Organization.

Wundt, W. (1905). *Grundzüge der physiologischen Psychologie*. Leipzig: Engelmann, 3.

Yarbus, A.A. (1967). *Eye movement and vision*. New York: Plenum Press.

Zajonc, R.B. (1984). "On the primacy of affect". *American Psychologist*, 39, 117-23.

Zealley, A.K., & Aitken, R.C. (1969). "Measurement of Mood". *Proceedings of the Royal Society of Medicine*, 62, 993-6.

Zenz, H., Brähler, E., & Braun, P. (1974). "Die Validität der On-Off patterns als Indikator für den psychotherapeutischen Prozess". *Zeitschrift für experimentelle und angewandte Psychologie*, 21, 326-38.

Zerssen, D. von, Köller, D.-M., & Rey, E.R. (1970). "Die Befindlichkeits-Skala (B-S) – ein einfaches Instrument zur Objektivierung von Befindlichkeitsstörungen, insbesondere im Rahmen von Längsschnittunersuchungen". *Arzneimittelforschung – Drug Research*, 20, 915-18.

Zipf, G.K. (1965). *Human behavior and the principle of least effort*. New York: Hafner (First published 1949).

Zuckerman, M., & Larrane, D.T. (1979). Individual difference in perceived encoding and decoding abilities. In R. Rosenthal (ed.), *Skill in nonverbal communication* (pp. 171-93). Cambridge, Mass.: Oelgeschlager, Gunn & Hain.

Zung, W.W.K. (1965). "A self rating depression scale". *Archives of General Psychiatry*, **12**, 53-70.

Zung, W.W.K. (1974). "The measurement of affects: Depression and anxiety". In P. Pichot (ed.), *Psychological measurements in psychopharmacology. Modern problems of pharmacopsychiatry*, vol. 7 (pp. 170-88). Basle: Karger.

Index of Authors

Subject Index